Sign language

Sign language interpreting

Linguistic coping strategies

JEMINA NAPIER

Coleford • England

8 St John Street
Coleford
Gloucestershire GL16 8AR
England
dmcl@forestbooks.com
www.ForestBooks.com

British Library Cataloguing in Publication Data
A catalogue record for this book is available from the British Library
ISBN 0-946252-37-8

Typeset in 10/14pt Monotype Albertina
Printed by Biddles Ltd, Guildford
Typography and cover by Ernst Thoutenhoofd

Contents

Acknowledgments

In addition to those people I specifically mention here, I would like to thank all my colleagues and friends for expressing an interest in my work, and for encouraging me to apply my interpreting experience in an academic field.

In particular I would like to thank Mary Brennan, David Brien, Judith Collins, Margo Currie, Peter Llewellyn Jones, Liz Scott Gibson, and Maureen Reed, who lectured on my Masters degree course, and inspired me to want to conduct further research on interpreting. Additionally, thanks go to Graham H. Turner and Kyra Pollit for engaging with me in many a conversation about interpreting, both linguistic and otherwise, and for their encouragement of my academic pursuits.

Special thanks go to Robert Adam, for helping me settle into a new country, and for being my friend and colleague. Robert introduced me to Renwick College at the Royal NSW Institute for Deaf and Blind Children, where I was provided with an office. Therefore, I would also like to thank Greg Leigh and all other staff members at Renwick College for making me feel welcome, and I would like to thank Rod Beattie for helping me out with applications for funding and development of a survey instrument.

Further thanks go to Roz Barker and Trevor Johnston, for their patience, diligence and unfailing support as supervisors. Cynthia Roy became my mentor, and I thank her for her support and encouragement, and for making me feel like I had something to offer.

For their financial support, I would particularly like to acknowledge the Australian Federal Government Department of Education, Training and Youth Affairs for the Commonwealth Scholarship that enabled me to move to Australia to study; the Victorian Services for Deaf Children for the grant that meant I could meet the expenses of my data collection and analysis; and the Macquarie University Postgraduate Research Fund and the Macquarie University Linguistics Department Postgraduate Research Fund, for funding towards my trip to the CIT convention in 2000, where I was able to present my research findings and get feedback. In addition, thanks to Renwick College and the Australian Sign Language Interpreters' Association (NSW) for their sponsorship of my attendance at the CIT (2002) convention to report the complete research findings.

I would like to thank all those people who were specifically involved in the research itself, namely, all the interpreters that responded to my survey; the ten interpreters who were involved in the analytical study; Colin Allen for being my research assistant; Adam Schembri and Della Goswell for doing reliability checks; Adam Schembri, Dani Fried and Andy Carmichael for piloting the interpreting tasks; Caroline Conlon, Leonie Jackson, Trevor Maggs and Darlene Thornton for being involved in the discussion panel; Michelle Maguire for interpreting the discussion panel; Peter Bonser and Viona Woodroffe for clarifying issues with regards to Auslan interpreters and interpreting; plus coordinators at all the Australian Deaf Society interpreting services, for helping me track down as many Auslan interpreters as possible.

I would like to give particular thanks to Adam Schembri, who gave me the idea for my research topic during one of our many discussions on linguistics and interpreting. He's been an excellent friend and colleague.

I would also like to thank all my family and friends for supporting me throughout the PhD research and adaptation of the book, including Melinda and Brian, Mark, Zoe, Karl, Bow, Cecy, Dylan, Adam and Joe, Amanda, Caroline, Colin, Della, Evie and Fabio, Peter and Michael, Robert, and Trevor, to name but a few.

Last but by no means least, thanks to Andy Carmichael. For making me believe in myself. I'd like to think that I could have done it anyway, but I really don't think that I could. Without you being there to share with, it wouldn't have been half as rewarding.

Prologue

When you know a language, you can speak to and be understood by others who know that language. This means you have the capacity to produce sounds that signify certain meanings and to understand or interpret the sounds produced by others…Deaf persons produce and understand sign languages just as hearing persons produce and understand spoken languages (Fromkin, Rodman, Collins & Blair, 1990, p.3–4).

Speculations over the numbers of languages used throughout the world have varied from 3,000 to 10,000, with the most regular evaluations citing numbers of 4,000 or 5,000 (Crystal, 1987). In addition to this, it has been estimated that half of the world's population can speak more than one language (Grosjean, 1982). The other half of the world's population, however, are monolingual. Typically it is these people that would rely on translators and interpreters for any formal contact and dialogue with persons from different languages and cultures. Yet although a large proportion of the world's population may have the ability to use more than one language, very few of them will have the competence to effectively translate between two languages (Grosjean, 1997).

Translating and interpreting

Translation is often used as a generic term to refer to the transfer of thoughts and ideas from one language (source) to another language (target) regardless of the form of either language (written, spoken or signed). When the form of the source language is either spoken or signed, the transfer process is referred to as interpretation (Brislin, 1976; cited in Cokely, 1992a, p.1).

It can be seen from the above quote that the term 'language' is pivotal in understanding what is meant by the translating and interpreting process. This is a supposition that anybody can make, and is consist-

ntly referred to in any literature related to the field of translation and
nterpretation. Accompanying the initial supposition is an additional
assumption that any translator or interpreter must be equally fluent in
the languages they work with. In order to transfer thoughts and ideas
from one language to another, however, it is not enough to just have
bilingual fluency.

Bilingualism

Several writers have considered the difference between bilingual
competence and translational competence (such as Baetens
Beardsmore, 1986; Hoffman, 1991; Isham & Lane, 1994; Romaine, 1995).
Grosjean (1997) studied bilingual individuals and stated that few
bilinguals are proficient translators and interpreters. He listed certain
factors that can influence a person's ability to perform as an interpreter.
These factors may include: unequal fluency in both languages; an accent
in her second language; late acquisition or learning of the second
language; lack of stylistic varieties in each language; undeveloped
transfer skills; or lack of pragmatic competence and cultural knowledge
about the two distinct groups. Grosjean made the distinction between a
regular bilingual and a *distinct* or *interpreter bilingual*, by clearly stating that
"interpreter bilinguals, unlike regular bilinguals, will have to learn to use
their languages (and the underlying skills that they have in them) for
similar purposes, in similar domains of life, with similar people. This is
something that regular bilinguals do not often need to do" (p.168). It can
be seen, therefore, that although balanced fluency in at least two
languages is essential, translators and interpreters are required to have a
wide range of knowledge and skills in order to effectively transfer
messages between two different languages.

Interpreting skills

According to Frishberg (1990), the art of interpretation requires "…an
understanding of the dynamics of human interaction…an appreciation
of social and cultural differences, the ability to concentrate and maintain one's attention, a good deal of tact, judgment, stamina, and above
all a sense of humour" (p.3), as well as competence in at least two
languages. The knowledge and skills listed above are only a few from

x   the gamut of those that translators and interpreters are expected to develop prior to, and maintain throughout, their career in order to effectively transfer a message from one language and culture to another. Other desired components of an interpreter's repertoire include the following list, derived from various literature on translating and interpreting (Frishberg, 1990; Napier, 1998a; Neumann Solow, 1981, 2000; Schein & Delk, 1974; Seleskovitch, 1978): interpersonal skills; public speaking skills; advocacy skills; 'listening' skills; effective short and long term memory; cognitive information processing skills; analytical skills; contextual knowledge; world knowledge; specialist knowledge; professionalism; flexibility; objectivity; self-discipline; responsibility; acting skills; independence; motivation; willingness to learn; self-confidence; ability to deal with situations encountered while interpreting; awareness of own limitations; and ability to provide peer support. After reading this extensive catalogue of interpreter skills requirements, it is possible to discern why Grosjean (1997) and others have determined that bilingualism alone is insufficient to guarantee effective interpreting skills.

In order to facilitate any discussion on interpreting, it is important to clarify several terms, which are familiar to those working in the field, and are consistently referred to throughout this book.

Terminology

Throughout any discussion of the interpreting process, references are made in the literature to key terms that are widely recognised by interpreters, interpreter researchers and interpreter educators. The most common terms compiled from several sources (such as, Frishberg, 1990; Neumann Solow, 1981, 2000; Seleskovitch, 1978; Simon, 1994) are presented here.

It is important to recognise the fact that interpreters work between two languages. Any research on interpreting needs to specify the difference between the language from which the message originates (*source language*), and the language into which the message is rendered (*target language*). The term *translation* refers either to the process of changing a written text in one language to a written text in another language, or is used as a generic term to discuss the process of transla-

tion and interpretation between source and target languages. The term
interpretation, however, refers specifically to the process of changing a
message produced in one language into another language, regardless of
whether the two languages are spoken or signed (e.g., English into
Spanish, Spanish to Spanish Sign Language, Spanish Sign Language to
Australian Sign Language[1]). With regards to the person who provides
an interpretation, the term *interpreter* is used generically throughout this
book since it is the most common referent for people working with two
or more languages.

The interpretation process can occur consecutively or simultaneously. *Consecutive interpretation* involves the interpreter providing the
interpretation after the speaker or signer has finished the presentation
of their message, which may occur after a phrase, a concept or an entire
speech. Alternatively, *simultaneous interpretation* is a process whereby the
interpreter renders the message at almost the same time it is conveyed
by the speaker or signer. There is often a short delay, called *decalage* or
lag time, since the interpreter needs time to hear or see the original
utterance before being able to process it.

Various studies of interpreting provide discussion from a
'psycholinguistic' or 'sociolinguistic' perspective, yet it seems that these
terms are sometimes used differently in interpreter research literature.
Interpreting literature tends to regard psycholinguistic and sociolinguistic analysis of interpreting as distinct processes, rather than just labels
for sub-disciplines in linguistics that are not necessarily mutually
exclusive. *Psycholinguistic analysis* of interpreting refers to the cognitive
processes involved in interpreting, and the language processing that
takes place (Ingram, 1985; Lörscher, 1996; Tweney, 1978). *Sociolinguistic
analysis*, however, refers to the consideration given to linguistic and
cultural factors that may influence interpreters in the language choices
they make (Cokely, 1985, 1992a; Pergnier, 1978; Roy, 1989a, 1992, 1996,
2000a). Although this book touches occasionally on psycholinguistic
issues related to interpreting, it is essentially reporting a sociolinguistic
study of sign language interpreters.

Interpreters who work between a spoken and signed language tend
not to engage in the task of written translation because signed languages are visual-gestural languages with no standard written orthogra-

phy. Sign language interpreters usually work simultaneously as there is no conflict between two languages being vocalised one over the top of another, and they cannot realistically take notes in order to interpret large consecutive chunks of information because they using their hands to interpret.

As interpreters work between two languages, any discussion of interpreters and interpreting should typically refer to both the languages being used, for example, Auslan/ English interpreter. This book incorporates discussion of interpretation between different sign languages, predominantly American Sign Language (ASL) or British Sign Language (BSL), and spoken English, as well as referring to interpreters of other spoken languages. For the purposes of expediency, however, references in this book will be to interpreters by the sign language, or language other than English, that they use. For example, Auslan/English interpreters will be referred to as Auslan interpreters, ASL/English or BSL/English interpreters as ASL or BSL interpreters, and French/English or Russian/ English interpreters as French or Russian interpreters.

Another convention that is used is in relation to gender reference. It is widely recognised that interpreters can be either male or female. The majority of sign language interpreters, however, are women (Atwood & Gray, 1985; Stewart, Schein and Cartwright, 1998). Therefore, again for expediency, in any discussion of interpreters throughout this book, if the gender of an interpreter is unimportant, the pronoun 'she' will be used.

Sign language interpreting: An emerging profession

Sign language interpreting has often been referred to as an "emerging profession" (Fenton, 1993; Scott Gibson, 1992). There is a dearth of research in this area, and little status afforded to those who choose to work in the field. To date North America has been at the forefront of professional development, with formal recognition of sign language interpreting as a profession in 1964 (Quigley, 1965), followed by the establishment of the Registry of Interpreters for the Deaf (RID), as well as the provision of specific training courses for sign language interpreters, and professional development for the trainers of interpreters under the umbrella of the Conference of Interpreter Trainers (CIT), which was established in 1979 (Simon, 1994).

As a result of the professionalisation of sign language interpreting in North America, research studies of ASL interpreting first began to appear approximately 25 years ago (Carter & Lauritsen, 1974; Dicker, 1976; Domingue & Ingram, 1978; Nowell & Stuckless, 1974; Sternberg, Tipton & Schein, 1973). The North Americans were closely followed by British researchers, writing about sign language interpreting as a unique language process (Hough, 1981; Kyle & Woll, 1985; Llewellyn Jones, 1981a, 1981b). Several writings on sign language interpreting emerged from other countries, such as Belgium (Demanez, 1987), Germany (Donath, 1987), Scandinavia (Hansen, 1991; Hassinen & Lehtomaki, 1986), and Japan (Kamata et al, 1989), to name but a few. Literature on sign language interpreting only began to appear in Australia, however, in the mid- to late-1990s (Bremner & Housden, 1996; Madden 2001; Ozolins & Bridge, 1999). Since the recognition of sign language interpreting as a profession, many researchers have carried out studies on various aspects of interpreting between signed and spoken languages, yet there is still a dearth of literature in the area.

An innovative study of sign language interpreters

This book discusses the findings of an innovative study of interpreters working between English and Auslan, and explores how the findings can be equally applied among sign language interpreters working with other sign languages, and possibly to spoken language interpreters.

The study focused on Auslan interpreters working in a university lecture. Through informal discussion with members of the Australian Sign Language Interpreters Association (ASLIA), it was noted that many Auslan interpreters have not completed a university education, have not undergone any interpreter training, yet regularly work in universities. Observations of, and discussions with counterparts in, the sign language interpreting professions in other countries such as the UK and USA, also revealed similar circumstances. This situation obviously raises many questions in relation to language fluency (both comprehension and production), service provision, ethical practice, the impact upon the educational experiences of Deaf[2] people, and the implications for the education and training of sign language interpreters. One of the key issues to consider, is the types of linguistic coping strategies used by

xiv   sign language interpreters while interpreting for university lectures, and the impact their formal educational background might have on their use of such strategies.

Coping strategies can be defined as those methods or techniques adopted by interpreters to ensure that they are best equipped to cope with the variety of different factors that may impact upon their interpreting. There are various sources of demand on interpreters, which arise from linguistic factors (associated with the languages being used) and non-linguistic factors, such as environmental, interpersonal and intrapersonal demands (Dean & Pollard, 2001). In general, coping strategies can be considered as those strategies used by interpreters to deal with the demands placed upon them by non-linguistic factors, for example, team-working and preparation techniques. Linguistic coping strategies, however, are those strategies that specifically deal with linguistic factors influencing an interpretation. Examples of linguistic coping strategies used by interpreters would include the application of linguistic and cultural knowledge, communication management, translation style, the use of linguistic transference, and the use of additions, substitutions and omissions within an interpretation.

This book reports on sign language interpreters' translation style and omission production as linguistic coping strategies while interpreting for a university lecture, and the extent to which educational background influenced translation style and the number and types of omissions produced.

Organisation of the book

In order to place this study within the wider scene of linguistic and interpreting research, it is worthwhile to examine and discuss theoretical and empirical literature that focuses on sociolinguistic issues relevant to interpreting, and those specifically pertinent to sign language interpreting.

Chapter one concentrates on sociolinguistic and sociocultural contexts of interpreting, thus providing a wider context for those significant influences on a sign language interpreter's ability to interpret a university lecture effectively. The beginning of the chapter introduces a framework for interpreting, providing an overview of information

that is fundamental to understanding the study, with a focus on the
interpreting process, models of interpreting, and interpreting techniques. Comparisons are then made between spoken and signed
language interpreters, in relation to bilingualism and the bimodality of
sign language interpreting. Finally, chapter one discusses the discourse
environment factors to consider, such as: the university lecture as a
discourse genre; situational variance of language register; typical
language features of university lecture text, and the challenges faced by
sign language interpreters when interpreting this kind of text.

Chapter two goes on to discuss the notion of coping strategies used
by interpreters, reviewing relevant research studies and thus defining
linguistic coping strategies, the use of translation style and omissions as
linguistic coping strategies, and the concept of metalinguistic awareness.
Chapter three provides an overview of discourse-specific studies on
interpreting relevant to the study, namely conference and educational
interpreting. Chapter four details the analysis of linguistic coping
strategies, by describing the methodology of the study. A technique for
defining lexical density of language is introduced, and an 'omission
taxonomy' used to analyse the participants' interpretations is outlined.

Chapter five discusses the findings of the study, with use of transcribed extracts from the videotaped interpreting task. Finally, Chapter
six provides discussion of issues to consider as a consequence of the
research findings in relation to the linguistic coping strategies of
interpreters working in a university lecture, and presents the perspective of Deaf university students and their expectations as consumers of
interpreting services. Chapter six also discusses the implications of this
research in relation to sign language interpreter training and education,
followed by discussion of the wider implications of this study regarding
interpreting in different contexts, and concludes with suggestions for
future research.

Notes

1. Hereafter referred to as Auslan.
2. Any discussion involving Deaf people concentrates specifically on sign
   language users who use sign language as their first or preferred language,
   and who perceive themselves as members of a linguistic and cultural

xvi   minority group, as opposed to persons with a hearing loss; therefore adopting the convention first proposed by Woodward (1972) and later developed by Padden (1980) of using the upper case 'D' to signify a deaf 'identity'. Whenever 'hearing' people are mentioned, this implies that the writer is referring to the majority of people in society who do not have any kind of hearing loss, and who are not necessarily familiar with the Deaf community, its culture and the concept of a Deaf identity.

Sociolinguistic and sociocultural contexts of interpreting

1.0 Introduction

In order to establish a context for the work of sign language interpreters, it is necessary to explore sociolinguistic and sociocultural factors that may influence their work. In understanding a framework for interpreting in general, it is possible to identify the unique nature of sign language interpreting in comparison with spoken language interpreting. Other sociolinguistic and sociocultural factors to consider include those relevant to the discourse environment and the challenges for interpreters when dealing with particular linguistic features of source texts.

1.1 A framework for interpreting

In order to effectively explore the linguistic coping strategies of sign language interpreters, it is necessary to establish a framework for the way in which interpreters work. By exploring the generic nature of an interpreter's work, it is possible to establish a context for the study. As a route to understanding the complexities involved in interpreting, it is essential to discuss not only the linguistic processes involved, but also the behavioural aspects of an interpreter's role.

The fundamental nature of interpreting as a process for transferring ideas from one language into another was introduced in the Prologue. The process involved in the transference of concepts between two languages is not, however, as straight forward as it would seem, hence the need for interpreters to maintain a multi-layered skills base. Cokely (1995) neatly summarises the various layers of the interpreting process:

> [the] competent and coherent use of one naturally evolved language to express the meanings and intentions conveyed in another naturally evolved language for the purpose of negotiating an opportunity for a successful communicative interaction in real time within a triad involving two principal groups who are incapable of using, or who

prefer not to use, the language of the other individual or group
(Cokely 1995, p.1).

As indicated by the above definition, interpreting is a highly complex
linguistic process involving "intriguing mechanisms by which the brain
is able to process two languages simultaneously" (Ingram, 1978, p.113).
Particular writings have presented a psycholinguistic perspective of the
cognitive information processes involved in interpreting (Flores
d'Arcais, 1978; Ford, 1981; Goldman-Gisler, 1978; Goldman-Gisler &
Cohen, 1974; Ingram, 1974, 1985; Isham, 1994; Isham & Lane, 1993; Le Ny,
1978; Lörscher, 1996; Massaro, 1978; Moser, 1978; Seleskovitch, 1976;
Tweney, 1978). A psycholinguistic approach often emphasises a linear
process of interpreting, whereby the information from the source
language is decoded, analysed, and re-encoded into the target language,
with an emphasis on memory. However, this approach has limitations
as it implies that the transfer process only takes place between two
languages, rather than between languages, communities and cultures.

Other authors (such as Cokely, 1985, 1992a; Frishberg, 2000;
Metzger, 1995, 1999; Neumann Solow, 2000; Pergnier, 1978; Roy, 1989a,
1992, 1996, 2000a) have stated that any study of interpretation should
apply a framework of sociolinguistic parameters, as interpreters can be
seen to mediate not only between two individual languages, but also
between communities and cultures. Any interpretation therefore needs
to be based on a linguistic and cultural understanding of the participants within an interaction, and their differing norms and values. Scott
Gibson (1992) asserted that interpretation is more than just comprehension of a message. She stated that any interpretation should re-express
the thoughts of one language into another, incorporating the same
intent and style as would be used by a native speaker of the second
language. Additionally, Scott Gibson emphasised that interpreters must
be both bilingual and bicultural, "for accurate transmission of information may take place only if based on a deep knowledge of both languages, both cultures, and the cultural differences involved" (p.255).

By adopting a sociolinguistic/sociocultural approach to interpreting,
the focus is not on the decoding and re-encoding of information in
different languages, but rather on the message that is delivered and the

meaning it conveys. A sociolinguistic perspective emphasises that the crux of any interpretation is to achieve 'dynamic equivalence' (Hatim and Mason, 1990), that is, to get the message right by ensuring that the target language audience derives the same meaning from a message as is intended by the source language presenter. Therefore, rather than the interpreting process being about language transmission and change, it is about the message within a sociolinguistic and sociocultural context (Pergnier, 1978).

In the sign language interpreting world, the focus on whether to 're-formulate language' or 'convey the message' has been greatly influenced by the various models of interpreting mooted over the last twenty years. Perspectives on the role of an interpreter have been defined in several ways, such as "service models" (Witter-Merithew, 1987, 1988), "images of the interpreter" (Frishberg, 1990), "philosophical frames" (Humphrey & Alcorn, 1996) and "models of interpreting" (Stewart, Schein & Cartwright, 1998). Lee (1997) stated that the interpreter's role is influenced by a multitude of different factors, yet there are established models which have been developed and improved upon as more research has been conducted in the field. Lee commented that "while we define our role to persons outside the field... we talk amongst ourselves, as professionals, about the model of interpreting that we work under" (p.41).

An interpreting model is considered as "a hypothetical representation of a process or object; it serves to display, verbally or graphically, an event, object, or series of events..." (Stewart, Schein & Cartwright, 1998 p.33). Early models gave little recognition for the sociolinguistic or sociocultural factors that may effect an interpreter's work, or the fact that interpreters will inevitably influence any communicative interaction with their presence. Proposed models included the *cognitive model,* (Stewart, et al, 1998), the *conduit model* (Neumann Solow, 1981), and the *facilitator of communication model* (Neumann Solow, 1981; Frishberg, 1990). Several writers recognised, however, that a metaphorical description of an interpreter as a conduit that does not impact on communication, does not account for human dynamics and the need for interpreters to be flexible (Humphrey & Alcorn, 1996; McIntire & Sanderson, 1993; Roy, 1993; Metzger, 1999).

20   A model of interpreting based on sociolinguistic paradigms is the best way to represent the complete dynamic of interpreting, whereby the interpreter engages in a complex linguistic and cultural process of transferring information between languages, with the recognition that they may contribute to, rather than hinder, any communicative interaction. The central focus of a *sociolinguistic model* is the human interaction between participants, whereby the various sociolinguistic factors that may influence an interpreter's work are acknowledged, and the effect that an interpreter can have on any interaction is also recognised. Rather than being 'invisible' and relying on understanding of language alone, a sociolinguistic or *bilingual-bicultural model* (McIntire & Sanderson, 1993) requires the interpreter to identify and consider the setting, the participants, the purpose(s), and the message within any interaction (Stewart et al, 1998). Interpreters have been recognised as being members of a 'third culture' (Atwood & Gray, 1986; Bienvenu, 1987; Napier, 2002a; Sherwood, 1987). This notion stems from the fact that interpreters are often the only people present within an interaction who can identify issues for representatives of two cultures coming together, and therefore use their understanding of those cultures to make appropriate language adjustments (Roy, 1993).

Cokely (1985, 1992a) has been one of the major advocates of a sociolinguistic model of the interpreting process. He defined a sociolinguistic approach to interpreting as being multifaceted through parallel, rather than linear, processing. In his proposed *sociolinguistically sensitive process model*, Cokely (1992a) posited seven key stages to the interpreting process. The pictorial depiction of the model implies that processing occurs sequentially, however, Cokely clarified this point by stating that "it is more helpful to think of the process as one in which there is multiple nesting of stages" (p.128). In this way the key processes and sub-processes can be described, but it is acknowledged that the major stages are not necessarily discrete entities and may overlap.

The seven major processes outlined by Cokely (1992a) include: (1) message reception, (2) preliminary processing, (3) short term message retention, (4) semantic intent realisation, (5) semantic equivalence determination, (6) syntactic message formulation, and (7) message production. Additionally, Cokely hypothesised that a range of sub-

processes and factors can influence the overall interpreting process. 21
These include cross-linguistic and cultural awareness, linguistic and
syntactic competence, physical and psychological factors, semantic,
syntactic and contextual knowledge, and cultural awareness.

Hence, rather than seeing the interpreter as an entity who does not
effect interaction, the interpreter is recognised as a human being who
can influence, and is influenced by, the participants, languages, cultures
and social norms of any interaction. Baker Shenk (1986) has stated that
it is impossible for sign language interpreters to be completely neutral,
as they are members of the hearing majority, and therefore members of
the society that has historically oppressed Deaf people. A sociolinguistic, bilingual-bicultural approach to interpreting provides the opportunity for interpreters to use their knowledge of both Deaf and hearing
cultures to address power imbalance, and provide the opportunity for
meaningful interaction (Page, 1993). The interpreter can be regarded as
an 'ally' of the Deaf community (McIntire & Sanderson, 1993), who takes
on the role of linguistic and cultural mediator to empower Deaf people
to gain equal access to information.

Taking Cokely's (1992a) model one step further, Stewart, et al (1998)
suggested an interactive model of interpreting, which gives consideration to extralinguistic, as well as sociolinguistic and sociocultural
factors that can effect the interpreting process. The components that
effect the interpreting process are grouped into categories: Participants,
Message, and Environment. The category of 'participants' refers to the
initiator of any interaction (also known as the source language presenter); the receiver of the message (also known as the target language
group/individual); and the interpreter, who processes the message. The
'message' category refers to the information being expressed by the
primary participants. The 'environment' category incorporates "the
physical and psychological context in which an interpreted discourse
occurs... [which subsumes] the social context of an interpreted discourse..." (Stewart, et al, 1998, p.34). The success of the model is dependent on the interactions that take place between each category which
implies the 'multiple nesting of stages' as suggested by Cokely (1992a).

This model incorporates all sociolinguistic factors as outlined by
Cokely (1992a), but also explicitly considers the nature of communica-

22 tive interaction. The interpreting process is defined, not just as a process of translating information between languages, but also between cultures and communities. The central focus is the fact that all language exchange takes place within an interaction, and that in order to effectively interpret between languages and cultures, the interpreter has to be considered as part of the interaction. As opposed to preceding models, the interactive model acknowledges that an interpreter brings something to any interaction, and can personally contribute to effective understanding between interlocutors using different languages, by conveying the meaning of a message so that it is culturally appropriate.

Other writers, such as Metzger (1995, 1999), Roy (1989a, 1992, 1996, 2000a), and Wadensjö (1998), have also maintained that an interactive approach is the only feasible way to adequately describe the interpreting process. An interactive model of interpreting, therefore, should be considered as the ideal framework for interpreting. By looking at the interpreting process from an interactional perspective, it is possible to determine the extent of, and reasons for, linguistically and culturally effective interpretations. Nonetheless, an interactive model can only be applied successfully when interpreters adopt a sociolinguistic and sociocultural approach to their work, and concede that every individual interpretation will vary according to the context of situation.

1.1.1 Interpretation: A sociolinguistic/sociocultural approach

…texts often depend on prior textual experiences in order to evoke significant meanings (intertextuality). When recipients of the discourse have not had experience with language and thus, the relevant prior texts, it becomes the responsibility of the translator to provide a translation that allows the recipients to infer the ideological stances intended in the source (Metzger, 1995, p.28).

In order for the interpreter to be able to provide discourse participants with a sociocultural framework in which to make inferences about 'ideological stances', it is necessary for the interpreter to be bilingual and bicultural. Being bicultural and bilingual is not enough, however, as interpreters need to have the tools to determine what something means to their target audience, and the best way for a message to be interpreted

in a meaningful way, in order for it to make sense with regards to the
audience's cultural norms and values. Therefore, not only do interpreters
need to understand sociolinguistic and sociocultural contexts of their
audiences' world view, but they also need to utilise appropriate interpretation methods to ensure that they have the facility to convey the
meaning of a message within a sociocultural framework.

According to the kind of experiences people have had throughout
their life, and the culture to which they feel they belong, they will
develop a set of assumptions about the world and the people with
whom they interact. *Frame theory* is one explanation for how people
categorise their knowledge based on their experiences with similar
situations, and thus may use lexical, grammatical and experiential
knowledge, consciously or unconsciously, to make judgments about a
discourse situation and its' participants. Several writers, including
Goffman (1974), Gumperz (1982), Hatim and Mason (1990), Metzger
(1995, 1999), Roy (2000d), Schiffrin (1993), Tannen (1979, 1993), and
Wilcox and Wilcox (1985), have referred to 'frame' or 'schema' theory in
relation to discourse. Schema theory is defined by Wilcox and Wilcox
(1985) as 'a theory about knowledge', which offers an explanation of
how comprehension takes place, and how it is influenced by prior
knowledge and contextual influences. Schema or 'frame' theory claims
that the meaning of a message is not decoded, as described in cognitive
models of language, but rather it is constructed.

Essentially, frame theory describes 'frames' of concepts, which
people use to 'hang' information on, and it is upon these frames that
people base their assumptions about objects, people and places. The
'frames' are constructed of different values, which will vary from person
to person depending on their life experience. When put together, the
values give rise to a concept. In the same way that individuals make
assumptions about people, objects and places, they do the same for
'unwritten' rules of behaviour in the form of 'scripts'. Schank and
Abelson (1977) defined scripts as a "standard event sequence" (p. 38),
whereas Hatim and Mason (1990) referred to scripts as "stabilised plans
with pre-established routines" (p.160). These 'scripts' are used to guide a
person through particular forms of social intercourse according to
certain expectations of behaviour within any particular environment,

24 which again, will depend on the types of social interactions that one has been exposed to while growing up.

New information is given based on an assumption of what is already known, and bridging inferences are made between frames and scripts to make further assumptions about information that is being received. Interpreters, therefore, when entering an interpreting assignment will come with their own frames and scripts about the people, the topic, and the event. All other participants, whether Deaf or hearing, will also have their own assumptions that may influence the interaction. As a consequence, the assumptions held by the interpreter will inevitably have some kind of influence over the interpretation itself, meaning that when considering models of the interpreting process, this must be a central factor.

As cited earlier, the interactive model, by adopting a sociolinguistic approach, has the capacity to incorporate the 'interpreter as participant' into the interpretation process, and therefore acknowledge that the interpreter, as well as primary interlocutors, will have an influence on any interaction that takes place. By using their contextual knowledge of both communities, their languages and cultures, and subsequently making assumptions and judgments about what their audiences mutually understand, interpreters can ensure they make any interpretation linguistically and culturally effective for all participants. Interpreters will make specific language choices according to their frames of reference, what certain concepts mean to them, and inferences they make about what concepts will mean to their source and target language audiences from a cultural perspective (Napier, 1998b, 1998c, 2000, 2001). Interpreters will therefore construct the meaning of a message according to the perspective of the listener/ receiver (Frishberg, 2000).

In order for interpreters to ensure that their audiences are making the same inferences about the message they are receiving, they need to search for linguistic and cultural equivalents. It is not sufficient to search for directly translatable words in each language, as sociocultural contexts may alter the way certain expressions are understood. Hatim and Mason (1990) stated that the interpretation process is "an evolving entity, a process whereby producers and receivers cooperate and communicate by making assumptions about a shared cognitive environ-

ment" (p.100). To best deal with the sociolinguistic and sociocultural
contexts of interpreting, interpreters therefore need to recognise their
linguistic abilities and cultural knowledge, and the fact that their
interpretations can be enhanced by using their knowledge. In this way,
interpreters can be seen to positively contribute to any communicative
interaction. It is posited here that the most appropriate and dynamic
interpretation method to utilise, in order to apply the fundamentals of
frame theory and perform effectively as a linguistic and cultural
mediator, is that of *free interpretation.*

1.1.2 Interpreting techniques

The principle of free interpretation centres on the concept of the
interpreter being more than just a conduit. It is not enough for an
interpreter to be extremely fluent in both languages; she must have a
deep understanding of the potentially opposing cultural norms and
values, and should make judgments about her interpretation accordingly. Although linguists would assume that fluency implies cultural
awareness, the application of this concept to interpreting is compara-
tively a recent phenomenon. Much of interpreting literature states that
an interpreter must use not only her cultural knowledge and understanding of the participants involved, but needs to use her metalinguistic awareness to judge the effectiveness of any interpretation.

According to McKee (1996) one of the biggest difficulties faced by
interpreters of any language, is the fact that interaction participants
who do not share the same language, may also not share any experiences, knowledge or familiarity with a particular situation. She stated
that interpreters will often accompany individuals into situations where
they are acquiring new information which is not culturally relevant, or
will be working in situations where participants know nothing about
each other's community, its language or cultural values. Therefore, "we
may feel that in our interpretation we have not made something clear,
but more often than not, the participants simply don't share the same
set of knowledge or assumptions, or ways of going about things"
(McKee, 1996 p.22).

Thus it can be argued that the interpreter has to be prepared for the
different assumptions held by the different cultures. Every interpreter

26   will take one piece of information and will interpret it differently, according to what that piece of information means to them; but what they also have to consider is what it will mean to the participants using the target language once the message has been translated.

In relation to free interpretation, the key is in the assumptions brought to, and the inferences made during, any interpreting assignment. In order to make assumptions about the target audience, the interpreter needs to be bicultural as well as bilingual. Familiarity with the community and its culture will expose the interpreter to knowledge such as the standard of education that people have received, the kind of information that community members will have been exposed to, and the nature of language use alongside cultural norms and values. By making assumptions about members of the audience, the interpreter can make considered choices throughout the translation, by making inferences about their cultural and linguistic understanding of the topic being discussed, and transpose cultural meaning appropriately (Hatim and Mason, 1990). Tajfel (1969) described how "enculturation acts as a reference point against which all else is measured and interpreted", therefore interpreters need to be aware of differing cultural perspectives and how cues may be acted upon or ignored (cited in Cavell & Wells, 1986, p.99). Too often interpreters focus too closely on a syntactical, lexical interpretation, relying on the form of the language. The ability to paraphrase the meaning of an utterance, and therefore impart cultural significance, can be more important than the ability to translate 'word-for-word' by concentrating on the form of the message. Free interpretation, therefore, can be regarded as a method of interpretation whereby "the linguistic structure of the source language is ignored, and an equivalent is found based on the meaning it conveys" (Crystal, 1987 p.344); as opposed to a *literal interpretation*, which means that "the linguistic structure of the source text is followed, but is normalised according to the rules of the target language" (Crystal, 1987, p. 344). For example, if interpreting from English into Auslan, the literal delivery of Auslan would incorporate English word order or lip-patterns while also using Auslan features. Much of sign language interpreting literature refers to literal interpretation as *transliteration* (Cerney, 2000).

The crux of any interpretation is to get the message right, and to

ensure that the target audience is receiving the same message as those
listening to, or watching, the source language presenter. Thus interpretation has to be more than mere word-for-word translation from one
language to another. The search should be for equivalent meaning,
rather than equivalent lexical items (Seleskovitch, 1978). The word
equivalence is central to the concept of free interpretation. During any
assignment, an interpreter will bring her own frames about the situation; she will have her own assumed knowledge about participants
involved, and will make inferences according to those assumptions. By
being both bilingual and bicultural, the interpreter should be able to
find equivalents between two languages, by understanding, and making
inferences about, what something means to a particular audience.
Hatim and Mason (1990) reinforced this point by stating that every
lexical item has several equivalents in another language, depending on
the *denotative meaning* (primary lexical meaning) and *connotative meaning*
(additional meaning beyond the primary meaning) that is imparted in
different contexts. Baker (1992) stated that it is not, therefore, just a
matter of knowing substitutable lexical equivalents in two languages,
but rather interpreters must be able to find terms "which will express
'the same thing' regardless of the words used in the original statement"
(p.87), that is, the 'sense' of any message (Seleskovitch, 1992).

On this premise, everything that is said in one language can be
expressed in another, provided that the two languages belong to
societies which have attained comparable levels of development.
Seleskovitch (1978) postulated that the only reason particular words are
deemed untranslatable is because different languages express concepts
in different ways, whereby exact lexical equivalents will not necessarily
exist. Different communities will, however, have similar frames of
reference, therefore "words, i.e., the concepts they represent are
'untranslatable' only when their referent does not yet exist in the society
using the target language" (p.88).

Seleskovitch (1978) noted therefore, that a necessary part of the
translation process might involve introducing a new concept into an
existing cultural framework, before formalising it in the target language
by giving it a name. Subsequently, during any assignment, an interpreter will use her language skills and cultural knowledge to make

28   decisions about whether a concept is new to the audience, and will therefore express the idea accordingly. The search for linguistic and cultural equivalence is fundamental to any interpreting process, in ensuring that all participants in any interaction all leave having received the same message. This equivalence presents a challenge when certain words or concepts may hold positive connotations for one audience, yet negative associations for another (Frishberg, 1990; Lane, Hoffmeister & Bahan, 1996), meaning that interpreters have to consider the 'culturally rich realities' of the interaction participants (Cokely, 2001).

The connotations of any concept must be reflected in the language choices that are made; it is not enough to interpret sign-for-word, or word-for-sign, without paying heed to the cultural values which are inherently embedded in certain signs or words. A skilled interpreter, adopting the role of linguistic and cultural mediator within an interactive model, should use free interpretation as a matter of course, as she should regard this as the only feasible way of translating between two languages and cultures. In recognising the influence of additional sociolinguistic factors, Crystal (1987) stated that in addition to being bilingual and bicultural, interpreters need a thorough understanding of the discourse being used in the interpreting context, and thus any social, cultural, or emotional connotations which may influence the intended effect of the message.

The concept of free interpretation is often alluded to in different writings, but has only been discussed specifically by Metzger (1999) and Napier (1998c, 2000, 2001), who defined the free interpretation as "the process by which concepts and meanings are translated from one language into another, by incorporating cultural norms and values; assumed knowledge about these values; and the search for linguistic and cultural equivalents" (Napier, 2001 p.31).

One other issue to recognise, however, is the appropriateness of using a more literal interpreting technique as a translation style in particular discourse environments, due to the formality of the environment and the needs of the target audience. This issue will be explored further in section 2.2.2.

1.2 Sign language interpreters and spoken language interpreters: A comparison

Discussion thus far has highlighted that interpreters work with people who cannot, or choose not to, use the same language. It has also been suggested that interpreters work as mediators between individuals who have different cultural experiences. Many interpreters will work with linguistic minority groups, and therefore will be working with communities who are not of equal status in society (Gentile, Ozolins & Vasilakakos, 1996). Interestingly, Gentile et al observe that "the interpreter is likely to belong to the same ethnic group as the client speaking the 'lower status' language", and that "these dynamics impinge directly on the interpreter" (p.21).

Although the essential processes of interpretation are the same, regardless of the languages used (Roberts, 1987), and sign language interpreters similarly work between communities of incomparable status; there are many issues that confront sign language interpreters, which are different to those faced by spoken language interpreters. For instance, if considering Deaf people as members of an ethnic group, it is impossible for sign language interpreters to truly belong to the same group by virtue of the fact that they can hear. This situation means that sign language interpreters are confronted with various linguistic issues in terms of their use of sign language, in relation to their membership of the Deaf community, and their bilingual status.

1.2.1 The Deaf community and its language use

Many writers (such as Brennan, 1992; Higgins, 1980; Ladd, 2002; Lane, Hoffmeister & Bahan, 1996) have discussed the concept of the Deaf community, and have defined Deaf people as a linguistic and cultural minority group who identify with one another based on shared language, identity, social and educational experiences.

Baker and Cokely (1980) defined four 'avenues' of membership to the Deaf community: audiological, political, linguistic and social. People satisfying all four avenues would be considered as 'core' members of the community, whereas other people may be considered as 'peripheral' members. For example, Padden (1980) stated that the inability to hear is

30 not a requisite of being a member of the Deaf community: "A deaf community may include persons who are not themselves Deaf, but who actively support the goals of the community and work with people to achieve them" (p. 41). Therefore, this definition can include interpreters and non-deaf family members, but only as peripheral members of the community. Thus, although people who can hear may be accepted by the community, they will never be considered as true members of the 'ethnic group'.

The Deaf community is often considered to be a disenfranchised group in society that has experienced oppression at the hands of the non-deaf majority. Several writers (such as Baker-Shenk, 1986; Lane, 1993) refer to Deaf people as an 'oppressed group' whose lives have historically been dictated and controlled by 'hearing' people. Deaf people have experienced the denigration of their language and cultural values, and have been stigmatised as being 'abnormal' (Higgins, 1980). Being members of a stigmatised group has had obvious implications on the social and cultural identity of Deaf people—they have been denied the right to use their language and have had their culture, traditions and beliefs devalued in a power struggle with the dominant members of society, that is, those that can hear (Humphrey & Alcorn, 1996).

According to Rawlings and Jensema (1977), only five to ten percent of children in deaf schools have Deaf parents (cited in Meadow-Orlans, 1990). For the majority of Deaf people, therefore, their first opportunity to identify themselves with other Deaf people, and develop a personal notion of deafness as a social identity, is when they enter the education system. Lane (1993) cited residential schools as being one of the most salient of Deaf cultural values.

Paradoxically, the education system seems to have been one of the most oppressive institutions in the experience of Deaf people. As a result of the 1880 congress for teachers of the deaf in Milan, the use of sign language was banned in schools, and the vast majority of Deaf children received their education through an 'oral' approach, where they were encouraged to use whatever residual hearing they had, lipread and develop their speech skills, rather than use sign language (Erting, 1994; Lane, Hoffmeister & Bahan, 1996). Thus Deaf cultural values continued to develop almost in spite of the education system, as

Deaf people relied on the residential schools to bring them together at
an early age and give them a sense of shared experience.

Over the years the education system has changed, with many
residential schools being closed down and Deaf children being placed
either in units within local schools, or fully integrated into schools with
non-deaf children. Thus due to the diverse educational experiences of
Deaf people, and the language or mode of their education, their use of
sign language may vary (Kannapell, 1989). Other factors that can
influence a Deaf person's sign language proficiency include whether they
used sign language in the home as children (regardless of whether their
parents were Deaf or hearing), whether they have a Deaf signing partner,
and whether they work in a Deaf or 'hearing' environment. Although a
person may use some form of signed communication, he or she may not
necessarily be a fluent user of a naturally occurring sign language.

Humphrey and Alcorn (1996), among others, have described a 'sign
communication spectrum' that may be encountered when interacting
with members of the Deaf community. The continuum includes manual
communication forms such as Signed English [3], contact varieties of
signed and spoken languages, and natural sign languages.

With the more recent introduction of bilingual education programs
for Deaf children, however, Deaf people may be just as comfortable
using a written form of spoken language, as they are with a manual
form of sign language. Even for those Deaf individuals whose first or
preferred language is a naturally occurring sign language, the sign
system that they choose to use or receive may vary according to the
context of the situation they are in.

Aside from implications of language use for interpreters, in that they
have to consider the background and educational experiences of each
Deaf client they meet, and the communication method they may prefer,
there is one other factor to consider. As a consequence of being
oppressed by the dominant members of society who can hear, there are
obvious ramifications for the working relationship between Deaf
people and sign language interpreters, as interpreters are members of
the majority group.

Although Padden (1980) has delineated how non-deaf people may
be members of the Deaf community, it seems that there are boundaries

32   to how far Deaf people will welcome hearing people into the fold. In order for interpreters to adequately enculturate themselves, and become proficiently bilingual, it is necessary for them to be accepted into the Deaf community.

Traditionally, hearing people have taken on paternalistic roles within the Deaf community. Corfmat (1990) and Scott Gibson (1992), among others, have described how interpreting for Deaf people was once considered an inherent part of the role of welfare workers for the Deaf, and how the majority of the time it was relatives of Deaf individuals who would fulfil these roles. Regardless of being able to hear, these people would have almost automatic entry to membership of the Deaf community, would be native or near-native in their sign language fluency, and therefore could be considered as bilingual.

The role of sign language interpreters was professionalised in an attempt "to liberate Deaf people from the yoke of paternalism and care" (Pollitt, 1997, p.21). Along with more research into the linguistic status of sign languages, more hearing people have become involved with the Deaf community through their interest in the language, rather than a sense of duty to 'help'. The process of professionalisation seemed to meet the demands of the Deaf community, yet Scott Gibson (1994) described 'the cult of professional expertise' as one of the most fundamental difficulties experienced by sign language interpreters, due to the divergent needs of interpreters and the Deaf community. Phillip (1994) discussed a lack of reciprocation from hearing interpreters for Deaf people allowing them to become members of the community. Due to improved societal attitudes towards sign languages (Burns, Matthews, & Nolan-Conroy, 2001), there has been a surge of interest in learning a sign language as a second language (some would even argue that it is 'trendy'), meaning there are far more hearing people choosing to train as sign language interpreters.

In highlighting the issues of sign language interpreting, language use and the education of Deaf people, Corker (1997) expressed anxiety at the power struggle enforced on Deaf people and interpreters by the fact that interpreters are often better educated about the Deaf community, its language and culture, and are often more proficient in sign language than a lot of Deaf people themselves. As a consequence of this di-

chotomy, Corker stated that interpreters are often "more sophisticated
in their ability to manufacture discourses using the rules of the dominant culture" (p.19).

Much of the literature that discusses the nature of the relationship
between Deaf people and hearing interpreters implies a fractious
interdependence (Napier, 2001). Interpreters rely on the trust and
generosity of Deaf people to let them into the community in order that
they can become bilingual and bicultural, and Deaf individuals rely on
interpreters to be bilingual and bicultural in order to mediate between
themselves and the wider majority. The literature indicates that Deaf
people do not want to be 'helped' by hearing individuals, yet they are
wary of anyone who has a genuine interest in working with the Deaf
community, if they have not grown up in that community themselves.
Pollitt (1997) attributed the current state of mistrust to the fact that
interpreters have adopted the professional values of the non-deaf
majority, and as a consequence have been "seen to eschew the precious
cultural values of the Deaf community, who in their own terms were not
clients, but teachers, mentors, family members and friends" (pp.21-22).

Interestingly, the professional values on which sign language
interpreters chose to model their own, were those of spoken language
interpreters (Pollitt, 1997). This seems like common sense as ultimately
interpreters perform the same function regardless of their working
languages. Yet it can be seen from the descriptions the Deaf community, its language, culture, and status in society, that the role of the sign
language interpreter is multi-faceted. Although the essential process of
interpretation is the same, regardless of the languages used, signed and
spoken language interpreting does not necessarily precipitate the same
working conditions, roles and boundaries (Swabey, 1992). It can be
argued that many of the required traits are similar, yet some issues for
sign language interpreters are unique.

1.2.2 Bilingual and bimodal interpreting

Some of the issues that sign language interpreters face in working with
the Deaf community have already been reflected upon, such as the
sceptical views of Deaf people as to what hearing individuals can offer
them, and the diverse forms of communication used in the Deaf

34   community. The issue of language variation has implications for the training of interpreters, as the only way that they can become native-like in their use of sign language is to enculturate themselves. Unfortunately, sign language interpreters cannot follow the path of spoken language interpreters and go and live in the country from which their second language is derived, as there is no "Deafland" that they can travel to and immerse themselves in. Their enculturation depends upon their ability to interact with members of the Deaf community, which has inherent difficulties as already outlined.

It was mentioned earlier that spoken language interpreters often come from the ethnic group for whom they are interpreting. This is obviously not the case for sign language interpreters, which has wider implications for their language use, and highlights yet another issue that differs from spoken language interpreters.

It is the general practice of spoken language interpreters that they will work into their 'mother tongue' or 'A' language (Baker, 1992; Bowen, 1980), that is, from their second into their first, native language. This pattern follows the assumption that people will always use their first language more competently, coherently and accurately. For sign language interpreters, however, this is often not the case (Frishberg, 1990). Unless an interpreter has been exposed to sign language from a very young age through parents or siblings, it is unlikely that she will acquire a sign language as her first language. Yet sign language interpreters are more likely to work consistently from, for example, English into Auslan or BSL, meaning that they are invariably working from their 'A' language into their 'B' language. Due to the power imbalance between Deaf and hearing people, interpreters are usually present at communication events where Deaf people are relying on non-deaf individuals for information, which means that the interpreting process often conveys messages one way.

Another language issue that effects the working practices of sign language interpreters is that of modality. Spoken language interpreters work between two linear languages, whereby one word is produced after another, and the message is built up sequentially. Sign languages, however, are visual-spatial languages that can convey meaning by creating a picture using space, location, referents and other descriptive

elements. Therefore sign language interpreters are constantly transferring information between two alternate modalities, which requires the
representation of information in very different ways. This process is
commonly referred to as *bimodal interpreting*.

It has already been noted that interpreters work at the interface of
bilingual, bicultural interaction, yet consideration needs to be given to
the bimodality of sign language interpreting and the impact this can
have on communicative interactions between Deaf and hearing
individuals. Brennan and Brown (1997) devoted much discussion to
interactional effects of bimodal interpreting in courtroom settings, but
the issues are pertinent to all situations where sign language interpreters
work. They suggested that the realities of bimodal interpreting "inevitably change the dynamics of live interactions" (p.125), due to the visual
nature of sign languages. Brennan and Brown listed certain elements for
consideration. First, the issue of eye contact was highlighted. In order to
receive the message, Deaf individuals need to maintain eye contact with
the interpreter, whereas in the norms of hearing interaction, participants engaging in the interaction would maintain eye contact with each
other. Therefore Deaf participants may miss out on visual cues given by
their hearing counterparts. Similarly, hearing individuals may focus
their attention on the interpreter, as this is where the 'voice' is coming
from, and miss out on visual-gestural cues given by the Deaf person.
Second, the vulnerability of sign language interpreters was raised in that
they are always visible to all participants in any situation, and therefore
may attract a great deal of attention (also commented on by Siple, 1993).
Third, Brennan and Brown (1997) stated that Deaf and hearing people
use gesture in very different ways, it would be easy for someone to
misconstrue the meanings and intentions of another person by referring to their own frames of reference for how gesture should be used.
Certain facial expressions that are intrinsic to the grammatical use of
sign languages may be misinterpreted by hearing people. When
receiving information, for example, Deaf people often nod their head to
indicate that they are understanding the signs they see, in the same way
that non-deaf English-speaking people might use "mmm, hmm" or "uh-
huh" to affirm they understand what they are hearing. The head nod,
however, may be misconstrued, as typically a head nod is a gesture for

36   agreement in wider Western society. Although a Deaf person might be nodding, it does not necessarily mean that he or she agrees with the information being received.

As sign languages express information in a visual-spatial dimension, Brennan and Brown (1997) postulated that they encode visual information as a matter of course, as the 'real-world' visual information pervades the grammatical features of the language. This element of sign language use therefore places certain demands on sign language interpreters, which may not be appreciated by spoken language interpreters. When hearing certain abstract concepts or generic descriptions, it is necessary for sign language interpreters to receive detailed visual information, which needs to be implicitly encoded visually into any interpretation. Brennan and Brown cited an example in BSL of the sentence 'X broke the window', indicating that the interpreter ideally needs to know what type of window it is, and how it was broken, in order to be able to accurately represent the window and how it was broken visually. Similarly if someone is 'murdered', is it done with a knife, gun, by strangulation or suffocation. All of these concepts require visual representation in sign language in order to make sense to the Deaf receiver.

Thus when interpreting for Deaf clients, sign language interpreters face the challenge of constantly having to visualise what they hear in a linear form, or create sequential meaning from a visual picture. This factor adds an extra dimension to the interpreting process, as the interpreters have to transfer meaning not only between two languages and cultures, but also between opposing modalities of language production.

The use of language also impacts on signed and spoken language interpreters differently in another way. In the long term, the demand for sign language interpreters will never cease. In comparison with spoken language interpreters, whose clients have the option to learn the majority language and therefore desist with their use of interpreters, the clients of sign language interpreters do not have that option. Deaf people will always be unable to hear, and subsequently will always rely on interpreters for access to information (Ozolins & Bridge, 1999). As Davis (1989, 1990a, 1990b) pointed out, Deaf people use interpreters

because they cannot hear, not necessarily because they cannot understand or use the source language.

Thus far, interpreting in the context of the Deaf community has
been discussed in order to give a clearer picture of the particular issues
faced by sign language interpreters. By identifying general sociolinguistic and sociocultural issues in working with this consumer group it is
possible to focus on the specific context of this study. When considering issues faced by sign language interpreters in their everyday work in
relation to managing communication, other issues can be highlighted
in relation to interpreting for university lectures. The skills employed by
interpreters have to be adapted to allow for conditions specific to the
university discourse environment. Interpreting, therefore, can be
considered as a *discourse process* (Roy, 2000a).

1.3 Discourse environment: Factors to consider

In order to adequately conduct any research on interpreting, it is
necessary to recognise and establish the sociolinguistic and sociocultural contexts of any situation, which may influence the language that is
used. Language variation obviously has an impact on interpreting as a
discourse process, as interpreters will need to adapt to the source
language they are receiving, as well as modulate their target language
production accordingly.

1.3.1 *The context of situation*

The functional grammar approach to linguistics focuses on the
purpose and use of language, and examines spoken and written
languages within the contexts of their usage. The relationship between
words used and meanings derived are not regarded as arbitrary. Rather,
language is determined as being functional, whereby meaning is created
through the choice of words and the syntactic structure through which
the words are produced (Gerot & Wignell, 1995).

Thus, the study of language from a functional perspective, and
therefore the study of interpretation of language, cannot be separated
from the situations where language use takes place (Hatim and Mason,
1990). Halliday and Hasan (1985) described context and text of language
(whether written, spoken or signed) as being aspects of the same process,

whereby the context acts as a "bridge between the text and the situation in which texts actually occur" (p.5). Many writers have discussed the relationship between language, communicative interaction and context (such as Brown & Fraser, 1979; Crystal, 1984; Halliday, 1978, 1993; Hymes, 1967, 1972; Ryan & Giles, 1982; and Sinclair & Coulthard, 1975), propounding the notion that all languages function within contexts of situations, and therefore are relatable to those contexts. With this in mind, Halliday (1978) stated that the purpose of defining the context is not to question idiosyncratic use of vocabulary, grammar or pronunciation; but rather to identify "*which* kinds of situational factor determine which kinds of selection in the linguistic system" (p.32).

Crystal and Davey (1969), Halliday (1978), and Hymes (1967) have proposed sets of concepts for describing the context of a situation. Hymes (1967) outlined factors for consideration when analysing language in context of situation: the form and content of the message; the setting; the participants; the intent and effect of the communication; the key points; the medium and genre; and the norms of interaction within that particular setting.

In further extending these factors, Halliday (1978) summarised general concepts for describing how linguistic features of communication may be effected by the context of a situation, under three headings: 'field of discourse', 'tenor of discourse' and 'mode of discourse'. The 'field' refers to the institutional setting where language use occurs, the subject matter, the participatory activity as a whole and the degree of emphasis placed on the language itself. The 'tenor' defines the relationship and interpersonal dynamics between participants; whereas the 'mode' describes the channel of communication adopted (i.e., spoken, written, signed), the 'speech' genre, and the spontaneity of the utterance. He stated that the impact of context of situation on language leads to a systematic relationship emerging between language and environment, with linguistic features being assigned to different components of the semantic system—features from the 'field' being assigned to the ideational component, the 'tenor' to the interpersonal component, and the 'mode' features to the textual component.

Crystal and Davey (1969) also suggested that contextual factors influence language use by describing three categories of linguistic features. These include 'province', 'status' and 'modality'. The first category focuses on the utterance that takes place and the extralinguistic factors which influence its use; the second category refers to the participants of an interaction and their social standing; and the third category considers the purpose of the utterance. According to Crystal and Davey, these linguistic features combine to cause speakers to follow expected conventions for particular types of discourse setting.

All of the conceptual breakdowns discussed thus far serve to illustrate the point that consideration of context of situation is paramount in describing language use. If the context of situation influences language use, and the linguistic choices that interlocutors make, the same context will inevitably influence the linguistic choices made by interpreters. According to Cokely (1992a), interpreters are engaged in a process of constantly assessing the components influencing the interaction participants and the source language they produce, in order to accurately account for these components within the target language production. He stated that by examining the components effecting communicative behaviour, it is possible for interpreters to "identify components that pertain to the context within which the interaction occurs and components that pertain to the nature of the communicative message itself" (p.19).

Drawing on the work of Halliday (1978) and Hymes (1972), and writing specifically on interpretation, Cokely (1992a) identified components that effect communicative behaviour as 'interaction factors' and 'message factors'. The interaction factors which may influence the context of situation, and therefore the work of interpreters, were defined within a taxonomy devised to include: setting, purpose and participants. The setting takes into account a range of environmental or extralinguistic factors which may influence interactive outcomes; whereas the purpose considers the activities, participant goals and subject matter which occur within an interaction. The 'activity' component accounts for the range of purposes that participants might be involved in an activity. The 'participant' component refers to characteristics of individuals, or characteristics of actual or perceived relationships between individuals, which may effect the communicative

40   interaction. In referring to the work of Hymes (1972), Cokely also highlighted the importance for interpreters to recognise how 'message factors' may effect an interaction. The message form and content is obviously a crucial component to consider, along with the message key, its channel and language form; the interaction norms and interpretation norms, and the discourse genre.

It can be seen, therefore, that by defining the nature of a communicative interaction, and establishing the context of situation, it is possible to predict what should be expected of interpreters when placed in those situations. In discussing the context of situation, it has been acknowledged that language use varies according to what situation a person is in, and the context of any interactional involvement they have. The language variation which arises as a consequence of contextual and situational diversity is the biggest consideration for working interpreters, as they must be prepared to adapt their language use accordingly.

1.3.2 *Situational language variation*

Situational variables are observable where the same person speaks differently in different environments. Studying language from this angle often means thinking about the role or function which language is playing in a situation. This in turn means that you can gauge the status and mutual familiarity of speakers, and their reason for needing to communicate, from the style or register which they use... (Wray, Trott & Bloomer, 1998, p.93).

In discussing language variety and situations of use, Finegan, Besnier, Blair and Collins (1992) used the term "linguistic repertoire" to describe language varieties exhibited in the speaking and writing patterns of a speech community. Others refer to "diatypic variation" when classifying language according to its use in social situations (Wray, et al, 1998).

According to Zimmer (1989), register or style variation involves differential language use that is sensitive to situational factors. Wardhaugh (1992) and Fromkin, et al (1990), however, made a clear distinction between 'style' and 'register'. Wardhaugh (1992) described styles as different ways of speaking either formally or informally, depending on the circumstances. He defined register, however, as "sets

of vocabulary items associated with discrete occupational or social
groups" (p.49). Styles are described by Fromkin, et al (1990) as 'situation
dialects', which range between two extremes of informal and formal
language use, and are influenced by the speaker's attitude towards the
receiver, the subject matter or the purpose of the communication.
Register is defined as language variety that is determined entirely by
subject matter. Fromkin, et al asserted that style or register variation
does not only include changes in vocabulary, but also an adaptation of
grammatical rules. For example, "in an informal style, the rules of
contraction are used more often, the syntactic rules of negation and
agreement may be altered, and many words are used that do not occur
in the formal style" (p.266). Different subject matters such as legal prose
or cooking recipes are given as examples of different register variation,
with the former using longer sentences, more archaic words, longer
adverbial elements and explicit repetition; whereas the latter uses short
simple sentences, verbs in the imperative mood, and prepositional
phrases. In summarising their concept of the linguistic repertoire of a
monolingual community, Finegan, et al (1992) stated that language
register is determined by a set of linguistic features, combined with
characteristic patterns of how the language is used in different situations, yet with all varieties of the language relying on essentially the
same grammatical system. In addition, they asserted that rules govern-
ing register variations accompany non-linguistic behaviour such as
standing, sitting, physical proximity and face-to-face positioning.

Many of these various definitions have developed as a consequence
of an established model of register devised by Joos (1967), which
postulated five different styles of communication, ranging through
different levels of formality. Halliday (1978) has criticised this particular
model by questioning the notion of 'formality' and what it means. It
should be acknowledged that by concentrating on finite styles, this type
of model can be limiting, because language is a living entity and is
therefore difficult to compartmentalise. Nonetheless, for the purpose of
analysing language production and the impact that this can have on
interpreters, it is worth exploring the definitions put forward by Joos
(1967), as they provide categories which can be generalised for discussion of language and interpretation.

42   Joos (1967) proposed five distinct registers or styles of language use: frozen, formal, consultative, informal and intimate. Each register has specific characteristics and unwritten rules that determine interactional norms, syntactical and sentence complexity, lexical choices, 'volume' of speech production, rate of speech production and appropriate subject matter for discussion. The characteristics of each register are now briefly introduced.

The frozen register incorporates texts which are the same each time they are used, and are usually ritualistic in their use. For example, recitation of the Lord's Prayer, or singing of the national anthem. In these instances, the meaning and intent is derived more from the purpose of use of the frozen text, rather than what the text itself actually says. That is, the ritual of people coming together in church to recite the Lord's Prayer would give more meaning than listening to the words of the prayer itself.

The formal register refers to situations where invariably there is one dominant speaker and a group of listeners, with virtually no turn-taking between the speaker and audience. Examples of situations where formal register is used would include a key-note address at a conference, a university lecture, or a presidential address. These types of settings are often distinguishable by physical and psychological separation between speaker and audience, whereby physical positioning and lighting psychologically emphasise the boundaries between speaker and audience. Certain characteristics of language use in a formal register would include: no turn-taking; less colloquialisms in lexical choices; more convoluted and complex sentence structure; slower and more deliberate rate of speech production; and amplified volume of speech production.

Consultative register is used during interactions when one interlocutor has 'expert' knowledge, and their advice or guidance is being sought. The difference between this and formal register is that interaction occurs between speaker and audience to ensure that communication is happening. Common examples include meetings between teacher and student, doctor and patient, or lawyer and client. There are certain unwritten rules for turn-taking and interaction which are expected to be adhered to, such as, a student raising his or her hand in the classroom before addressing the teacher, or a patient not interrupting when a

doctor is giving a diagnosis. Language characteristics include the use of   43
complete, compound sentence structures, and specialised or technical
vocabulary pertinent to the subject matter being discussed. Individuals
will change their role according to the knowledge being sought, and
their ability to provide that knowledge. Humphrey and Alcorn (1996)
give an example of an interaction between a lawyer and a plumber.
Depending on whether it is legal advice or a quote for plumbing that is
required, this will dictate whether it is the lawyer or the plumber who
takes on the role of 'expert' in that particular interaction.

The use of informal register tends to imply the equal status of the
interaction participants. Turn-taking is more fluid, and acceptable levels
of interruptions are allowed. Sentences tend to be shorter, which
therefore leads to a faster rate of delivery. Use of colloquialisms, slang
and less punctilious use of grammar are often observed in informal
discourse. Common examples of this register of language use, would be
interactions between neighbours, students, or work colleagues.

Intimate register is used by individuals when interacting with others
with whom they share one or more common experiences. Due to
assumed knowledge, the communication dynamics change in that
information does not necessarily need to be clearly presented. This
register would most often be used between friends, parents and children,
siblings, and couples; and is identifiable by rapid turn-taking, the use of
incomplete sentences, and lack of specialised vocabulary or terminology.

Although these registers were presented by Joos (1967) as discrete
entities, observation of language use demonstrates that overlap does
occur. For example, speakers at formal functions may incorporate
consultative or informal register norms into their presentations in order
to create more of a rapport between themselves and their audiences.
Similarly, teachers may use a more formal style and discourage interaction, even when they are in the consultative setting of a classroom
(Humphrey & Alcorn, 1996). Therefore, although it is useful to refer to
the work of Joos (1967) as a basis for describing language, the context of
situation also needs to be taken into account, adopting more descriptive
techniques as suggested by Halliday (1978).

The concept of language registers and styles presents a challenge for
interpreters, in that they need to be familiar with the norms of interac-

44   tion and language use for different situations, and adapt their interpretations accordingly. In searching for linguistic and cultural equivalents,
interpreters need to be aware of appropriateness of language use in
relation to context of situation. For instance, a perfect equivalent may
be found but its use would only be appropriate for informal conversation, and not for a formal lecture presentation.

The concept of register variation or 'diglossia' in signed languages
has been debated, and there is a general agreement within the literature
that it does exist (Davis, 1989; Deuchar, 1979, 1984; Fontana, 1999; Lee,
1982; Llewellyn Jones, Kyle & Woll, 1979; Lucas & Valli, 1989, 1990;
Stokoe, 1969; Woodward, 1973; Zimmer, 1989). There has been some
disagreement, however, about the salient characteristics of a sign
language register. Zimmer (1989) stated that register "is an abstract
notion that is not easily definable, and any given speech event may be
difficult to categorise as a variant" (p.257).

The main issue for sign language researchers has been the 'continuum' of sign language varieties which can exist simultaneously
within one Deaf community, and whether one form of signed communication should be considered as more 'formal' than another. It is
widely accepted that sociolinguistic variation exists in signed languages
across age, social class, gender, ethnic group, religious affiliation,
educational background, and geographical location in the form of
accents and dialects (Lucas, Bayley, Valli, Roser, & Wulf, 2001; Sutton-
Spence & Woll, 1998), but the notion of variation according to language
use within particular situations has given rise to different theories.

Earlier notions of diglossia in signed languages were discussed by
Stokoe (1969) and Deuchar (1979), who distinguished between a 'high'
variety of sign language used at formal functions, and a 'low' variety
used informally. Deuchar stated that the high variety that she observed
in BSL was actually a form of Signed English, with the low variety being
a purer form of BSL with no English interference. This theory does not
deserve much credence, however, due to the perjorative undertones of
superior versus inferior language use, especially as in a later publication,
Deuchar (1984) commented that the Signed English she had previously
observed tended to be the variety of sign language used by hearing
people involved with the Deaf community, rather than that of Deaf

people themselves. More appropriately, Woodward (1973) suggested a 45
diglossic continuum rather than two distinct varieties. Llewellyn Jones,
Kyle and Woll (1979) accepted the notion of two varieties of sign
language (that is, BSL and Signed English), but suggested that Signed
English is not commonly used amongst members of the Deaf community, but rather as a form of communicating with hearing people. Thus
Llewellyn Jones, et al perceived that the British deaf community were
not diglossic in their language use, because those who used the 'high'
variety were marginal to the community or part of its elite, and therefore had privileged access to a more formal variety of language, which
was inaccessible to the majority of the community.

Lawson (1981) stated that Deaf people had not yet become adjusted
to the idea of using BSL as the language of formal meetings, hence the
reliance on Signed English. Llewellyn Jones (1981a) demonstrated,
however, that a formal register exists in BSL by videotaping Deaf sign
language users in different environments, including formal meetings. In
retrospect, it is possible that the use of Signed English observed by
Deuchar (1979, 1984) and Llewellyn Jones (1981a) was in fact a contact
variety of BSL used in formal situations.

Thus it can be seen that it is feasible to consider sign languages as
having their own form of situational language variation. Examples of
situations where more 'formal' registers of signed languages are used,
are academic lectures, business meetings, banquets and church (Baker &
Cokely, 1980; Lee, 1982).

Zimmer (1989) presented findings of a study, which demonstrated
that situational language variance does exist within ASL. Although this
is only one study, and is not necessarily conclusive that all sign languages demonstrate situational variance, it is worth considering as an
overview of the linguistic characteristics of a signed language register.
In Zimmer's study, a Deaf native signer was videotaped in three
different situations: a lecture, an informal talk, and an interview; and his
sign language output was analysed for phonological, lexical, morphological and syntactical differences.

Zimmer (1989) stated that there was a phonological distinction in
the use of space between the three situations. In the lecture, the Deaf
person used a much larger signing space (volume), whereas in the other

46 two he used a more neutral space. Body movements were also more pronounced when lecturing, with more switching of signs between the dominant and non-dominant hand. In the lecture, there was no overt evidence of assimilation of signs (whereby signs assimilate features of other signs immediately preceding or following each other), and no use of anticipation (whereby the base handshape is in place before the dominant handshape begins to make the sign). Also there was infrequent use of perseveration (whereby a non-dominant base handshape stays in place after the dominant hand has moved onto making the next sign).

Lexical and morphological differences noted included the use of particular signs used in the lecture, which were not used in the informal talk or interview; plus colloquial signs were used in direct speech, but not in the body of the lecture. A certain type of morphological inflection was noticeable in the lecture presentation, where Zimmer (1989) suggested the exaggerated movement of a sign was used instead of some non-manual features.

Syntactically, the lecture made extensive use of rhetorical questions, made more use of metaphorical signs and metaphorical description, less topicalisation and more boundary marking with use of the lexical item 'now'. Although this data was only collected from one Deaf signer, it is sufficient to illustrate that sign languages incorporate marked differences in the production of the language, according to the context of situation. Sign language interpreters, therefore, are faced with the same challenge as spoken language interpreters in dealing with the variety of language registers they may come across in different interpreting situations. Zimmer (1989) noted that knowledge of language register variation is critical for interpreters to be able to effectively reproduce an equivalent message, as an interpretation can be accurate content-wise, but lacking if an inappropriate register is used.

From my own observations of Deaf people using Auslan and BSL in different contexts, it would seem that situational variance does occur. As a working interpreter, I have interpreted in a variety of different situations, from meetings, to conferences, to performances, and have noted a difference in sign language output of Deaf participants, according to the formality of the situation. It is my opinion, therefore, that

characteristics of language contact between signed and spoken lan- 47
guages are prevalent in formal discourse environments, such as university lectures. As this comment is not based on any empirical research,
the statement should be regarded merely as an anecdotal observation.

Nonetheless, the issue of language contact has been recognised in the
sign language research field, and merits consideration. Lucas and Valli
(1989) stated that "one of the major sociolinguistic issues in the deaf
community concerns the outcome of language contact" (p.11), in the fact
that a specific kind of signing exists as a result of contact between signed
and spoken languages. The majority of studies of language contact in the
Deaf community have taken place in the USA, however one more recent
study explored the situation in Italy (Fontana, 1999), and observed that
similar phenomena are present in other Deaf communities.

Woodward (1973) claimed that this contact variety is a pidgin, which
results from interaction between Deaf and hearing people. Cokely
(1983b), Lucas and Valli (1989, 1990), and Davis (1989), however, refuted
this claim. Cokely (1983b) referred to criteria normally required as pre-
conditions for the development of a pidgin language (asymmetrical
spread of the dominant language; relatively closed network of interaction; and attitude of a significant number of users that the emerging
variety is a separate entity), to illustrate that language contact between
ASL and English has not necessarily led to the emergence of a pidgin.
Instead, Cokely argued that the dynamics of 'foreigner talk' [4], judgments
of proficiency, and learners' attempts to master the target language
results in a continuum of language varieties within ASL.

Lucas and Valli (1989, 1990) described the characteristics of language
contact between ASL and English as code-switching and code-mixing,
whereby English words are mouthed on the lips or manually coded
(fingerspelled) while the signer is still using linguistic features of ASL.
They also noted that contact signing yields "idiosyncratic syntactic
constructions... that fit neither the ASL nor the English grammatical
system" (p.30).

Lucas and Valli (1989, 1990) and Fontana (1999) suggested a variety
of sociolinguistic factors which influence the use of code-switching and
mixing between a signed and a spoken language, including lack of
familiarity between participants, and more the formality of a situation.

48   According to Lucas and Valli (1989, 1990), more English 'interference' occurs in more formal situations, when technical or specialised terms are used, and thus are incorporated into ASL in the form of mouth patterns or fingerspelling.

Davis (1989, 1990a, 1990b) adopted the same perspective on language contact as Lucas and Valli (1989, 1990), and referred to code-switching and code-mixing between ASL and English as 'interlingual transference'. He explored the use of these language contact phenomena in interpretations of English into ASL, and found that the mouthing of English words and the use of fingerspelling is patterned. Typically, he found that "English mouthing marks fingerspelled words, most lexicalised fingerspelling is used for emphasis, lists, numbers, and question words" (1989, p.101); and all of these features were identified as being appropriate to ASL. In relation to fingerspelling, Davis stated that an English word might be fingerspelled because an equivalent ASL sign does not exist. Alternatively he observed that a 'multi-meaning' ASL sign can be prefaced, or tagged, with a fingerspelled word. In such cases, Davis noted that "the fingerspelled words are flagged in very specfic ways, for example, mouthing, eye-gaze, indexing, labelling, quotation markers, and palm orientation" (1989, p.102).

Davis' (1989, 1990a, 1990b) study showed that interpreters used contact varieties of sign language appropriate to the situation they were interpreting in, which was a lecture. These findings thus agree with the conclusions of Lucas and Valli (1989, 1990), that the formality of a situation influences the use of language contact phenomena in sign language. Davis (1989, 1990a, 1990b) also demonstrated that the sign language interpreters in his study reflected the typical language use of Deaf people in this type of situation. Napier and Adam (2002), in a linguistic comparison of BSL and Auslan interpreters, drew similar conclusions. After comparing the sign language output of five BSL and five Auslan interpreters interpreting for the same formal presentation, they found that the interpreters' use of language reflected the language use of the Deaf communities for whom they were interpreting. For example, in relation to fingerspelling, "Auslan exhibits a greater degree of fingerspelling use than does BSL…and this is reflected in the use of fingerspelling in the five Auslan interpreted texts" (p.28). When consid-

ering the notion of language contact and sign language variation, the
discussion highlights the need for interpreters to appropriately reflect
the language used by Deaf people when participating in formal interactions, and to observe the 'rules' of the discourse genres in which they
are interpreting.

1.3.3 Discourse genres

Discourse analysis can be applied to any form of communicative
interaction in an attempt to identify various discourse genres. Studies of
alternative discourses have included genres such as: narratives (Chafe,
1980); jokes (Sacks, 1974); and conversations (Schegloff, 1972; Tannen,
1984b). Discourse analysis is relevant to the study of both monologue
and dialogue (Longacre, 1983); therefore lectures, as typical monologues, can be considered as a distinct discourse genre. Cokely (1992a)
noted, however, that very few descriptive studies have focussed on the
particular monologic discourse of lectures. Instead, general observations have been made about the characteristics of lectures. Before going
on to discuss these characteristics, it is necessary to define what is
meant by the term 'a lecture':

> A lecture is an institutionalised extended holding of the floor in which
> one speaker imparts his views on a subject, these thoughts comprising
> what can be called his "text". The style is typically serious and slightly
> impersonal, the controlling intent being to generate calmly considered
> understanding, not mere entertainment, emotional impact, or
> immediate action (Goffman, 1981, p.165).

Lakoff (1982) defined lectures in a similar way to that of Goffman (1981),
whereby one participant in the interactive discourse is in control, selects
the subject matter, and decides when the discourse should start and
finish (cited in Cokely, 1992a). Therefore it can be seen that lectures can
be characterised as non-reciprocal monologues, or "expository monologues" (Cokely, 1992a, p.27).

In drawing on the work of Longacre (1983) and applying discourse
analysis to expository monologues in general, certain characteristics
can be identified as being distinct from those of narratives. A typical
expository monologue relies on topical or logical linkage, as opposed

50   to the inherent chronological nexus often observed in narratives. The focus of expository monologues tends to be on a theme or set of related themes, rather than on participants, such as in narratives. Plus more tension, that is struggle or polarisation, can be found in an expository monologue than in a narrative. Longacre noted that effective expository discourse should inherently incorporate an effort to ensure clarity of information, especially when people receiving the discourse may not have the necessary background knowledge.

In focussing on characteristics of a lecture, and the language production within this discourse genre, Goffman (1981) highlighted three different modes of speech production which establish presenters on a different 'footing' [5] with their audience. These modes are: memorisation; aloud reading; and fresh talk. He stated that lecturers often choose to read aloud from prepared texts, which influences the reception and responsiveness of an audience. According to Goffman, people may choose to read out printed text, rather than spontaneously provide 'fresh talk', due to different dynamics of written and spoken texts, which imply that written language has more status:

> consider the effect of "high style", even if issuing from a patently read address. Elegance of language—turns of phrase, metaphor, parallel structures, aphoristic formulations—can be taken as evidence not only of the speaker's intelligence..., but also of his giving his mind and ability over to the job he is now performing (Goffman, 1981, p.189).

Goffman (1981) asserted that the register of language used in a lecture is important in defining the relationship between speaker and audience. Therefore although perceptions of 'good writing' and 'good speaking' are systematically different, people will often choose to 'read aloud' previously prepared texts when delivering a lecture, as printed text tends to be more coherent than spontaneously produced spoken text.

This finding has implications for interpreters who are working in university lectures, as Halliday (1978) suggested that academics often deliver lectures using a written language structure of speech production. Halliday argued that academics are so influenced by their environment and the assumption of literate intelligence of university students, that they produce lexically dense spoken text when lecturing. Lexically dense spoken text is characterised by its conformity to typical written 51 language structure, with a higher number of lexical words than grammatical words.

Before discussion of lexical density can take place, however, it is necessary to consider characteristics of a lecture provided in a signed language rather than a spoken language, and whether there are any marked differences. Sign language interpreters working in lectures would need to consider the expectations of spoken and sign language users when attending a lecture, and the language use they would expect to receive.

As mentioned earlier, Zimmer (1989) noted marked differences in signing style between a lecture environment and two other less formal environments. Kluwin (1985) studied the ability of Deaf students to acquire information from a signed lecture, and found that the salience of the information presented had an impact on the amount of recall. However, this impact was seen to depend not only on the sign language fluency of the presenter, but also that of the receivers. Christie, Wilkins, Hicks McDonald and Neuroth-Gimbrone (1999) compared the visual representations of discourse structures of ASL, spoken English and written English in order to facilitate the development of Deaf students' academic bilingualism. Students were asked to create a formal narrative in ASL, incorporating appropriate discourse features of ASL formal register. The features highlighted were the same as those previously discussed by Roy (1989b).

Roy (1989b) conducted a study looking at particular discourse features of an ASL lecture. In a general context, Roy stated that lectures are discourses with particular goals in mind, which tend to be mono-logues that satisfy informational goals, and are content-oriented. She claimed that lectures require the use of linguistic devices to give the listener a clear idea of how an utterance fits into the lecture process as a whole. The linguistic elements are not part of the content, per se, but are used as a guide by listeners as to how they should interpret the information they are receiving. Words and phrases used as cohesive, structural devices can contribute to the listener's ability to distinguish between major and minor points, old and new information, and shifts in the flow of topics. Roy described the lecture as adhering to a particu-

52   lar construct, whereby the organisational structure incorporates a
natural chain of events linking sub-topics. She stated that there is
general agreement in society that most lectures open with an introduction and some explanation of the purpose of the lecture, followed by
the main body of the lecture and an obligatory summary. The naturally
occurring segments of a lecture are also referred to as 'episodes', which
can be distinguished by the use of certain discourse markers.

In the ASL lecture, Roy (1989b) found that the sign for 'now' was
most often used as a discourse marker, as it was used to mark a shift
into a new subtopic, rather than just indicating the present time in an
ongoing discourse. The sign for 'now that', however, was used to signify
a shift into a group of episodes within the discourse. Bienvenu (1993)
described similar features of formal ASL discourse to those outlined by
Roy (1989b), in terms of 'opening, middle and closing features'; 'developmental episodes'; and the need for repair strategies (cited in Christie,
et al, 1999).

Although it is acceptable that signed language lectures would adhere
to a particular construct in much the same way as spoken lectures, it
could be argued that the discourse markers suggested by Roy (1989b)
are not characteristics of a formal register, but rather idiosyncratic use
of formal language. It is inevitable that lectures presented in signed
languages will incorporate discourse markers to indicate the formality
of the situation, but the characteristics may vary from person to person.
Lecturers may therefore conform to shared notions of organisational
structure of a lecture, indicative of a formal register, such as pausing or
repetition, but may use individual preferences for signs to indicate a
shift in topic or sub-topic. For example, with reference to the signs
'now' and 'now that' mentioned by Roy, it is possible that people may
choose to sign 'okay', 'right', 'well' or 'so', in much the same way as
people might use these words as discourse markers in spoken English.

Nonetheless, sign language interpreters need to incorporate their
knowledge and understanding of the lecture as a discourse genre into
any interpretations they provide, taking into account the linguistic
features of the language register, in particular, the potential for the
lecture source text to be 'lexically dense'.

1.3.4 *Lexical density*

Lexical density represents the complexity that is typical of written language (Crystal, 1995; Halliday, 1985; Gerot & Wignell, 1995), and can be used as a measure of difficulty of a piece of text (Richards, Platt and Platt,1992; O'Loughlin, 1995). The notion of lexical density is discussed here in the context of university lectures, and how information is presented. It has been established that lectures are often 'read aloud', whereby the presenter will read verbatim from a written text; or alternatively due to environmental influences, academic lecturers may present spoken language using a written language structure. Halliday (1985) made the distinction between spoken and written English by asserting that "most written English does not sound too good in speech" (p.77). He contended that although they are both kinds of the same language, written and spoken English have different characteristics, yet speech is no less structured than writing:

> Spontaneous speech is unlike written text. It contains many mistakes, sentences are usually brief and indeed the whole fabric of verbal expression is riddled with hesitations and silences (Halliday, 1985, p.76).

Lakoff (1979) suggested that some of the major factors influencing differences between spoken and written discourse are the 'informality', 'spontaneity' and 'inconsequentiality' of speech in comparison with writing (cited in Beaman, 1984). Typically spoken text has complex sentences with simple words, whereas written text has complex words in simple sentences, which Halliday (1979) suggested is because writing is static, compared with speech, which is dynamic. As a consequence, spoken language tends to be less lexically dense than written language. Ure (1971) stated that in English, the lexical density of a text is a function first of the medium (i.e., spoken or written), and second, a function of the social environment (i.e., pragmatic language use). This statement highlights how academic lecturers may be influenced working in an environment where pragmatic language use is often based on technical research, and therefore allows their spoken language production to be influenced by the written language medium.

54   Language can be divided into lexical items (content words) and functional items (grammatical words), therefore counting the number of lexical and functional items in a text implies lexical density. A lexically dense passage, for example, would feature a higher number of lexical items than functional items. Halliday (1985) stated that, typically, written language is dense and spoken language is not, in that "there is a characteristic difference between spoken and written language. Written language displays a much higher ratio of lexical items to total running words" (p.61). Therefore, "the more 'written' the language being used, the higher will be the proportion of lexical words to the total number of running words in the text" (p.64).

Grammatical words in a language function in closed systems of the language, that is, they can be identified as determiners, the majority of prepositions, conjunctions and some classes of adverbs and finite verbs (e.g., the, has, to, on). Content words, however, operate in open systems of the language, where different classes of the language cannot be closed off (e.g., door, gate, window, etc.). As content words, lexical items can be constituents of variable length, and therefore can consist of more than one word, for example, the term 'stand up' functions as one lexical item. Modal verbs, such as 'always' and 'perhaps', are on the borderline between lexical and functional items; thus for the purpose of any analysis, a decision needs to be made about which category the modal verbs will be incorporated into, and for there to be consistency in the counting. One generally identifiable difference between lexical and functional items is in the spelling. Lexical items usually have a minimum of three letters, whereas functional items can have only two.

In reporting lexical density of text, calculations can be presented in the following way: If a piece of text has a ratio of twelve lexical items to eight functional items, the proportion of lexical items can be seen to be 12 out of 20, therefore the lexical density of that particular piece of text would be 60%.

Ure (1971) used the above application to analyse alternate spoken and written texts, and developed a list of typical density percentages. The various spoken texts (including informal dyadic conversation, story telling, radio interview and sports commentary) were found to have a range of lexical density from 23.9% to 43.2%. The written texts (including school essays, children's stories, manuals and newspaper reports), however, had a range from 35.8% to 56.8%. Therefore Ure found that spoken text has an average lexical density of 33%, and written text has an average lexical density of 46%. In relation to the spoken texts, he found that all the texts with a density of 36% or more were monologues, whereas all those under 36% involved some form of interaction. Ure found that a typical spoken lecture had a lexical density of 39.6%.

1.4 Interpreting for lexically dense text

According to Messina (1998), previously prepared texts that are read out verbatim create more problems for interpreters than spontaneous speech. He cited the "peculiarities of written texts and how they are usually delivered by speakers" as being the main reason for effecting an interpreter's performance (p.148). In this regard, Messina is referring not only to the grammatical simplicity and lexical density of written text, but also to the prosodic features of speech delivery when reading text aloud. Some examples include monotonous intonation, faster rate of delivery and lower frequency of pauses.

Balzani (1990) studied interpreters' performances when working from a written text which was read out, and found that more mistakes were made (cited in Messina, 1998). The key issue for interpreters when dealing with lexically dense text, is "higher risk of impaired understanding and interpretation as the interpreter's processing capacities reach saturation" (Messina, 1998, p.156). The notion of text being read out, however, is not the only difficulty for interpreters. Spoken texts which are not necessarily read out, but which are prepared, may also be lexically dense, and thus provide a challenge to interpreters.

Interpreters, therefore, may face difficulties in interpreting for any spoken text that is more lexically dense than usual, that is, has a lexical density of more than 33%. A university lecture is a good example of the kind of source text that may prove challenging for an interpreter working with any language. It is important to remember the point made by Halliday (1978), that academics often deliver lectures using a structure of language more typical of written than spoken language.

1.4.1 *Sign language interpretation of lexically dense text*

In addition to challenges faced by interpreters in dealing with the delivery style of a lecture (such as speed, less pausing, etc.), the lexical density of university lectures has implications for how Deaf people will access information through sign language interpreters. As sign language has no conventional written orthography, a Deaf audience may have no frame of reference for what a 'lexically dense' interpretation into a sign language should look like. This situation presents a challenge for sign language interpreters in that they have to decipher the meaning of a text, and decide which lexical items are the most important to convey. Sign language interpreters have to take into account the following issues: The language contact situation of interpreting between spoken and signed languages; what the norms of sign language production would be for a lecture in general; what cultural relevance certain lexical items may hold, and thus what their linguistic and cultural equivalents may be; as well as deciding what linguistic coping strategies should be adopted in order to ensure that a Deaf audience receive the same message as a non-deaf audience. The contextual force or relative impact (Isham, 1986) of the message on the receiver ultimately should be as much as possible the same for both Deaf and non-deaf audiences.

Nida (1998) summarised the sociolinguistic and sociocultural contexts which require consideration throughout an interpretation, into four categories: (1) the appropriate language register to be used in the context; (2) the expectations of the target audience as to the type of translation they expect to receive; (3) distinctive sociolinguistic features of the source text; and (4) the medium employed for the translated text (i.e., written or spoken).

For sign language interpreters working with Deaf students in a university lecture, there are additional sociolinguistic and sociocultural factors to consider, as well as the lexical density of the text. Educational interpreting is unique to sign language interpreters (Bremner & Housden, 1996), and requires special skills (Saur, 1992), as Deaf students have differing needs compared to those from other non-English speaking backgrounds (Ozolins & Bridge, 1999). Typically in relation to education, spoken language interpreters may be used to facilitate discussion between parents and a teacher. For Deaf people, however, interpreters are used in the classroom in order to provide students with access to the actual teaching process itself.

When considering the issues faced by sign language interpreters in their every day work in relation to managing communication, other issues can be highlighted in relation to interpreting for university lectures. The skills employed by interpreters have to be adapted to allow for conditions specific to the university discourse environment, so that educational interpreters can effectively contribute to the academic achievement of deaf students (Paul & Quigley, 1990). The interpreter needs to consider her role in an educational environment, and the fact that Deaf people may be disadvantaged when compared to other university students. Although all university students may attend lectures without any background knowledge to the subject, and thus have lack of familiarity with subject-specific terminology, the interpreter is faced with the task of deciding how to provide an interpretation that is linguistically and culturally sensitive, incorporating meaningful equivalents, while still providing Deaf students with the opportunity to access specialised terminology that may be important for them to know in order to fully understand the subject of the lecture and pass examinations.

This context presents sign language interpreters with a dilemma of whether to freely interpret the content of a lecture, or whether to establish a language contact situation that occasionally relies on the fingerspelling of English words and possible use of literal interpretation. In the light of the interpreter's knowledge of the consumer's language and her knowledge of the topic and its terminology, the interpreter needs to decide which concepts should be interpreted into a sign language equivalent, and which terms should be rendered literally. Thus, the interpreter will also need to judge the importance of lexical items presented in the lecture source text, and when it might be appropriate to omit information for clarity. The interpreter's decision-making will be influenced by how she perceives her role in this discourse environment.

As discussed earlier, the current thinking is that interpreters should present themselves as bilingual and bicultural mediators, who make

58   linguistic decisions based on their cultural knowledge of the groups for whom they are interpreting, and their knowledge of interactional norms. In making decisions as to whether Deaf students need to access subject-specific terminology, interpreters should not perceive their role as educators, but rather as linguistic decision-makers. Through this process of decision-making, it is inevitable that interpreters will make omissions, some of which may be accidental, and others that may be made as part of the linguistic decision-making process. Thus the interpreter will aide her decision making by employing key linguistic strategies.

    I would suggest that sign language interpreters working in university lectures should switch translation style, between free and literal methods, as a linguistic coping strategy to enhance their decision-making process and their interpretation output. Use of this coping strategy would therefore give Deaf students access to specialised vocabulary when appropriate (through incorporation of fingerspelling in literal interpretation), while providing a meaningful, conceptually accurate and culturally relevant message (through free interpretation). In order to enhance this process, another linguistic coping strategy would be for interpreters to employ the use of omissions strategically and delete irrelevant or redundant information, to effectively convey the message and intent of a university lecture. The notion of linguistic coping strategies of interpreters, and how they use them, is defined and discussed further in Chapter two.

Notes

3.   Australasian Signed English is the manual representation of English word for word. Several methods for manually representing English have been used over the years. "Some use just twenty-six hand configurations to represent the letters of the alphabet, others use a combination of signs used by the deaf and fingerspelling, others use a combination of deaf signs, fingerspelling and contrived signs. They all have in common the aim of manually representing English, word for word, if not morpheme by morpheme" (Johnston, 1989, p.473).

4.   'Foreigner talk' is the simplified register often identified as being appropriate for addressing foreigners or 'outsiders' (Fontana, 1999). Certain features that characterise foreigner talk include: short sentences; lack of function words; avoidance of colloquialisms; repetition of lexical items; slow and exagger-

ated enunciation; and less use of inflections (Ferguson & DeBose, 1977; cited in Cokely, 1983b).

5.   "A change in footing implies a change in the alignment we take up to ourselves and the others present as expressed in the way we manage the production or reception of an utterance. A change in our footing is another way of talking about a change in our frame for events" (Goffman, 1982: 128)

CHAPTER TWO
Coping strategies of interpreters

2.0 Introduction

The aim of this chapter is to elaborate on the notion of 'coping strategies', in order to provide a clear definition of what is meant by the term linguistic coping strategies. By discussing the generic concept of coping strategies of interpreters, the detail of how translation style and omissions can be used by sign language interpreters as linguistic coping strategies can then be explored in more detail.

2.1 Coping strategies

The term coping strategies is an 'umbrella' concept, that is, one that can encompass a plethora of discretionary facets according to individual interpretation. Little has been written on this explicit term, and alternative labels have included those such as, coping tactics (Gile, 1995), "strategies for the management of the communication event" (Roy, 1996, p.63), coping mechanisms (Moser-Mercer, Kunzli & Korac, 1998) and creative problem-solving (Mackenzie, 1998). Gran (1998), in fact, wrote about tactics as the interface between strategies and creativity. Alternative coping strategies can be used at different stages of the interpreting process. In describing the different stages, it is possible to provide a context within which to place linguistic coping strategies, and the consideration of translation style and omissions as potential linguistic coping strategies.

2.1.1 Stages of coping

Coping strategies may be incorporated into any stage of the interpreting process, whether at the preparatory stage, during the assignment (in-situ), or retrospectively (Napier, 1996; Witter-Merithew, 1982), and can be defined as:

...those methods or techniques adopted by interpreters to ensure that: (1) they are able to carry out the task as fluidly as possible; (2) intrusion or misunderstanding occurs as little as possible; (3) external factors are controlled; and (4) comfort and confidence is retained throughout the interpreting assignment (Napier, 2001, p.72).

Preparatory strategies may include: Obtaining papers and other preparation materials before an assignment; researching particular topics of assignments and familiarising oneself with key terminology (through books, journals or the Internet); keeping up with current affairs; consultation with co-workers in advance of an assignment with regard to tandem interpreting procedure,[6] or liasing with clients to establish working practices (e.g., lengths of working periods, seating arrangements, lighting, etc.). These are only a few examples of lengths that interpreters may go to before they start working, to ensure that they have as much background knowledge about the assignment as possible and can therefore predict and deal with any possible difficulties (Shaw, 1997).

Mackenzie (1998) emphasises the need for thorough preparation, and for interpreters to ask the right questions in order to locate and define any potential problems: "this requires an analysis of the situation in which the need for translation has arisen. On the basis of this analysis the translator can decide what specific questions need to be asked…" (p.202). Turner (2001) suggests that all interpreting assignments have a dimension of 'preparability', whereby "the more preparable an assignment is… the less complex it might be considered" (p.68). He proposes a schema of twelve dimensions for interpreters to consider in order to decide whether they will have the strategies to cope with an interpreting assignment, and therefore whether to accept an assignment, including aspects such as the interpreter's familiarity with the language and context, the potential language diversity of consumers, the technicality of the language that will be used, and the sensitivity and perceived difficulty of the assignment. By identifying various sources of demand in interpreting assignments, interpreters will be in a better position to control their input (Dean & Pollard, 2001), and therefore be better prepared to cope with any challenges that may arise within that assignment.

Retrospective techniques can combine any approach that an interpreter might use to reflect on an interpreting assignment, whether

62   that means talking to clients or co-workers and obtaining feedback on
      her performance, watching or listening to a recording of an assignment
      and applying some form of critical analysis, or just generally pondering
      over the effectiveness of an assignment and remembering key issues for
      future reference. Many authors (such as Humphrey, 2000; Labath, 1998;
      West, 1994) have commended the use of reflective journals as a strategy
      for retrospectively considering the strategies used in interpreting
      assignments, and how one coped in a particular setting. When in-situ,
      however, other problems may arise which the interpreter may have to
      deal with spontaneously, regardless of the amount of preparation
      carried out, which will require the interpreter to implement other
      coping strategies.

2.1.2 *Spontaneous problem-solving*

Coping strategies are needed in-situ in response to a range of problems,
which can arise spontaneously due to distinct factors. These factors
could include: linguistic interference, such as comprehension, productive and receptive language skills of the interpreter and clients; sociolinguistic influences from the discourse environment, such as accent,
dialect, or register of language; metalinguistic awareness of the interpreter; as well as internal or external extralinguistic interferences, for
example, poor prediction skills, fatigue, assumed knowledge of
interpreter and clients, environmental distractions, and effectiveness of
the co-working relationship. Attention has been brought to these
factors in many different discussions, some of which have proposed
resolutions, others simply raising issues for deliberation (Anderson,
1978; Blewett, 1985; Brasel, 1975; Cooper, Davies & Tung, 1982; Darò,
1994; Gerver, 1974).

     In considering spontaneous problem-solving skills of interpreters,
Gile (1995) surmised that it is inevitable that problems will arise during
interpreting assignments, regardless of interpreters' amount of experience. He identified that spontaneous problems may occur due to
"processing capacity limitations, errors in processing capacity management, and gaps in the interpreters' knowledge base" (p.191). Atwood
(1985) described one particular extralinguistic factor that may require an
interpreter to use spontaneous coping strategies, in the form of envi-

ronmental distractions in interpreting. Within his paper, he referred specifically to verbal interjections that an interpreter may receive from a co-worker while they are working, which contributes to a "loss of equilibrium" for the interpreter (p.94). He suggested different methods for resolving disagreements between co-workers by discussing appropriate phrases to use for clarification, as well as appropriate times and places for confrontations of this nature. The issue of auditory interjection while working has potentially huge linguistic ramifications for any interpreter, in that it can interfere with the language interpretation process. Unfortunately, Atwood only touched on this issue very briefly, as he chose to concentrate on extralinguistic strategies for working in tandem, such as those mentioned above.

Fischer (1993) detailed more positive methods for interpreters working in tandem, by focussing on pro-active rather than reactive measures. Guidelines were given to ensure that interpreters can work effectively together to provide a satisfactory service, taking into account other extralinguistic influences such as fatigue, techniques for feeding information and working conditions.

Mackenzie (1998) distinguished between two types of problem that may occur (open- and close-ended), but only gave an explanation for the concept of open-ended problems. She postulated that many interpreters encounter open-ended problems, where there is no pre-determined solution, which can be consciously solved through the use of controlled conditions. Rather, Mackenzie suggested that open-ended problems require the use of creative problem solving strategies. Although it can be agreed that coping strategies require interpreters to be creative in dealing with spontaneous problems, it can also be argued that problems can be solved consciously if interpreters have the ability to monitor their language choices, that is, if interpreters possess a level of metalinguistic awareness about the interpretation process.

Scheibe (1986) elaborated on the notion of creative problem-solving by suggesting several steps including assessment of the problem, recognition of areas needing change and analysis of group dynamics. Her conclusions, however, were rather unsophisticated as she recommended the development of curiosity and allowing time to daydream as strategies for creative problem-solving, without any recognition for the

64 multi-layered linguistic processes involved in interpreting and the
actual problems that may occur.

Riccardi (1998), however, asserted that the creative behaviour of
interpreters could be regarded as a problem-solving strategy, as the
interpreting process is intrinsically creative by its nature. She gave
credence to problem-solving being part of a conscious process by
describing two specific strategies which are applied according to the
type of difficulties being faced. First she referred to skill-based strategies,
which are automatic responses that are stored and can be carried out
routinely as part of the interpreting process (such as typical conference
proceedings including greetings, thanking, running through an agenda,
motions, etc.). She then discussed knowledge-based strategies, which
require a different approach as they are implemented in new situations
relying on conscious analytical processes and "stored knowledge"
(p.174). According to Riccardi, knowledge-based strategies require much
more effort than skill-based strategies, as information processing
throughout the interpretation is controlled and conscious.

It is this level of consciousness and analytical attention, or
metalinguistic awareness, that is imperative in the decision-making
process of selecting coping strategies when in-situ. One focus of this
study is the level of metalinguistic skill that sign language interpreters
have during the interpretation process. The metalinguistic, analytical
abilities of any interpreter will influence the particular strategies chosen
at any one time.

2.1.3 Metalinguistic awareness

The concept of metalinguistic awareness is usually discussed within the
context of language acquisition and development of literacy skills.
Several writers have discussed the metacognitive skills that children
acquire, the metalinguistic awareness they have about their own language development, and how this impacts upon their literacy skills
(Clark, 1978; Karmiloff-Smith, 1986; Perner, 1988; Tunmer & Bowey,
1984; Tunmer & Herriman, 1984). Malakoff and Hakuta (1991) specifically discussed the translation skills and metalinguistic awareness of
bilingual children. Garton and Pratt (1998) defined metalinguistic
awareness as "the ability to focus attention on language and reflect upon

its nature, structure and functions" (p.149), and stated that "those who work with language must be able to focus attention on it" (p.150). Therefore, the concept can be applied to interpreters and the skills they have to self-regulate and monitor their abilities in the languages they interpret between (Peterson, 2000; Smith, 2000). Perner (1988) postulated that in order for an ability to be metalinguistic, individuals must be able to focus their attention on their language use, and reflect on it, as well as appreciating the fact that it is language that they are reflecting upon (cited in Garton & Pratt, 1998). Bialystok and Ryan (1985a, 1985b) and Bialystok (1991a, 1993) asserted that metalinguistic awareness involves key skills. These skills include ability to analyse linguistic knowledge into categories, capability to control attentional procedures that select and process specific linguistic information, as well as facility to intentionally consider what aspects of language are contextually relevant.

It can be argued therefore, that in order to function interpreters should have highly developed metalinguistic awareness, as they are constantly having to analyse the linguistic structure of language, as well as having to consider sociocultural contexts of language use and individual message impact. According to Garton and Pratt (1998), the development of metalinguistic awareness provides skills of choice and control of language, and in addition serves to facilitate communication. As a consequence, they believe that metalinguistic awareness depends upon social interaction, as people need to gain access to feedback on their language use. When applying this concept to the work of interpreters, it can be seen that they would rely on some form of interaction in order to develop their metalinguistic awareness. Interpreters will typically receive feedback from Deaf clients, in the form of a head nod or other affirmative sign that they understand. If the feedback is negative, rather than positive, interpreters will need to be aware of what linguistic choices they made, and how to repeat or change them to make the interpretation understandable. This concept has been alternatively referred to as 'meta-competence' (Nord, 2000), or the use of 'meta-strategies' (Hoffman, 1997).

One of the interests of this particular study was the level of metalinguistic awareness or metacognition (Peterson, 2000) that sign language interpreters had about linguistic choices they made while

66 interpreting in a university lecture, in particular in relation to the types of omissions they made and why. Darò, Lambert and Fabbro (1996) noted that the conscious monitoring of attention during simultaneous interpretation may effect the number and types of mistakes made by interpreters. Thus, the aim of the research study was to demonstrate what types of omissions were made by interpreters, and whether they were applying 'metacognitive strategies' (Smith, 2000) in making certain omissions, or whether the process was an unconscious one.

At this point, I would like to assert that coping strategies are not necessarily used to resolve problems, as has been the implication far. Coping strategies can be regarded as different techniques that may be used to ensure that the interpretation is as effective as possible. Although some strategies may be reactive, they can often be pro-active and enhance an interpretation, rather than just dealing with something that has gone wrong. So far, none of the literature that has been discussed has made any reference to the nature of coping strategies as part of a linguistic process. It is these coping strategies, used as part of a linguistic process intrinsic to any piece of interpretation, that are the central focus of this book, that is, linguistic coping strategies. It is strategies of this kind that can contribute to the effectiveness of an interpretation as opposed to being used solely for crisis management.

2.2 Linguistic coping strategies

Most studies that refer in some way to the use of coping strategies as part of the linguistic interpretation process have been sociolinguistic studies focussing on interactive communication events. All of the studies, however, have a different approach to the concept of coping strategies, which are open for interpretation. Two authors analysed interactive discourse (Roy, 1989a, 1992, 1996, 2000a; Metzger, 1995, 1999), one concentrated on particular linguistic strategies (Davis, 1989, 1990a, 1990b), whereas another focussed on the use of free interpretation in relation to culturally bound information (Napier, 1998b, 1998c). These studies can be grouped according to the use of linguistic and cultural knowledge as a linguistic coping strategy, or the use of translation style as a linguistic coping strategy.

2.2.1 Use of linguistic and cultural knowledge as a coping strategy

Roy's thesis (1989a), which was further developed in papers written in 1992 and 1996, and a book published in 2000, looked at how an ASL interpreter can impact upon the turn-taking sequences of a face-to-face dialogue. This impact would occur when the interpreter "manages each turn through knowledge of the linguistic and social meaning beyond what appears in the surface form…" (1996, p.40). Thus, the study looked at what coping strategies an interpreter used in order to control the turn-taking involved in a face-to-face interaction, from a sociolinguistic point of view.

The original study (1989a) involved Roy videotaping and transcribing a tutorial session between a university professor and a student, analysing the video footage, as well as interviewing all three participants involved (the professor who could hear, the Deaf student and the interpreter) about their perceptions in relation to particular turn-taking sequences, and any confusion or misunderstanding which occurred. In the discussion of the results, Roy focussed on studying the interpretation as a successful communication event, and investigated what the interpreter did successfully rather than what he did wrong. It was found that, because the interpreter was bicultural as well as bilingual, he was able to use his knowledge of conversational interaction norms amongst hearing and Deaf people to ensure that the flow of communication was not constrained in any way. This factor meant incorporating a range of strategies, such as, taking his own turn, prompting the student to take a turn, acknowledging the power differential involved by occasionally yielding turns to the professor, and using lengthy time lags before interpreting certain utterances.

Analysis of the transcript revealed that the interpreter did not rely solely on the primary participants to control the turn-taking, although regular turns in the interpretation did take place which "resemble regular turns in ordinary face-to-face conversation" (Roy, 1996, p.47). In the retrospective interview, where the videotape was played back with Roy asking the interpreter why he had made certain decisions, she was able to elicit that the interpreter was making conscious choices about what coping strategies to use, for example, when there was an overlap

68   in conversation. Although the central focus of the study was not about
the interpreter's consciousness of the linguistic decisions made about
his interpretation, it can be seen that the interpreter was using his
knowledge of linguistic and cultural dynamics, and his metalinguistic
awareness about that knowledge, to formulate coping strategies in
relation to turn-taking exchanges. Roy (1996) summarised:

> Turns taken by the interpreter were shown to be a mixture of the
> interpreter's decisions as well as the primary speakers' tacit agreement
> to accept those decisions… [Interpreters are] involved in interpreting
> conventions for language use and in creating turn exchanges through
> their knowledge of the linguistic system, the social situation, and the
> discourse structure system (Roy 1996, p.63).

Thus Roy (1996) asserted that interpreters need to be not only compe-
tent bilinguals, but also knowledgeable about ways of speaking in social
situations, as well as possessing "strategies for the management of the
communication event." (p.63).

Qian (1994), writing on spoken language interpreting, used a similar
approach to that of Roy (1989a) and described how an interpreter effects
the communication process. Two situations were discussed where the
interpreter was deemed to have stepped out of role and therefore
inappropriately effected the communication. Qian (1994) stated that
interpreters must "suppress instincts or impulses to interact with the
participants of a communication event" (p.218) in order to remain
professional. Roy (1989a, 1992, 1996, 2000a), however, would encourage
interpreters to recognise those instincts and utilise them appropriately
in order to enhance the effectiveness of the communicative interaction.

Metzger (1995, 1999) also looked at the influence that ASL interpreters have on interactive discourse between Deaf and hearing participants, but focussed on slightly different parameters and collected her
data from within another kind of interpreted interaction. Whereas Roy
(1989a, 1992, 1996, 2000a) concentrated on how the presence of an
interpreter impacts on turn-taking, Metzger (1995, 1999) focussed on
what she called the paradox of neutrality. By using this term she was
referring to the ideal that professional interpreters are expected to
remain impartial throughout any interpreting assignment, and faith-

fully interpret every utterance; whereby "impartial rendering of the participant utterances helps ensure that interpreters do not selectively omit portions of other participant utterances" (1995, p.9). The aim of Metzger's study was to 'deconstruct the myth' of this neutrality (1999) by demonstrating that interpreters cannot remain completely impartial, thereby illustrating that the notion of neutrality is unrealistic.

Metzger (1995, 1999) argued that due to the very nature of their work, and the fact that interpreters are bilingual and bicultural, they are bound to use the knowledge they possess to make assumptions about their source language and target language audiences, and to make inferences about what an utterance will mean linguistically and culturally to each audience. This view implies, therefore, that it is impossible for them to remain completely neutral within any interpreted interaction. She based this argument on the construct of 'frame theory', and the notion that everybody has their own developed frames of reference for different concepts which have been shaped by their life experiences. As a consequence, interpreters will make specific choices within their interpretation as to what something means to them, and also what they assume it will mean to the interaction participants. In doing so, they are able to provide equivalent messages to each cultural group, thus making any utterance meaningful in a sociocultural context.

In order to validate her argument, Metzger (1995) conducted an interactional sociolinguistic analysis of two interpreted medical interviews, one was a role-play performed by an interpreting student, and the other an actual medical appointment involving a professional interpreter. The former interview was recorded as part of an interpreter training program, with a copy given to Metzger at a later date with the permission of the participants. The interview took place in a large classroom with three participants, two hearing women and one Deaf man, and the encounter lasted for just over seven minutes. The latter interview involved Metzger being present at a real medical consultation and videotaping the interaction. The interview was held in a doctor's office with six participants—the doctor (male), nurse (female), interpreter (female), mother (female), child (male) and researcher (female), and lasted for approximately 26 minutes. The interviews were compared in order to establish the extent of the interpreters' influence on the interactive discourse, and whether they brought their own frames of reference to the communicative events.

Although Metzger (1995, 1999) acknowledged certain sociolinguistic influences on the study, such as having a researcher and/ or video camera present, the language contact influence on the Deaf participants, and the differing lengths of each interview, other factors that may have effected the validity of her study were not raised. For example, the fact that each encounter involved different numbers of people, gender differences which may have influenced the dynamics, and the fact that the interviews recorded following different procedures under alternate conditions may have seriously skewed the comparability of the two cases. Another issue that needs to be taken into consideration is that comparison was made between only two interpreters, and these interpreters were at completely different skill levels. One was an interpreting student who was learning ASL as a second language, the other was a native ASL user with extensive experience as an interpreter. Thus the validity of juxtaposing two case studies which present differ-ent data can be questioned. Nonetheless Metzger's findings highlight important qualities of an interpreter's work, which can be identified as linguistic coping strategies and therefore still merit consideration.

Metzger (1995, 1999) found that a variety of linguistic features served as evidence of frames of reference, which included prosody, discourse sequences (such as question-answer pairs), topic initiation and repairs. In each case study the linguistic features used indicated that some of the participants' and interpreters' frames for events were mutual, whereas other frames were not shared. The interpreters were found to influence the interactive discourse in each case study in different ways through, for example, interruptions, clarifications, and responding to directed questions from either the hearing or Deaf participants. Metzger con-cluded that interpreters do bring their own frames of reference and assumed knowledge to any interpreted encounter, and therefore influence the dynamics of the interaction, and that some interpreters are more aware of this influence than others. She stated that because an interpreter's choice to include certain non-renditions might be con-scious, she will inevitably make choices about linguistic code and consequently influence the outcome of any interaction.

When another perspective is applied to the research carried out by
Metzger (1995, 1999), it is possible to assert that interpreters use their
assumed knowledge and make inferences as part of their repertoire of
linguistic coping strategies. If they are making conscious decisions
about finding equivalence between two languages and cultures, this
implies that they have a certain degree of metalinguistic awareness
about the interpretation process, and are therefore able to justify any
decisions that are made. The decision-making process employed by
interpreters in applying their linguistic and cultural knowledge to make
strategic decisions to cope with a communication event, has ramifications in that interpreters will invariably use their translation style as a
linguistic coping strategy.

2.2.2 Use of translation style as a coping strategy

For my first piece of research I conducted a study of free interpretation
and its use by BSL interpreters (Napier, 1998b). I adopted a similar
approach to that of Metzger (1995), by applying the concept of frame
theory to the process of interpretation, and questioned the ability of
BSL interpreters to remain completely neutral. Methods of 'free' and
'literal' interpretation were discussed, and I made the assertion that
interpreters should use the former if they regard themselves as linguistic
and cultural mediators.

I agreed with other writers (such as McDade, 1995; Phillip, 1994;
Pollitt, 1997; Scott Gibson, 1994), that the professionalisation of sign
language interpreting services has led to interpreters and Deaf people
having different perceptions of what it means to be a professional
interpreter, and that interpreters may no longer be meeting the needs of
the Deaf community (Napier, 1998b, 1998c). In relation to this point, I
suggested that this phenomenon has led to feelings of mistrust between
Deaf people and interpreters, in that interpreters are not trusted to do
their job without having their translations checked, and interpreters feel
vulnerable about their skills base. I then speculated that this mistrust
manifests itself in literal interpretations being used by the majority of
BSL interpreters, as this gives Deaf members of any audience the licence
to check their interpretation choices by lip-reading them, and then
comparing the message with that of the original speaker.

72   I tested my theory by videotaping and analysing the output of five
BSL interpreters working from English into BSL. Each interpreter was
asked to simultaneously translate a six-minute video clip that presented
"culturally bound" [7] information (Napier, 1998b, p.60). It was more than
likely that the source text was lexically dense due to the fact that it was
prepared text read aloud. All of the interpreters were given the opportunity to watch the clip through once before their task began, but were
not told anything about the purpose of the research. Analysis of the
results showed that only two of the five interpreters provided what I
defined as "culturally effective" interpretations (Napier, 1998b, p.66), by
rendering the message using a free method of interpretation. The other
three provided much more literal translations, and were found to make
a larger number of inappropriate miscues.

The purpose of the study was to look at working practices of BSL
interpreters in relation to their role as linguistic and cultural mediators,
and to evaluate whether they meet the needs of the Deaf community. I
argued that in order to effectively complement the requirements of
Deaf people, interpreters should use their sociolinguistic and sociocultural knowledge of both the Deaf community and wider society to
ensure any interpreted message is culturally, as well as linguistically,
relevant to Deaf people's frames of reference. Although the study is an
interesting one in terms of the use of free interpretation as a translation
style, and the exploration of the relationship between BSL interpreters
and Deaf people, in hindsight I can identify that the analysis was carried
out subjectively. Although I proposed that culturally effective interpretations were born out of using a free interpretation approach, I did not
provide any rationale for how the cultural effectiveness of the interpreted renditions was specifically defined. This weakness was taken into
account for the study reported in this book, with the classification of
translation 'styles' of interpreters described in detail. The participants in
my first study were not interviewed to determine the level of consciousness about their linguistic choices and how much was based on their
sociolinguistic and sociocultural knowledge, therefore only assumptions can be made about the interpreters' metalinguistic awareness of
the interpreting process. Nonetheless, in applying the notion of
linguistic coping strategies, it can be contended that the use of free

interpretation should be considered as a technique for coping linguistically with the dynamics of interpreting between two languages and
cultures. This is a strategy that some interpreters will employ, and
others will not (as demonstrated by Napier, 1998b). In utilising frame
theory, assumed knowledge and by making inferences, interpreters
should be able to make judgments about the linguistic and cultural
meaning that needs to be equalised between two language communities. Therefore by using this knowledge, and employing a variety of
approaches in dealing with the sociolinguistic and sociocultural
information, sign language interpreters can be seen to be using linguistic coping strategies to enhance the effectiveness of their translations.

Davis (1989, 1990a) also explored influences on translation style, but
gave consideration to different linguistic features of a translation. Davis
discussed language contact phenomena in ASL and the impact on
interpreters' translation style when interpreting in a language contact
environment, by analysing the linguistic interference and transference
that took place when two lectures were interpreted from English into
ASL. He used a videotape produced by Sign Media Inc. entitled Interpreter Models: English to ASL as the source of data for his analysis, in
which two ASL interpreters could be seen to simultaneously interpret
two 30 minute lectures without any rehearsal or interruptions. The
interpreters were working in a language contact environment, with a
mixed audience of five Deaf and nine hearing people. The audience was
divided so that each interpreter was interpreting for a separate audience.
Each interpreter could see the speaker and his or her audience, but could
not see the other interpreter. Both interpreters were native users of ASL,
and were experienced, well regarded interpreters in their profession.

Davis (1989, 1990a) defined linguistic interference as the rules of one
language being transferred to the other, as opposed to linguistic
transference which was defined as the transfer of material from the
source language while the rules of the target language are maintained.
Davis explained that for sign language interpreters working simultaneously between spoken English and ASL, some interference should be
expected due to the highly divergent nature of the two languages. He
surmised that "it is conceivable that a lack of ASL proficiency on the
part of the interpreter can significantly contribute to linguistic interfer-

74 ence" (1989 p.91). He then made the assumption that native ASL users who work as interpreters will experience minimal English interference when they are interpreting into ASL, due to more thorough assimilation of both languages. However, this assumption seems naïve on Davis' part, as it is likely that some level of interference would be inevitable for all interpreters processing two languages at the same time, regardless of their language fluency, especially when fatigued.

In his analysis of the data, Davis (1989, 1990a) focussed on the occurrence of code-switching, code-mixing (switching within a sentence or clause) and lexical borrowing within the interpretations of the lectures, and found that linguistic interference happened far less than linguistic transference. He identified that there is a rule-governed approach to code-mixing (transference) as both of the interpreters used it in very similar ways when making their language choices. For example, the interpreters used the mouthing of English words simultaneously with the production of ASL signs for nouns, question words, numbers and fingerspelled words. In relation to fingerspelling, Davis noted that the interpreters used a strategy of 'nonce' fingerspelling for borrowing particular lexical items. In this case when the speaker introduced a word for the first time, the interpreters would fingerspell the lexical item, representing each letter (or ASL morpheme). The more the word was repeated the interpreters either deleted or assimilated morphemes so that the fingerspelled word resembled a lexicalised sign rather than "a fingerspelled representation of an English orthographic event" (1989, p.98). Davis described the participants, topic and setting as altering the extent of interlingual transference, due to the fact that some Deaf members of the audience may have been more bilingual than others, so the interpreters had the option to encode some spoken English words into the visual mode of ASL.

Davis' study (1989, 1990a) can be seen to effectively demonstrate how linguistic transference and interference occur throughout the process of sign language interpretation in a language contact environment. Nevertheless, it should be acknowledged that Davis' data was limited in that only two interpreters were studied, and both were native signers. Careful deliberation is needed, therefore, before extrapolating Davis' findings to the sign language interpreting population as a whole.

In order to provide a more balanced perspective, an ideal study should
incorporate use of both native and non-native signers. Yet it is still
worthwhile considering the issues raised by Davis, as he made some
interesting notes that can be discussed in relation to coping strategies.

In another paper which developed his initial ideas, Davis (1990b)
described code-mixing, or transference, as a linguistic strategy which is
used to avoid any vagueness or ambiguity within an interpretation, with
interpreters encoding English forms in their ASL output, thus switching
to a more literal translation style. He noted that when interpreters
encoded English forms visually, they used systematic markers to
elucidate discontinuities between ASL and English. For example,
interpreters used the ASL sign for 'quotation markers' before and after
fingerspelling a lexical item in order to emphasise a lexical item that
was not ASL. On the other hand, Davis described 'interference' as the
incorporation of encoded English into ASL output, which actually
interferes with the propositional content of the message, and are
"sporadic and unsignaled" (p.308), without the patterning noted with
the systematic use of markers when fingerspelling and mouthing.

It can be argued, therefore, that the transference skills that Davis
(1989, 1990a, 1990b) highlighted can be regarded as linguistic coping
strategies, in that interpreters made conscious decisions about the
language choices they made in order to clarify information within the
interpretation, and thus adapted their translation style accordingly. The
selections made within the interpretation had to be conscious to some
extent, as both interpreters used code-mixing in similar ways, and
according to established rules of transference. Davis did not, however,
follow up this theory in any of his discussions, therefore there is no way
of knowing the extent of the interpreters' metalinguistic awareness
about their own interpretation and the linguistic strategies they
employed.

Various strategies that may be used to achieve cultural transfer were
discussed by Ivir (1998), and include techniques such as borrowing,
literal translation, substitution, addition and omission [8]. Ivir stated that
a translator's decision to select certain strategies is regulated by linguistic and communicative considerations, and translators' strategies are
therefore determined by a decision-making process, with each decision

76 "made on its own merits, taking account of the context of the situation in which the translational act of communication takes place" (p.138). For the purposes of this book, the focus is on linguistic coping strategies which require the incorporation of linguistic and cultural knowledge into an interpretation, and therefore give rise to a range of techniques that can be used to ensure that linguistic and cultural equivalence is achieved. The metalinguistic awareness that interpreters have about the strategies they employ, and the reasons they employ them, are also considered in relation to the use of translation style and the strategic use of omissions as part of a linguistic decision-making process.

2.3 Use of interpreting omissions

One dictionary definition defines an omission as "something that has not been included or not been done, either deliberately or accidentally" (Fox, 1988, p.547). Another describes omissions as "the action or an act of neglecting or failing to perform something, especially a duty" (Brown, 1993 p.1994). In terms of omissions being used by interpreters, it would seem that the former definition is more appropriate as it makes a more positive statement about things not being included, rather than using negative connotations of failure.

The first definition also identifies that the act of omission can be accidental or deliberate, or to put it another way, unconscious or conscious. An example of an unconscious omission in interpreting may be that the interpreter simply does not hear a particular utterance and thus does not include it in the translation. Conscious omissions, however, would be those that are made, either deliberately or not, by an interpreter for a variety of reasons. An interpreter may be conscious of the fact that they have made an omission, but it was not necessarily a deliberate decision. For example, the interpreter may not understand the meaning of a word, or the interpreter does not immediately translate a word or concept as she is waiting for further elaboration, but as a consequence of waiting the information gets lost as more information is received. Alternatively, an interpreter may make a deliberate decision to consciously omit something as a result of evaluating the source message for cultural meaning, and determining its equivalence in the target language and culture. A conscious strategic decision can be

made not to embrace certain concepts within the interpretation, that is,
to omit those that have no relevance to the receivers of the interpretation, or those that are not central to the message and would prove more
detrimental to understanding if left in. It is these strategic omissions
that can be considered as strategies used by interpreters to cope with
lexical density, linguistic and cultural relevance.

There has been little research looking at this specific area of interpreting, nonetheless a few studies have been found which are reviewed here.
Although it has been established that omissions can be used as a positive
strategy to ensure effective interpretations, it is worthwhile comparing
literature that looks at omissions from different perspectives. The studies
which are reviewed here can be categorised as follows: those that place
interpreting omissions within the context of errors or mistakes; or those
that regard omissions as linguistic coping strategies which are intrinsic
to an interpreter's work.

2.3.1 Omissions as errors

In order to discuss omissions as errors, it is helpful to explore the
concept of error and language interpretation in general. Kopczynski
(1980) concentrated a large part of his writing on errors made by
interpreters. In establishing a context, he defined an error as "any utterance of the speaker-learner which deviates from the adopted norm"
(p.63). He identified two different kinds of errors: those which violate the
rules of the norm that are not known to the learner (systematic errors);
and those which violate the rules known to the learner (mistakes).
Systematic errors were defined as those errors committed regularly by
people at the same level of proficiency and with the same learning experience, also referred to as errors of competence. Mistakes, however, were
categorised as occurring due to other influencing factors such as inatten-
tiveness, stress and fatigue; otherwise known as errors of performance.

In introducing the notion of error analysis, Kopczynski (1980) stated
that the only utterances that can be considered as erroneous are those
that violate the known rules, (i.e., errors of performance). Kopczynski
used a taxonomy of errors, originally proposed by Barik (1975), which
distinguishes between three major types of errors where an interpreter
may depart from the original source language message. These are

78 omissions, additions and substitutions, each of which are broken down
into certain types. Additions include qualification, elaboration, relationship and closure additions; whereas substitutions incorporate mild and
gross semantic errors based on lexical items or chunks of speech (such as
phrases or sentences). The omission taxonomy detailed four types of
errors: skipping (of a single lexical item); comprehension (omission of a
larger unit of meaning as a result of an inability to comprehend the
source language message); delay (omission of larger unit of meaning due
to lagging too far behind the speaker); and compounding (conjoining
elements from different clauses or sentences).

Kopczynski (1980) noted that Barik (1975) studied the number and
type of omissions made by professional and amateur interpreters. Barik
found that both groups omitted approximately the same amount of
material when working into their dominant language, as they did when
working into their second language. He also identified that prepared
translations experienced more omissions than those rendered spontaneously, with greater time lags resulting in a larger number of omissions.

Kopczynski (1980) conducted his own study, using Barik's (1975)
error analysis taxonomy, in an attempt to determine the borderline
between correct and erroneous translation. He selected a piece of text
giving political toasts from a diplomatic reception and asked eight
students of interpreting to perform the task of translation between
English and Polish. The study used a lexically dense piece of text relying
on formal register of language, which Kopczynski described as the
"type of text that may be classed as a written monologue intended for
oral delivery" (p.76).

The findings of Kopczynski's (1980) study detailed different types of
error which occurred within the translations, including syntactic and
phrasal errors of competence, lexical errors, errors of performance (e.g.,
hesitation, repetition, etc.), additions and omissions. In concentrating on
omissions, it is worth noting that Kopczynski made the distinction
between "obligatory" and "optional" omissions which arose as a result of
differences between the structure of the two languages being interpreted (p.85). These types of omissions were deemed more or less
appropriate according to whether key words within a piece of text were
translatable. The results demonstrated that more omissions were made

than additions, regardless of the piece being translated simultaneously or consecutively. When omissions of whole or parts of sentences were looked at more closely, however, a much higher proportion of omissions took place within the consecutive interpretations. In his summary, Kopczynski defined omissions under both umbrellas of errors of performance and errors of receptive competence. He claimed that omissions could be regarded as performance errors because they can be effected by memory lapses, failure to choose the optimal moment of interpreting, time pressure and fatigue. He also asserted, however, that they can be regarded as receptive competence errors if they occur due to failure to understand the source language message (on the part of the interpreter).

In detailing Kopczynski's (1980) perspective on omissions, and how and why they occur, it is clear that he regarded omissions as errors or mistakes that occur during an interpretation. Apart from a fleeting mention of 'optional' omissions, no indication is given within his writing that omissions may be used as a conscious part of the interpreting process, or as a linguistic coping strategy. There is no consideration that omissions may be used effectively to ensure that cultural equivalence is obtained as part of a successful interpretation. In order to gain insight into the interpretation process, it is possible to break down any interpretation and analyse for meaning and accuracy. Thus Kopczynski should be commended for his detailed analysis and comparison of different interpretations, nonetheless it should be recognised that a more positive analysis can be done, still breaking down any interpretation into smaller components, but looking at the success of the interpretation rather than the mistakes. Other writers (such as Altman, 1989; Moser-Mercer, Kunzli & Korac, 1998; Russell, 2002) have adopted a similar approach to Kopczynski (1980), in that they have looked at errors made by interpreters, and omissions have been categorised as mistakes rather than strategies. This study highlights the different types of omissions made by interpreters, those which could be defined as strategic, and others which could be identified as potential errors.

Cokely (1985, 1992a, 1992b) conducted qualitative linguistic analyses on interpreters working between English and ASL, and developed a similar analysis technique to that of Barik (1975), refining it for the purposes of analysing sign language interpretation. The technique is

80   known as a miscue taxonomy, which by its very name has negative
connotations, as the term implies that the taxonomy is looking for
mistakes or errors made by interpreters. Miscues were defined by
Cokely as being "deviations from the original text" (1992a, p.73) and five
general miscue types were identified. These included additions, omissions, substitutions, intrusions and anomalies. Omission miscues were
then broken down further into morphological, lexical and cohesive
omissions.

In a specific study of the effects of time lag on interpreter errors,
Cokely (1992b) applied his miscue taxonomy to the analysis of four
videotaped individual interpretations from English to ASL in a conference setting. Cokely identified that two of the interpreters maintained
an average time lag of two seconds, whereas the other two maintained a
consistent lag time of approximately four seconds. He then compared
the number of miscue occurrences in relation to the amount of lag time
used by the interpreters.

In terms of omission occurrence, Cokely (1992b) found that lexical
omissions were the most prevalent for both groups, followed by
cohesive omissions and a much smaller number of morphological
omissions. Interestingly, the study shows that those interpreters using a
two-second time lag made more omissions than those with a longer lag,
with over twice as many total miscues. This point is worthy of note as it
contradicts the findings of Barik's earlier study (1975) which demonstrated that a longer time lag led to more omissions being made. Cokely
(1992b) stated that a naïve assumption of simultaneous interpreting
would be that fewer omissions are made with a shorter time lag. He
asserted, however, that "a compressed lag time places the interpreter in
a quasi-shadowing task, in which differences in speech articulation and
sign production rates may result in increased omissions, as the interpreter strives to 'keep up' with the speaker" (p.54). Alternatively, Cokely
argued that an increased time lag augments the overall comprehension
of the source language message, which therefore sanctions the interpreter to "determine the informational and functional value of morphological and cohesive as well as lexical units" (p.54).

Although Cokely (1985, 1992a, 1992b) recognised that interpreters
may use additional lag time to make decisions about the interpretation,

therefore implying a level of metalinguistic awareness, his various
studies all referred to omissions as errors, with discussion of possible
causes for the miscues; thus inherently recommending ways to prevent
omissions occurring within a piece of interpretation.

The benefit of studying interpretations for success and effectiveness
has been established earlier in this chapter. This section has discussed
studies that count the number of mistakes, as opposed to looking at
omissions as successful strategies. As long ago as 1973, Enkvist questioned whether analysis of interpretation should count the number of
errors or measure the success in communication. In supporting a goal-
oriented approach to analysis, Enkvist (1973) suggested the concept of
contextual appropriateness as a 'yardstick' to assess the seriousness of
an error, by looking at the appropriateness of an utterance in the
context of situation. Enkvist claimed that as a consequence of interactions being goal-related, errors should only be considered as such in
relation to functionally relative objectives, rather than just as errors
themselves. Baker (1992) has also recognised the occasional need for
interpreters to 'translate by omission', therefore recognising that the use
of omissions can indeed be strategic.

2.3.2 Strategic omissions.

In giving an account of interpreter-mediated communication, Wadensjö
(1998) explored the responsibilities of the interpreter and the expectations of both the participants and the interpreter involved in the interaction. She analysed the interpretation of an interaction between a police
officer and a Russian immigrant applying for a residency permit, which
took place at a hearing at the immigration department of a police station
in Sweden. Wadensjö discussed the concept of community interpreting,
the role of an interpreter, interactional norms, the premise of communication and the interpreter's influence, turn-taking, and linguistic and
cultural equivalence. This study has been highlighted in relation to
strategic omissions, because Wadensjö suggested her own taxonomy for
use in determining the successful outcome of an interpreted event. She
developed a taxonomy which incorporated similar components to those
of Barik (1975) and Cokely (1985, 1992a, 1992b), yet she used an alternative terminology which has more positive connotations.

82   First of all, Wadensjö (1998) established the interpreter's utterance as
a 'rendition', which relates in some way to the immediately preceding
original utterance. The relation between the rendition and the utterance
of the originator was classified into distinct sub-categories. She stated
that source texts can be considered as "context(s) in a chain of utterances" (p.106), which condition and influence additional discoursal and
contextual development. Wadensjö claimed that although 'original'
utterances are heard (or seen in sign language) in a particular context, it
is necessary for interpreters to de-contextualise each original utterance
to a certain extent, so that it is a separate unit and can be re-
contextualised as a new utterance in the "flow of talk" (p.107).

Thus, in order to compare interpreters' utterances with the originals,
Wadensjö (1998) defined a taxonomy of eight sub-categories of renditions. These included close renditions, expanded renditions, reduced
renditions, substituted renditions, summarised renditions, multi-part
renditions, non-renditions and zero renditions. These sub-categories
enable the analyst to explore the successful nature of an interpretation,
by looking at the appropriateness of particular renditions in the context
of the interpreted interaction.

In relation to strategic omissions, the category of most interest is
that of reduced renditions, similarly referred to by other authors as
condensing strategies (Sunnari, 1995) or selective reductions (Hatim and
Mason, 1990). Wadensjö (1998) defined reduced renditions as "less
explicitly expressed information than the preceding 'original' utterance"
(p.107). It has been noted that omissions can be regarded as strategies
whereby a conscious decision is made to leave something out, or to
reduce the amount of information included from the source language
message into the target language interpretation. Ergo, Wadensjö's
approach, of an interpreter deciding to provide a reduced rendition,
applies positive connotations to the concept of making deliberate
omissions.

Wadensjö (1998) argued that the interpreter in her study used
reduced renditions in order to meet the communicative goals of the
interaction. This coping strategy involved the interpreter using her
linguistic and cultural knowledge about the participants and their
communities, as well as her knowledge of communicative norms in

different situations. Wadensjö gave an example of a reduced rendition
which involved the source language message (in Russian) saying:
"…and anyhow if—even if I live in the USSR, to my mind I am anyhow
not Russian I am Greek, anyhow, so officially I am Greek." (p.114); to
which the interpretation into Swedish was as follows: "… even if I have
been living all of my life in the USSR I am anyhow counted as a Greek,
and not as a Russian." (p.114). Wadensjö explained that this interpretation was contextually, linguistically and culturally appropriate as the
communicative goals of the original statement were achieved in the
interpreter's rendition of the message. She stated that the reduced
rendition placed emphasis on the most recently articulated of the two
communicative goals indicated in the original utterance. She justified
the interpreter's decision to focus on the second goal, because the
information met the needs of a police officer, "to record quickly and
unambiguously the facts of the case (rather than, for instance, his
possible wish to understand the ways in which the applicant in front of
him is reasoning)" (p.115).

Thus Wadensjö (1998) justified the omission made on the part of the
interpreter by explaining why the translation was appropriate, and how
it enabled the interaction to be maintained without cognitive disso-
nance occurring for any of the participants. Again, Wadensjö did not
explore the metalinguistic awareness that the interpreter had about the
strategic omissions or reduced renditions that she was making. Nonetheless, it can be assumed that if the interpreter was aware of the
necessity to omit certain utterances in order to deliver an equivalent
message to the receiver, the strategic omissions made must have been
conscious to some extent.

2.3.3 A new omission taxonomy

The previous section discussed various types of omissions that could be
made by interpreters, as suggested by different researchers, which
include omissions at the morphological, lexical, syntactical, cohesive,
and contextual levels. It has been established that interpreters may
make conscious or unconscious omissions while they are processing
information from the source into the target language, which can be
respectively considered as strategies or errors. As a consequence of the

84   research study reported in this book, a new omission taxonomy has been developed, identifying potential interpreting omissions based on levels of consciousness and strategic-ness (Napier, 2001):

1. Conscious strategic omissions—omissions made consciously by an interpreter, whereby a decision is made to omit information in order to enhance the effectiveness of the interpretation. The interpreter incorporates his or her linguistic and cultural knowledge to decide what information from the source language makes sense in the target language, what information is culturally relevant, and what is redundant.

2. Conscious intentional omissions—omissions made which contribute to a loss of meaningful information. The interpreter is conscious of the omission and made it intentionally due to a lack of understanding of a particular lexical item or concept, or due to an inability to think of an appropriate equivalent in the target language.

3. Conscious unintentional omissions—omissions made which contribute to a loss of meaningful information. The interpreter is conscious of the omission and made it unintentionally, whereby he or she heard the lexical item (or items) and decided to 'file it' before interpreting it, to wait for more contextual information or depth of meaning. Due to further source language input and lag time, however, the particular lexical item (or items) was not retrieved and therefore omitted.

4. Conscious receptive omissions—omissions made that the interpreter is aware of, but he or she cannot properly decipher what was heard due to reported poor sound quality.

5. Unconscious omissions—omissions made which contribute to a loss of meaningful information. The interpreter is unconscious of the omission and does not recall hearing the particular lexical item (or items).

These omission categories were developed as a consequence of the task reviews conducted with the interpreters, and as a result of the comments they made about their levels of consciousness about the omissions they made, all of which are discussed further in chapter four, which focuses on the methodology of the study.

This chapter has introduced the notion of coping strategies, in order to provide a context for the study of translation style and omissions as linguistic coping strategies. It has been suggested that different strategies are used by interpreters during different stages of the interpreting process, either before, during or after an interpreting assignment, in order to cope with various linguistic and extralinguistic factors that may effect their interpreting performance. As well as being used as a reactive measure for spontaneous problem-solving, it has been mooted that coping strategies can also be used as a pro-active measure to enhance an interpretation. Several studies have been presented that explore linguistic coping strategies used by interpreters, incorporating use of linguistic and cultural knowledge and use of translation style. It has been argued that interpreters may choose to use these processes as linguistic coping strategies, in order to enhance the effectiveness of their interpretations, and to ensure that the 'meaning potential' of any utterance is achieved. In order for interpreters to engage in this decision-making process, and actively select linguistic strategies, it has been suggested that they must have a level of metalinguistic awareness. By drawing on their metalinguistic aware-ness, interpreters will monitor their language use and their language choices, and thus make adaptations to the interpretation accordingly, and select the appropriate strategies to use to cope with the linguistic demands of the discourse environment.

Further studies that evaluated the occurrence of interpreter omis-sions have been discussed, and it was pointed out that the majority of studies focus on omissions as errors. It has been argued that as well as being erroneous, omissions can be used as a linguistic coping strategy, whereby interpreters deliberately choose to omit information in order to ensure that the target language rendition is linguistically and cultur-ally relevant. To be able to make the decision to use this omission type, interpreters must be engaging in a conscious metalinguistic process of strategic selection. Thus this omission type has been named a 'con-scious strategic omission'.

As a consequence of being metalinguistically aware, interpreters may be conscious of making erroneous omissions, although they may not have been intentional. A taxonomy was introduced, therefore,

86   which places conscious strategic omissions within a spectrum of omission types.

Now that the notion of how an interpreter copes linguistically has been discussed, and it has been established that this study focuses on the translation style and types of omissions produced by interpreters when interpreting for a university lecture, it is worth examining the discourse environment in more detail. In giving consideration to discourse-specific research, it is possible to identify the linguistic features of discourse environments comparable to university lectures. Conferences are renowned for using high registers of language, and often provide similar environments to that of university lectures, whereby the source text will often be written initially, then read out to an audience. Chapter three reviews various literature investigating conference interpreting, before discussing the area of educational interpreting, and exploring issues faced by sign language interpreters when interpreting in university settings.

Notes

6. Tandem interpreting is a term generally used to describe two interpreters working together on the same assignment, whereby one will be active and work for a stretch of approximately twenty to thirty minutes, while the other is passive but provides on-going support. This arrangement has become the norm for the majority of assignments lasting longer than two hours, and has transpired as a result of research illustrating that the optimum period for interpreting is twenty minutes, after which the quality of the interpreting service will decline. If only one interpreter is used, regular breaks should be provided.

7. The source material was deemed to be "culturally bound" in that it was taken from a British current affairs program which makes assumptions about the levels of language and life experiences of its viewers, which may not be compatible with the language levels and frames of reference of members of the Deaf community. Therefore as the information presented in the videoclip was 'bound' to the source language and culture, in order to find cultural equivalence when interpreting a piece such as this, free interpretation would be the most effective method. Similarly referred to by Cokely (2001) as "culturally rich" information.

8. For further discussion on additions and substitutions, see Cokely, (1985 & 1992a); and for further elaboration on borrowing and literal translation, see Ivir, (1998).

CHAPTER THREE

Discourse-specific research: An overview

3.0 Introduction

This chapter gives an overview of research that has been conducted in the types of discourse environment relevant to this study. Although this study focuses on interpreters working in university lectures, literature is also reviewed which looks at interpreters working in conference settings. It is worth reviewing literature on conference interpreting because interpreters often have to work under similar conditions to those encountered in universities, in that they are having to deal with more formal registers of language, precise social discourse expectations, and will also invariably be working unidirectionally. The similarities between these discourse environments have been recognised in the field of sign language interpreting for over 25 years, with Sutcliffe (1975) stating that the same translation style should be adopted in conference and university settings. Thus, consideration is given first of all to conference interpreting, followed by discussion of educational interpreting in general, and then more specifically, university interpreting.

3.1 Conference Interpreting

Conference interpretation officially began during the First World War as a result of negotiations taking place between people who could not converse fluently in the diplomatic language of French. Initially it is thought that interpretation was provided consecutively, using a sentence-by-sentence process (Gentile, Ozolins & Vasilakakos, 1996; Herbert, 1978). The process of simultaneous interpretation was formally introduced to conferences for the purposes of the Nuremberg trials in 1946 (Gentile, Ozolins & Vasilakakos, 1996; Moser-Mercer, Kunzli, & Korac, 1998), where equipment such as booths and headphones were used to avoid the need for protracted consecutive translation. Over the years many papers have been written on the issues faced by simultaneous conference interpreters (Gerver, 1969; Kopczynski, 1994; Kurz, 1993; Moser, 1978; Paneth, 1957). A seminal work in relation to conference interpreting, however, is that of Danica Seleskovitch (1978). Written from the perspective of an extremely accomplished conference inter-

88   preter, Seleskovitch gives anecdotal examples from her own experiences to emphasise the need for conference interpreters to search for the meaning within any message, and to find equivalents between languages and cultures. Seleskovitch raises intelligibility of language as one of the major barriers that conference interpreters must face. She stated that:

> Intelligibility, which is the goal of the spoken language, is not merely expressed by a greater or lesser degree of explicitness—it takes other forms as well... The speaker's desire to accommodate, to adjust to the situation, leads him into error... (Seleskovitch 1978, p.20).

As well as errors made by producers of the source language message, interpreters have to deal with conference terminology or 'jargon', which may also make the source language unintelligible. Seleskovitch (1978) equated this difficulty to the feelings of isolation experienced when people are in a situation where they know nobody else, when the language used often assumes familiarity with the subject and context. She gave examples of family members or work colleagues who can understand one another although they may use "elliptical expressions and imprecise terms" (p.21). Familiarity such as this will often give rise, for example, to the use of acronyms, or at Deaf conferences the use of name signs [9], which an interpreter may not be familiar with, and will obviously have a bearing on the interpretation she is able to provide. To compensate for this unknown element of language use, Seleskovitch maintained that interpreters need to sustain a wide range of general knowledge, and must be prepared to devote time to preparation and research before a conference in order to raise awareness over topics that may be discussed. She asserted that, first and foremost, interpreters must concentrate on analysing the meaning of any message, and should use their knowledge of the subject to support, rather than take over, the interpreting process.

Seleskovitch (1978) described how interpreters are generalists, who need not have expert knowledge at the same level of specialists, but must understand everything. As interpreters do not originate information, but rather they organise information rationally, they should not judge "the accuracy, the originality or the cogency of the message"

(p.62). Instead they should assess what the message seeks to prove, and
for this they must have a "comparable level of intellectual ability" (p.63)
to that of the speaker. According to Seleskovitch, interpreters can be
faithful in their renditions of the source language utterances primarily
through logical analysis, and secondarily through familiarity with the
subject. She stated that it is this power of reasoning, rather than the
command of the facts, which must correspond with that of the
speaker.

Thus it can be seen that Seleskovitch (1978) has highlighted the need
for conference interpreters to use their linguistic and cultural knowledge, as well as any specialist knowledge they may have, to ensure a
more effective interpretation. She identified language use as one of the
most challenging aspects of conference work. The same analogy can be
applied to interpreting in university settings, whereby the interpreter
may flounder if she does not have some awareness of the specialist
topic being discussed (Harrington, 2001a). Additionally, she should be
prepared to draw on her own knowledge of the languages and cultures
involved to provide a meaningful interpretation. The intelligibility of
language will always be a factor as university lectures tend to be
delivered in a more formal register, and certain assumptions will be
made about the knowledge of the target audience. Seleskovitch mentioned 'comparable level of intellectual ability', which when applied to
university settings, can be argued to mean that interpreters should have
completed university education themselves before being able to work in
that environment. As a result, they should then be familiar with
language use in universities, and be able to anticipate how language use
in that setting may influence their interpretation process.

Sanderson, Siple and Lyons (1999) referred to the need for interpreters to be suitably qualified for working in postsecondary education with
Deaf students. This should include, as well as having studied in a
university environment in a spoken language, a demonstrable equivalent communicative competency in a sign language. Cummins' (1980)
categories of 'cognitive/ academic language proficiency' (CALP) and
'basic interpersonal communicative skills' (BICS) can be applied to the
linguistic proficiency of sign language interpreters. It is necessary for
interpreters to have achieved sociolinguistic communicative compe-

90   tence at a level of CALP in, for example, both English and Auslan in
order to effectively interpret for university lectures.

To return once more to the issue of language use at conferences,
Llewellyn Jones (1981a) explored the phenomenon of BSL as a naturally
occurring language and whether it is a suitable language to use in
conference settings. At the time of writing his paper, there was great
debate amongst the British Deaf community over whether BSL made
use of a formal register, and therefore whether it was an appropriate
conference language. Llewellyn Jones referred to work by Deuchar
(1979) which stated that the diglossia of sign language use in Britain
dictates that Signed English is regarded as the most prestigious form of
sign language, with BSL being the lowest. Llewellyn Jones (1981a)
argued, however, that Signed English is not necessarily used amongst
the Deaf community, and queried the authenticity of Deuchar's (1979)
data, as she observed Deaf people using BSL in a local Deaf club
(informal) and a hearing person using Signed English in a religious
environment (formal). In his own study, Llewellyn Jones (1981a)
demonstrated that there is in fact "a 'repertoire' of styles within BSL"
(p.51), after recording interaction amongst Deaf people in formal, semi-
formal and informal settings and noting a significant difference in their
sign language production. The differences included such factors as
increased use of fingerspelling and lip-patterns within the formal
setting. This language contact variety of BSL is now commonly referred
to as 'Sign Supported English' (SSE), which incorporates English syntax,
and is regarded as the code-mixing of two languages to produce an
inter-language (Corker, 1997).

As a consequence of his findings, Llewellyn Jones (1981a) postulated
that for interpreters working in conference settings, the decisions made
regarding target language output are a lot more complex than simply
differentiating between BSL (informal) and Signed English (formal). To
illustrate his point, he checked the comprehension levels of pre-
lingually Deaf sign language users when observing BSL interpreters at
work. The findings revealed that a high rate of incomprehension
occurred when the interpreters chose inappropriate target language
production forms. Llewellyn Jones noted that those interpreters who
did not have an extensive enough repertoire in BSL (i.e., competency in

both BICS and CALP) resorted to a manually coded form of Signed
English, rather than code-mixing to produce a formal SSE variety of
BSL, which resulted in misunderstanding on the part of the consumer.
In conclusion he stated that in order for Deaf people to gain equal
access to information at conferences and formal meetings, interpreters
must produce an interpreted rendition of the message in the form of
language "most meaningful to the majority of the deaf community" (p.
59). Llewellyn Jones' conclusion can be equally applied to the interpretation of university lectures for Deaf university students.

Moser-Mercer, Kunzli and Korac (1998) investigated the 'coping
mechanisms' which conference interpreters use when dealing with
stressful situations, and the impact on the quality of the interpreting
service. They introduced their study by establishing the working
practices of conference interpreters, which have been established "to
alleviate fatigue and help ensure high quality of output" (p.48). Working
conditions for conference interpreters incorporate key recommenda-
tions that interpreters work alone for a maximum of 40 minutes when
interpreting a single speech, or if working in tandem at an all day
meeting, should take turns approximately every 30 minutes.

The investigation looked at the quality of interpreters' output, the
physiological and the psychological stress levels that interpreters
experience after prolonged turns of over 30 minutes; as well as looking
at how interpreters' coping mechanisms manifest themselves in an
experimental situation. The subjects of Moser-Mercer, et al's (1998)
study were experienced conference interpreters who had worked as
interpreters for a minimum of 12 years between the languages of
English and German. They were asked to interpret four speeches given
by German politicians to determine quality of output, as well as being
asked to fill in a questionnaire to determine psychological reactions to
the environment, and donate saliva samples to ascertain physiological
levels of the stress-induced secretion of the hormones cortisol and
immunoglobulin.

Moser-Mercer, et al (1998) developed a taxonomy to evaluate the
quality of the interpretations based on rating scales used by other
researchers (such as Barik, 1971). The taxonomy focussed on meaning
errors, and its categories include contre-sens (saying exactly the

92   opposite of what the speaker said); faux-sens (saying something
different from what the speaker said); nonsense (not making any sense
at all); and imprecision (not capturing all of the original meaning). As
well as these categories, the study also included analysis of omissions,
additions, hesitations, corrections, grammatical mistakes and lexical
errors.

The qualitative findings of the study indicated that the more
prolonged the interpreting task, the higher the number of errors, with
omissions being the most frequent. The number of omissions rose
from 59.5 during the first three minutes, to 80 when the interpreter had
been working for over 60 minutes. Moser-Mercer, et al (1998) concluded that interpreters' metalinguistic ability to judge the quality of
their interpreting output was extremely unreliable after longer periods
of interpreting. They found that the interpreters were generally
unaware of the decline in the quality of their work, especially as three
out of the five subjects continued to interpret for a further 30 minutes.
The interpreters decided to stop only when they were so fatigued that
they could not continue to interpret.

In summary, Moser-Mercer, et al (1998) emphasised the effectiveness
of the study in demonstrating the qualitative coping strategies of
conference interpreters when working for prolonged periods of time.
They claimed that due to the number of meaning errors increasing in
accordance with interpreter fatigue, and the fact that the interpreters
were not aware of the decrease in their qualitative output, "interpreters,
at least on prolonged turns, cannot be trusted to assess their performance realistically" (p. 61).

They attributed this lack of awareness to cognitive overload, and
hypothesised that interpreters only become aware of the decreased
quality of their output when their fatigue reaches such a level that they
can no longer mentally process the source language message. As a
result, Moser-Mercer, et al (1998) recommended shorter turns to be
taken by conference interpreters to ensure a consistently high quality of
output. This study can be equally applied to interpreters working in
university settings, as they often have to work through two or three
hour lectures with minimal breaks. A coordinator for interpreting
services at an Australian university confirmed that it is very rare for

universities in Australia to consider providing more than one interpreter per lecture (V. Woodroffe, personal communication, December
8, 1999), therefore this practice will obviously have an impact on the
quality of service provided.

Although the study conducted by Moser-Mercer, et al (1998) revealed
that interpreters have a lack of metalinguistic awareness when it comes
to their interpreting performance, it needs to be remembered that these
findings can only be applied to interpreters working under stressful
conditions. This is not to say that interpreters, when working under
optimum conditions, will never have a certain level of metalinguistic
awareness. In the context of this particular study, it can be argued that it
is appropriate for Moser-Mercer, et al to discuss the incidence of errors,
as they have demonstrated that fatigued interpreters are not able to
make judgments about their output. Thus any omissions, additions or
hesitations that are used are unlikely to be part of any conscious
linguistic strategy, and can therefore be regarded as mistakes.

In looking at qualitative outcomes of conference interpreting from
another perspective, Moser (1996) conducted a survey that explored the
expectations of users of spoken language conference interpretation.
Moser sought to prove his hypothesis that different user groups would
have different qualitative expectations of a conference interpreter,
particularly for highly technical conferences. In administering a
questionnaire to approximately two hundred participants attending
conferences and seminars of alternate typologies, Moser found that the
responses covered a range of requirements.

Forty five percent of respondents expected any interpretation to be
faithful to the original source text, with 34% stating that regular
delivery, absence of hesitation, correct grammar, use of complete
sentences and clarity of expression, gave the impression of a good
interpreter. In addition, over one third of the respondents mentioned
that interpreters should demonstrate the features of a lively, non-
monotonous voice with clear enunciation in order to effectively convey
the feeling of the original message. The findings also demonstrated that
approximately one third of respondents found it irritating when the
interpreters' time lag was too long, and felt that it was important for
interpreters to retain synchronicity (that is, keep up with the speaker).

94   Moser (1996) correlated the amount of experience that people had of
attending conferences, with the different expectations they held.
Although those with less experience rated good voice, synchronicity
and good rhetorical skills as being just as important as those who were
more experienced users of interpreters, there were significant differences in expectations about the faithfulness of an interpretation. Of the
more experienced group, 53% stated the importance of a faithful
interpretation, compared to only 35% of less experienced respondents:

> It would appear that users who do not often have occasion to use
> interpretation rank synchronicity, voice, rhetorical skills and faithful-
> ness to meaning more or less equally whereas highly experienced
> users rank content match a long way ahead of the other factors (Moser
> 1996 p.157).

Some respondents stated a preference for completeness of renditions, whereas others flagged the importance that the interpreter should
concentrate on the expression of the essentials of any message. Older,
less experienced respondents had a stronger expectation that the
essentials should be conveyed. When asked their opinion on how long
interpreters should work before letting another interpreter take a turn,
over half the respondents stated 30 minutes as the optimum time. Not
surprisingly, a large proportion of respondents rated terminological
accuracy as being important, with women attending technical conferences being the greater advocates of this feature. Moser (1996) found
that less literal interpretations were preferred, with more importance
attached to interpretation of the meaning of a message, regardless of
whether respondents were at general or technical conferences.

Although Moser (1996) highlighted potential flaws in the validity of
the data due to different circumstances, two general conclusions can be
made about the results of the survey. First, experienced users of conference interpreters had higher expectations of the service they should
receive and what it should entail; and second, participants at different
types of conferences do not necessarily require alternative methods of
interpretation. Moser's original hypothesis assumed that the more
technical the conference, the more respondents would prefer a literal
interpretation incorporating technical terms. The survey results

demonstrated, however, that the conference delegates involved in his study preferred faithful interpretations, which conveyed the meaning of the message.

In applying these findings to Deaf consumers of conference interpretation, it can be assumed that survey results would be very similar in that they would prefer to receive a high quality interpretation that focuses on meaning. Universities provide an analogous setting in that, as mentioned earlier, information is often presented in a similar way to how it is presented at conferences. It is possible, therefore, to assume that users of interpreters in a university lecture would have similar expectations to those users of conference interpreters. The studies of conference interpreting that have been reviewed establish the comparability of service that interpreters are expected to provide when working in universities. It is now possible, therefore, to review any literature that specifically looks at interpreters working in educational settings generally. It has been noted that there is a dearth of research in the sign language interpreting field, yet within the research that exists, a large number focus on educational interpreting. One can surmise that this is due to the fact that educational interpreting is unique to sign language interpreters.

3.2 Educational interpreting

According to Stewart, Schein and Cartwright (1998), "more interpreters practice in schools than in any other setting" (p.189). There is high demand for the provision of sign language interpretation in educational settings, ranging from primary through to tertiary educational institutions (Ozolins & Bridge, 1999), and some interpreters carry out the majority of their work in educational institutions (Chafin Seal, 1998; Hayes, 1992; McIntire, 1990). For those Deaf children who require sign language interpretation, they will invariably receive their education in an integrated setting, usually in some kind of special unit for 'hearing impaired' children within a mainstream school (Bowman & Hyde, 1993; Chafin Seal, 1998). A task force on interpreting provision for Deaf students in the USA described educational interpreting as "an enabling factor" in integrating Deaf students with their hearing peers (Stuckless, Avery & Hurwitz, 1989, p.1). The issues facing interpreters working in

96   primary and secondary schools are different from those they are confronted within postsecondary institutions. Stewart, et al (1998) described the different demands placed on sign language interpreters when working with children. These demands include: adaptation of their linguistic output; the types of information they will be expected to interpret (e.g., story reading); their role as support workers; their ability (or inability) to remain completely impartial; and potential lack of knowledge of subjects taught at secondary school level (e.g., biology and geometry). These issues may equally apply to interpreters working with Deaf adults in universities, especially the matter of inadequate background knowledge of the subject being interpreted. Paul and Quigley (1990), for example, have questioned what subjects educational interpreters should study before working with Deaf students.

     Greenhaw (1985) focussed on educational interpreters working with older Deaf students. In response to a lack of research at that time, Greenhaw administered a survey to postsecondary educational institutions providing interpreting services to hearing-impaired students in the USA. The survey covered a gamut of questions in an attempt to collect data on every aspect of educational interpreters' work, including employment conditions, interpreter reliability, interpreter/student ratios, specialisations, evaluation of services, supervisory issues, and costs. In her summary of the findings, Greenhaw stated that "the survey indicates a lack of programmatic standardisation… in all aspects of interpreting services in the postsecondary setting. This situation causes dilemmas for interpreters…" (p.53). Although Greenhaw did not elaborate on the resulting dilemmas for interpreters, it can be assumed that she is referring to their roles and responsibilities, as mentioned by Stewart, et al (1998) in relation to younger children.

     Many writers (such as Compton & Shroyer, 1997; Dahl & Wilcox, 1990; Harrington, 2001b; Scheibe & Hoza, 1986; Stewart, et al, 1998) have suggested that the role of an educational interpreter incorporates the need for a range of skills and knowledge, which can be in contradiction with the conventional role of an interpreter working in other settings, and that interpreters are not always prepared enough for interpreting in education. Hayes (1992) conducted a survey of 32 educational interpreters in Western Pennsylvania, USA to ascertain how these interpreters felt about their work, and any problems or concerns they may have had. She found that the majority of educational interpreters were under-qualified for the job, and generally did not understand their roles and responsibilities. Jones, Clark and Soltz (1997) also conducted a survey of educational interpreters to collect their demographic characteristics and their perspectives on their responsibilities. The findings were similar to those of Hayes (1992), they found that the majority of respondents to the survey had insufficient training to meet the needs of their role. Wells (1996), however, looked at the role of the educational interpreter from a different perspective, by discussing consumer awareness of the responsibilities of an educational interpreter, and identified a need to educate consumers about the role of the educational interpreter.

Siple (1993, 2000) acknowledged issues faced by interpreters working in college classrooms, in relation to working with college teachers or lecturers who may not have an adequate understanding of the interpreter's role. She identified issues such as the different communication needs of deaf students, the visual 'distraction' for other students of having an interpreter in the classroom, use of visual aides in the classroom, difficulties in interpreting for rapidly paced presentations, and strategies for interpreting classroom discussions to avoid more than one person speaking at a time. Siple suggested that teachers should regard having an interpreter in their classroom as an opportunity to enhance the communication dynamics, and should perceive the role of the interpreter as a contributor rather than an unnecessary distraction.

In addition to the complicated role of an educational interpreter, another complex aspect requiring consideration is the skills base of educational interpreters. The notion of a 'skills base' has been explored from several different perspectives, with individual writers focussing on alternative competencies that an educational interpreter is required to develop. Taylor (1993, 2002), in writing about skills which are required of sign language interpreters in any given situation, delineates the concepts of 'knowledge-lean skills' and 'knowledge-rich skills'. The former are required in portions of an interpretation and refer more specifically to technical language and interpreting skills, whereas the

98 latter are requisite throughout the whole of an interpretation and rely on contextual knowledge of the communities and cultures involved within any interaction.

More specifically in relation to educational interpreting, however, Maroney and Singer (1996) discussed the development of a tool for assessing the skills of educational interpreters. Four areas of skill were identified: message equivalency, linguistic competency, fluency and process management. In developing an assessment tool, Maroney and Singer asserted that it is possible to improve and maintain quality interpreter services for deaf children, increase the number of qualified educational interpreters, encourage appropriate placement of these interpreters, and feed into a professional development structure for educational interpreters. Unfortunately, they were frustrated with the initial application of the tool, due to interpreters' anxieties at being videotaped, lack of a Deaf target audience for the interpreters to sign to, and the criteria used to identify message equivalence.

Schick, Williams and Bolster (1999) explored the skills of educational interpreters in terms of what should be considered the minimum skill level requirement for interpreters before they can work in the North American public school system. A pool of interpreters was assessed using a specific tool developed by Schick and Williams (1994) to evaluate the performance of educational interpreters. They found that less than half the interpreters assessed in their study "performed at a level considered minimally acceptable" (p.151). They argued, therefore, that educational interpreters should be properly trained and accredited before working with Deaf children, as they can have a major impact on the effectiveness of a Deaf child's educational experience.

Cokely (1983a) applied an alternative analysis technique to looking at a different set of skills. Cokely analysed the skills that interpreters possess in effectively conveying metanotative qualities when interpreting from English into ASL. He defined metanotative qualities as "the perceived qualities of messages and speakers rather than the literal or implied meanings of messages"; that is, metanotative qualities are seen as "those non-content characteristics that influence or determine a person's overall impressions of the speaker" (p.16). In order to demonstrate the extent to which interpreters accurately conveyed the

metanotative qualities of speakers, Cokely presented the analysis of two
interpreters who were asked to interpret a series of five lectures delivered in English. A group of Deaf and hearing raters were asked to make
judgments about the speakers by filling in a questionnaire, with the aim
of determining whether the same speaker was perceived differently
when interpreted by different interpreters.

Cokely (1983a) found that there were different perceptions of the
speaker according to which interpreter was being watched. For example, "deaf raters perceived Speakers 1 and 2 more positively than the
hearing raters when [interpreter] 1 was working" (p.20). Cokely concluded that this result could have occurred for two reasons: (1) Interpreters are not aware of the effect of some of their behaviours and
therefore consciously or unconsciously display mannerisms that
conflict with the metanotative qualities of the speaker. (2) Interpreters
may not be aware of how metanotative qualities can be conveyed by
certain linguistic features of sign language, and therefore may use
grammatically correct linguistic features which do not accurately
express the qualities of the speaker. These findings obviously have an
impact on Deaf students, as their perceptions (as well as understanding)
of college lecturers may be skewed by relying on the potentially
inaccurate metanotative qualities conveyed by their interpreters.

The skills of an interpreter also need to be considered in relation to
skills in translation. Livingston, Singer and Abrahamson (1994) compared the effectiveness of ASL interpretation (free interpretation) versus
transliteration (literal interpretation), in giving college students access to
lectures. They defined transliteration as working "between spoken
English and one of several contact varieties that incorporate linguistic
features from both English and ASL" (p.2), whereby interpreters will
tend to follow English word order using signs for individual words and
concepts. Conversely, interpretation was classed as the process for
digesting meaning from the source language and reproducing it in the
target language, therefore ignoring the individual words used.
Livingston, et al stated the need for Deaf students to receive appropriate
interpretation, otherwise they will not have access to the same kind of
instruction as their hearing peers. They determined that one reason why
interpreters might use transliteration was that Deaf students would get

100 access to the same pool of vocabulary as hearing students, as well as potentially helping them to improve their knowledge of English.

The study involved 43 students, divided into those who expressed a preference for one translation style or another, watching a lecture presentation either interpreted or transliterated by experienced interpreters, and answering questions on the information received. The results showed that the students understood more when the information was interpreted into ASL freely, rather than literally. This was the case even for those students who had expressed a preference for the latter method of signing, but who watched the lecture in the former.

In analysing successful interpretations of the lecture, Livingston, et al (1994) noticed that omissions did not necessarily lead to less understanding of the message. In fact, they reinforced the concept of omissions being used consciously as part of a strategic linguistic process. They explained that certain information might be omitted from an interpretation for two reasons. First, the interpreter may make a conscious decision to delete information because she feels that an equivalent message would be difficult to find. Second, the interpreter makes an omission based on her estimation of what would be meaningful to the particular audience she is serving. Therefore in asserting that interpretation, rather than transliteration, is a more effective method of conveying information to Deaf students to ensure higher levels of understanding, Livingston, et al condoned the use of omissions as part of a strategic linguistic process which can enhance an interpretation. They stated that "omissions were not necessarily indications of a poor interpretation. For this interpretation, it appeared to be just the opposite" (p.28).

In taking a more positive view of transliteration (or literal interpretation) and its usage, Winston (1989) also studied transliteration of a lecture, but in her study, analysed one interpreter who regularly worked with the same Deaf student in a university course. Winston wanted to focus on the features that occur in a transliteration when an interpreter is familiar with both the subject and the client, in order to discuss "conscious strategies used by transliterators during analysis and production of the target form, rather than random productions or errors" (p.152). She hypothesised that transliterations incorporate a

language contact mixture of English such as word order and mouthed
English words, and ASL features such as lexical items, head and body
shifting, and use of location. She highlighted particular strategic
choices, which are used to achieve certain types of transliteration. These
strategies included conceptual sign choice, use of additions and omissions, restructuring, and mouthing.

Winston (1989) borrowed from the work of Casagrande (1954) in
order to define four different types of transliteration. The first type is
'Pragmatic transliteration', whereby the source message should be
translated "as efficiently and accurately as possible, with a focus on the
meaning rather than on the form of the message" (p.151). The second
type, 'Linguistic transliteration', is described as a translation where
grammatical concerns, rather than meaning, influence the target
language output. The goal of the third type, 'Aesthetic-Poetic transliteration', is to achieve an aesthetically similar form in the target language,
to that which was produced in the source language. Finally, 'Ethnographic transliteration' seeks to include explanations of cultural
background and text from one language to the other. Winston stated
quite clearly that these transliteration types are not mutually exclusive,
but should be combined within any translation in order to achieve a
balance of all the stated goals.

To prove her hypothesis, Winston (1989) transcribed 25 minutes of a
lecture presented in English and transliterated into ASL, then chose two
particular segments for further analysis. She then consulted with the
transliterator about her reasons for incorporating particular linguistic
features, in order to retrospectively identify whether her strategies were
conscious, "as opposed to being randomly or erroneously produced"
(p.148). She also recognised the importance of checking the consumer's
comprehension of the transliteration to validate its adequacy, and
accepted the "apparent satisfaction" of the consumer involved in the
study as a valid measure (p.153).

In her analysis of omissions, Winston (1989) found that certain
portions of the source language that were redundant in the target
language were omitted. She claimed this strategy was used to achieve
the transliterative goal of efficiency, to provide a pragmatic translation,
even though direct lexical equivalents for transliteration purposes were

102   available. Redundancies noted included: repeated past tense markers; plural markers; linking verbs, such as 'be'; prepositions, such as 'of'; and previously established subject pronouns. Thus, the omission strategies outlined by Winston can regarded as 'conscious strategic omissions'. Although the study was carried out specifically on transliteration, rather than interpretation, the conclusions are equally relevant.

Siple (1995, 1996) further investigated Winston's (1989) findings, but focussed solely on transliterators' use of additions. She stressed the appropriateness of transliteration as a method of interpretation to be used in educational settings, and wanted to demonstrate that interpreters used additions strategically in order to clarify the message, and provide cohesion and emphasis where necessary, as well as rendering the message in a visually appropriate manner. Siple sought to identify different types and frequencies of additions by analysing and comparing the transliterations of a lecture of 15 experienced and 15 novice interpreters. The interpreters were asked to imagine that they were transliterating to three Deaf individuals who were known to them, and "all possessed PhDs, were professionals in the academic environment, and had strong English language skills (reading, writing, and sign), and preferred a more English-like transliteration" (1996, p.33).

As a consequence of her analysis, Siple (1995, 1996) defined five categories of additions: (1) cohesion, where an addition provides discoursal links; (2) clarification, where an addition makes the message clearer with less ambiguity; (3) modality adaptation, where an addition visually communicates an auditory aspect of the message; (4) repetition, where an addition provides emphasis by repeating a key word or phrase; and (5) reduplication, where an addition requires the re-formation of a sign to indicate pluralisation. The most common additions were those in the first three categories.

In her discussion of the results, Siple (1995, 1996) gave specific examples of words or concepts in English, and how they had been transliterated into ASL. She stated that the transliterated texts often contained information that was not present in the source text, which therefore proved that interpreters utilised additions strategically to "provide supplemental information in recognition that a verbatim message would be incomplete" (1996, p.39). This statement is based on supposition, however, as Siple did not interview the interpreters on completion of the interpreting task. There is no recognition in her discussion of the different factors that may effect an interpreter's linguistic decision-making process. Nevertheless Siple's study is commendable due to the focus on interpreter strategy, rather than interpreter error.

Viera and Stauffer (2000) discussed the expectations of Deaf consumers in relation to the use of transliteration. In their paper, they asserted that transliteration is a complex process, which requires more than a verbatim rendering of the message from spoken into manually coded English. Viera and Stauffer recognised the imperative that interpreters utilise additions and omissions strategically in order to elucidate meaning, whether they are interpreting or transliterating. They conducted a small survey of a range of consumers with different levels of deafness in the USA, and found that a high percentage preferred to receive transliteration, rather than interpretation. The survey was sent out, however, to colleagues of one of the authors, the majority of whom were employed in a professional capacity. Thus the results may be misrepresentative, because if the majority of the survey respondents were professionals, they were more likely to be bilingual as they would need university qualifications to do their job. If they were bilingual they would therefore be more likely to be comfortable with, or require, transliteration so they could access English terminology. Nonetheless, Viera and Stauffer's study does raise a valid point in relation to why transliteration may be preferred, which is especially relevant to the study reported in this book.

Viera and Stauffer (2000) asked survey recipients what they hoped to achieve when using a transliterator, rather than an interpreter, in a meeting, and found one of the most typical answers was that consumers wanted to be able to access the English language that their peers were using. In doing so, they could therefore participate in the discourse using the same language, and thus ensure mutual understanding of terminology. The survey respondents stressed the importance for interpreters to have an excellent command of the English language, at graduate level proficiency, with a wide vocabulary. Viera and Stauffer's findings may also be applicable to Deaf university students, in that they

104   may prefer to receive information through a more literal interpretation, (i.e., transliteration), in order that they can access the subject-specific terminology and academic English used in the university discourse environment. This requirement would necessitate interpreters working in university settings to have the appropriate level of language proficiency (CALP), and to be suitably qualified to work in such an environment.

It can be seen from the various studies reviewed thus far, that there has been great interest in the field of educational interpreting in general. All have touched on research conducted in primary, secondary or post-secondary college settings. Fewer studies have focussed, however, on sign language interpreters working in university settings.

3.3 University interpreting

One of the major considerations for interpreters working in universities, according to Stewart, et al (1998), is subject matter. In an ideal world it would be possible to place interpreters with Deaf students according to their background knowledge. Unfortunately in reality, with the shortage of available interpreters, this is not the case. Due to the wide range of subjects studied by Deaf students (Bremner & Housden, 1996), interpreters are often assigned to interpret for subjects they know nothing about, and are given very few opportunities for preparation.

Lawrence (1987) conducted a study of 10 educational interpreters with fewer than 300 hours of interpreting experience, and 10 with over 1500 hours experience, in order to document differences in prepared and unprepared interpretations. Five interpreters from each group were provided with specialised training on terms and concepts related to the subject 'cell division', and the next day all 20 of the interpreters translated this topic in a university lecture on cell biology. Lawrence analysed the interpreted renditions of the lecture for the number of achieved 'semantic equivalent units', and compared the mean number of each group. His findings showed that out of a total of 50 available semantic equivalent units, the less experienced interpreters achieved an average of 10.2 units without preparation, and 24.8 units with preparation. The more experienced interpreters, however, achieved 22.2 units without preparation, and 42.0 units with preparation.

The results demonstrated that preparation, and therefore some knowledge of subject matter, does lead to more accurate interpretations. In summary, however, Lawrence (1987) noted that although knowledge of subject matter is important, skill level has a major influence on achievement of accuracy. He suggested one reason why the advanced interpreters achieved a higher level of accuracy than the beginners, was that the advanced group "had already acquired many 'tricks of the trade' and needed only to be shown how to apply those skills to the subject" (p.89).

In some respects, one could argue that the role of interpreters in university settings is a lot clearer than in other educational settings. As they will be working with Deaf adults who have made the choice to further their education, it can be assumed that consumers will have clear expectations of interpreters, their role and their linguistic output. Nonetheless, interpreters have to deal with other issues, such as: how to interpret the meaning of something if they cannot understand it themselves; being confronted with highly specialised terminology; constantly working within formal registers of language and having to expand their own vocabulary; adapting to students' individual signing styles; and working for long periods of time without a break, to name but a few. This phenomenon leads one to ask questions about the levels of education and interpreter training that interpreters should be required to attain before being allowed to work in university settings. Eighinger (2000) clearly stated that although interpreters are often required to interpret for Deaf students studying towards a tertiary level degree, they should never accept work which involves interpreting at an educational level higher than they have achieved themselves.

Harrington (2000) stated that it is not possible to guarantee that interpreters have attended university themselves, or that they have knowledge and/or experience of the subjects that they may be expected to interpret in university lectures. He referred to the fact that the examination and assessment board for BSL interpreters (CACDP [10]) suggests that only five percent of educational interpreters in the UK possess a graduate level qualification. This cited figure raises questions about under-qualified interpreters' abilities to adequately understand and translate a university lecture in order to make it accessible for a Deaf student.

106   Chafin Seal (1998) argued that "as educational interpreters, learning should be held at a premium" (p.193). This point is reinforced by Roy (2000b), who commented that interpreters should ideally have a general 'liberal arts' university level education, which should include the four literacy strands of reading, writing, listening and speaking. She stated that an education, especially in the liberal arts, is about reading, composing, analysing, and interpreting text. By understanding the process of creating text, interpreters are thus able to interpret text more effectively. It would be pragmatic therefore, to suggest that interpreters should have a university level education generally, but especially before being encouraged to work in university lectures. Patrie (1993) outlined the relationship between the education of sign language interpreters and interpreting in educational settings. She cited the need to follow the lead of the spoken language interpreting profession, where interpreter training programs usually "accept only students who have a university education in place, world knowledge appropriate to the consumers they will be interpreting for and full language proficiency in at least two languages" (p.9).

It is surprising, therefore, that more research has not been done in a university setting, as it is probably the one area that provides more of a challenge for sign language interpreters than almost any other environment (Napier, 2002b). Ozolins and Bridge emphasised this point by stating that due to the diversity of subjects undertaken by university students, interpreters need to be aware of the potential challenges they face:

> The interpreter here is in a complex linguistic environment which requires subject and discipline specific knowledge and a native like fluency in the sign language which allows adaptation and creativity in order to cope with specific terminologies and concepts (Ozolins & Bridge, 1999, p.54).

In addition to subject and linguistic knowledge, understanding of the discourse environment and its' language use is imperative. Roy (1987) studied the outcomes of an interpretation of a videotape of a university lecture translated from ASL into spoken English, and the impact of the message on two different audiences. The first audience was a group of interpreting students that listened to the interpretation 'live', who congratulated the interpreter on the efficacy of her interpretation, in achieving accuracy and dealing with a difficult text. When Roy played a tape recording of the interpretation to another audience who were not familiar with sign language, and who were not aware they were listening to an interpretation, however, the response was quite different. Although the second audience clearly understood the content of the message, when asked for whom they thought the message was intended, the overwhelming response was 'children'.

Through further analysis, Roy (1987) found that the lexical choices and intonation used by the interpreter were characteristic of children's storytelling, rather than an academic lecture. Roy stated that the interpreting students had probably made judgments about the interpretation according to what linguistic choices they would have made, as they were 'listening out' for appropriate English equivalents for the ASL signs they had seen presented in the original discourse, rather than listening for how the interpretation sounded. The second group of listeners, however, only made judgments according to how the message sounded, with reference to familiar discourse types. Roy's study therefore demonstrates the importance for interpreters to consider the discourse environment, and the relationship between the discourse environment and language register, in order to make appropriate linguistic choices within an interpretation. This issue applies to the interpretation of signed language into spoken language, and vice versa. With regards to the interpretation of a university lecture, it is important for interpreters to consider the 'global' message and the intent of the lecturer, as well as the information presented.

Jacobs (1976) studied the efficiency of sign language interpretation to convey lecture information to Deaf students. Hearing students with no knowledge of sign language, and Deaf students who would normally rely on an interpreter, were subjected to watching the same university lecture delivered in English. Jacobs found an imbalance of knowledge acquisition between the hearing and Deaf students, with those relying on sign language interpretation receiving 16% less information than those receiving the information auditorily through English. It is not clear, however, how Jacobs defined the information received, and what was or was not accurate. It can be argued that if he was looking for

108   exact representation in the target language of words used in the source language (i.e., a literal interpretation), it is understandable why he concluded that less information was received by the Deaf students. Yet if he focussed on equivalence of meaning (i.e., a free interpretation), and this was not obtained, then the study raises a pertinent issue with regards to Deaf students accessing information in a university lecture.

Murphy (1978) conducted a study of the 'transmission' skills (sign language production) of interpreters working in a university setting, and found that the skills of interpreters at different levels of experience were essentially the same. In a follow up study, however, Murphy tested the receptive skills of interpreters in reading sign language (i.e., voicing-over for Deaf students), to determine how well information would be conveyed if a Deaf student were in an interactive university lecture. Murphy's study was based on Jacobs' (1976) original research and reached different conclusions. Interpreters were asked to watch a lecture given in ASL, then answer ten questions on the content of the lecture. The results were then compared to the scores of the original groups in Jacobs' study. The interpreters were also sub-categorised as having minimal level (less than 300 hours), moderate level (600 to 900 hours) or maximum level (over 900 hours) experience.

Murphy (1978) found that those interpreters with minimum level experience, attained receptive comprehension scores equal to the Deaf students in Jacobs' (1976) study. The comprehension scores of the moderate and maximum level interpreters were higher than those scores of the Deaf students. Interestingly, Murphy found that the scores of the hearing group from Jacobs' study were higher than the scores of the minimum level interpreters in his study, yet the moderate and maximum level interpreters' results were approximately the same as the original hearing group's. Therefore, although the amount of experience did not seem to effect interpreters' abilities to produce information in sign language effectively, it did appear to influence their receptive abilities. However, Murphy used his results to demonstrate that Jacobs' conclusions may be incorrect. He argued that sign language can effectively convey the content of university lectures, and that the discrepancies in scores between Deaf and hearing participants found in Jacob's study, should not be attributed to deficiencies in sign language.

Murphy (1978) explained that the deficiencies are more likely to come from poor educational backgrounds or the basic language of Deaf people, rather than the incapacities of sign language to transmit a meaningful message. Murphy's study is significant to any research conducted on the use of sign language interpreters in universities, as it implies that interpreters are capable of getting the content of lectures across to Deaf students. As a consequence, Murphy's study validates the further examination of research that looks at the performance of interpreters in this setting.

As a result of being a Deaf student studying at university and using interpreters regularly, Johnson (1991) became interested in the perform-ance of ASL interpreters in universities. She focussed on interpreters' ability to facilitate communication in classroom interaction, as well as their ability to convey the content of a lecture. In order to analyse the extent of miscommunication in university classrooms, Johnson transcribed and analysed 32 hours of videotaped classroom sessions, and monitored the data for discrepancies between what was said by the hearing person, and what was received by the Deaf person through the interpreter. She found that miscommunication or confusion does occur between Deaf and hearing people in a university classroom when relying on the use of sign language interpreters.

The criteria used to check whether the interpreters had interpreted the lecture correctly included checking for omissions of sentences or passages, misspelled words (in fingerspelling), incorrect conveyance of concepts, and inaccurate use of signs. Johnson (1991) noted that the most consistent problems occurred particularly when interpreters were unfamiliar with the subject, and also when it was necessary for them to render a verbal description of a diagram into ASL.

As a consequence, Johnson (1991) argued that Deaf students are often left out of classroom interaction, or misinterpret the content of lectures. The points raised by Johnson are extremely noteworthy, although she focussed on errors and mistakes, rather than positive strategies used by interpreters. This is understandable as students at university rely heavily on interpreters to get access to information at a crucial time of their lives, therefore it can be argued that it is important to know what kinds of mistakes are made. Johnson acknowledged, however, that not all

110   differences in Deaf/ hearing interaction are problematic for interpreters, which introduces the way for the present study.

Harrington (2000) presented initial findings of a similar study to that of Johnson (1991), whereby he analysed the relationships and dynamics that exist between university lecturers, Deaf and hearing students, and BSL interpreters. The express goal of his study was to identify access issues for Deaf students in university settings, and whether interpreters were adequately meeting the needs of Deaf students. He asserted that the aim of the study was to evaluate the dynamics of a university classroom, and to assess the strategies employed by lecturers, interpreters and students in fulfilling each of their roles in the learning process, rather than a critical analysis of interpreter errors.

Harrington (2000) videotaped 15 different lectures from a range of subject areas, which comprised a total of 32 hours of interpreting data. Within the settings recorded, 11 individual Deaf students and nine different interpreters were involved. The gathering of evidence involved the use of two video cameras placed strategically in the classrooms in order to film not only the interpreters, but also the Deaf and hearing students and the lecturers. Wherever possible, participants were also interviewed to ascertain their views on how they felt about the particular lecture, whether they felt that everybody had equal access to the information that was provided, and whether there was anything they would have changed about the situation.

Harrington (2000) recognised the bi-modality of a university classroom, and the distinct dynamics that may arise within any given classroom as a consequence of a variety of influences. The influences he listed include: the number of participants as a whole; the ratio of hearing to Deaf students; the ratio of Deaf students to interpreters; whether the lecturer was Deaf or hearing; the duration of the lecture; and extralinguistic factors, such as the physical environment, use of audio-visual equipment or poor acoustics.

Ultimately, however, the focus was on what he called 'the interpreted event', and the ways in which the spoken message was rendered into the target language by interpreters. Harrington (2000) observed various issues that affected the interpreters' abilities to successfully communicate the message, and therefore had an indirect impact on the general

interaction within the classroom. One example involved interruptions
from hearing students when the lecturer was addressing Deaf students,
and the dilemma interpreters experienced when more than one source
message was being received at the same time, and which should be given
priority for translation. Another example was in relation to a Deaf
student asking for clarification of a sign used by an interpreter. By the
time the interpreter had explained and repeated his lexical choice, and
the student asked a question about the concept, the lecture had moved
on considerably, thus the question raised was regarded as an unnecessary distraction. Harrington stated that the interpreter's unfamiliarity
with the subject of the lecture may have contributed to the breakdown,
and noted that a common issue raised within the study was a lack of
preparation materials for educational interpreters.

As the study itself was incomplete at the time of discussion in his
paper, Harrington (2000) did not make any concrete conclusions. But
in summary, he made a significant point that difficulties experienced by
interpreters in a complex linguistic environment such as a university
lecture, are usually only noted when things go wrong, which therefore
raises concerns about what mistakes or misunderstandings may be
unobserved because they have less serious consequences.

Locker (1990) studied lexical equivalence in transliterations performed in university settings. Locker built on the work of Fleischer
(1975), who described research with 40 Deaf students that determined
the amount of lecture information they received from watching interpreters with or without subject-specific knowledge, and who interpreted
into ASL or Signed English. Fleischer concluded that the students' level
of bilingualism influenced their receptive abilities, but that ultimately,
students better understood information interpreted into ASL.

Locker (1990) looked specifically at the effectiveness of transliteration (literal interpretation) for accurately conveying the content of a
university lecture, and identified three types of errors that frequently
occurred. These errors were defined as misperception of the source
message, lack of recognition of the source form, and failure to identify a
target language equivalent. The categories identified by Locker are
almost synonymous to some of those developed as a result of the study
reported in this book. The category of 'conscious intentional omissions'

112 incorporates lack of recognition of the source form, as well as failure to identify a target language equivalent. Misperception of the source message is comparable either to 'conscious receptive omissions' or 'conscious unintentional omissions', depending on whether the misperception is based on the interpreter being unable to hear the source message properly, or whether she mishears it. Locker focussed her analysis on the identification of errors that interpreters made, therefore no definition was suggested for any category analogous to that of 'conscious strategic omissions'.

Locker (1990) drew on Cokely's (1985) seven-stage model of the interpreting process and miscue analysis technique, to analyse the empirical data presented by the participants of her study. She videotaped six interpreters working in half an hour segments with three different Deaf students, two studying graduate courses, and one studying an undergraduate course. The videotapes were then analysed for "non-equivalent meanings resulting from lexical choices in the target form of the message" (p.174), where Locker found that only three of the interpreters produced lexical errors. It was these three subjects that Locker focussed on for the rest of the study. She points out with interest that those three who did not produce any lexical errors had a university qualification (i.e., a Bachelor's degree), whereas those that did produce errors had not studied at university level.

The next stage of the study involved Locker (1990) re-testing the three interpreters who had made lexical errors, then conducting a follow-up interview where the participants were shown their original and second translations, and asked to comment on their reasons for making the original choices. This process thus allowed Locker to determine the types of errors made, and the category in which the errors fit. She found in the original test, 17% of miscues were misperception errors, and 83% were sign-choice errors. The results of the retest showed that 49% of errors were corrected in the second translation. Of those errors that were not corrected the second time, Locker elicited information from the participants as to what the problem had been. She found that 44% of the uncorrected errors occurred due to not understanding the source language message, and 66% occurred due to failure to identify a target language equivalent. Locker noted that the

lexical items that interpreters had problems with were not necessarily   113
subject-specific terminology, but rather typical use of academic English.
This point was emphasised in relation to the fact that the three interpreters did not have a general university education, and were therefore
unfamiliar with the academic discourse environment. Locker (1990)
emphasised the issue, therefore, that the rate of lexical errors noted
could be linked to interpreters' level of formal education, and whether
they were educated in the topic, or even generally university educated.
She emphasised the ideal for interpreters to familiarise themselves with
the subject matter of lectures they will interpret, at least to acquire
'conceptual familiarity' with terminology and typical language use.
Another implication noted by Locker is that interpreters should have
"at least a bachelor's level of education, in addition to bilingual fluency
as a prerequisite… so as to be equipped for all the contexts in which
they might work" (p.180).

This chapter focussed on research both relevant and specific to the
discourse environment of interest in this book, namely university
interpreting. By incorporating discussion of research in conference
settings, which is a similar discourse environment to that of university
lectures, this chapter has considered linguistic issues for sign language
interpreters in dealing with complex, formal language. The discussion of
general educational interpreting research has identified specific considerations for interpreters in the educational discourse environment.

Several studies of conference interpreting were considered which
highlighted issues for interpreters working in conference and university
settings alike, due to the similar nature of interpreting in those contexts,
for example, the formality, lexicon and register of language. In particular, the need for interpreters to have 'comparable intelligence' to that of
source language presenters at conferences was raised, which highlights
an equivalent ideal requirement for interpreters working in university
lectures to have completed a university education themselves.

In relation to conference interpreting, another issue raised was the
expectations of consumers, and how these expectations can vary
according to the length and type of experience in using interpreters.
Nonetheless, it would seem that conference attendants count on
receiving a quality interpretation, which accurately reflects the meaning

114 and intent of the original message. This presents another comparable situation for Deaf consumers relying on the use of sign language interpreters in a university lecture, whereby one would expect them to demand a similar outcome.

The theme of educational interpreting has been discussed in depth, with an overview given of different facets of the educational interpreter's work and the issues involved, including their role, language skills and interpretation techniques. The few studies on university interpreting have described research on the comparative differences between prepared and unprepared interpretations, on the impact of interpreters on classroom interaction, as well as the effectiveness of sign language interpretation and transliteration techniques in conveying the content of university lectures presented in spoken English.

Now that an overview has been provided of the theoretical grounding for the study of interpreters' linguistic coping strategies, and the discourse environment of university lectures has been explored in depth, it is possible to discuss the results of a study of sign language interpreters' use of omissions and translation style as linguistic coping strategies while interpreting for a university lecture.

Notes

9. The use of name signs in sign languages have been discussed by Meadow (1977) and Mindess (1990), among others, and can be described as identity symbols in the Deaf community. As Deaf people rely on a visual-gestural language, it is common for them to identify each other through 'visual' names that they give to each other, as well as their orthographic name. These name signs may be descriptive, in that signs will be used to describe a particular feature of that person, e.g., large nose or curly hair. Alternatively the signs may be arbitrary, in that there is no visual reference to the person, and there will usually be some kind of story behind why they were given a particular name sign. Therefore if an interpreter is unfamiliar with name signs of Deaf people in their locality, it can be difficult to follow a conversation as they may have no idea whom is being talked about.

10. Council for the Advancement of Communication with Deaf People.

CHAPTER FOUR

Linguistic coping strategies: An analysis

4.0 Introduction

The empirical study that I conducted for my PhD research (Napier, 2001) involved the analysis of data obtained from a pool of professionally accredited Auslan interpreters. The analysis concentrated on the translation style and types of omissions produced by the interpreters when interpreting for a lexically dense university lecture, and the extent to which the interpreters were metalinguistically aware of the omissions they made, and why they made them. The study then focussed on the impact of interpreters' educational backgrounds on their ability to effectively interpret a lexically dense university lecture, and whether a university level education, or familiarity with the lecture topic, influenced the type of translation style used and types of omissions produced as linguistic coping strategies.

4.1 Research questions and hypotheses

The key research questions and hypotheses were as follows:

1. How do sign language interpreters use translation style as a linguistic coping strategy in the interpretation of a university lecture?
2. How many omissions do sign language interpreters produce (within the omission types defined as part of this study) when interpreting for a university lecture?
3. Does the translation style of sign language interpreters effect the number and type of omissions that they make?
4. Do sign language interpreters use conscious strategic omissions as a linguistic coping strategy in the interpretation of a university lecture?
5. To what extent are sign language interpreters metalinguistically aware about the types of omissions that they make while interpreting for a lexically dense university lecture?
6. To what extent do the linguistic features of the source text (that is, lexical density, subject-specific terminology, academic English)

influence use of the translation style and occurrence and types of omissions produced by sign language interpreters?

7. Do sign language interpreters feel that their educational background impacts upon their ability to interpret for a university lecture?

8. What are the expectations of Deaf university students in relation to the translation style, omissions made, and educational backgrounds of sign language interpreters in this discourse environment?

Initially, I believed that the interpreters involved in the study would switch between using free interpretation and literal interpretation methods, and that their educational background would influence the pattern of switching. From a theoretical point of view, I felt that interpreters who had studied at university would be better equipped to employ a more free translation style to effectively interpret a university lecture, as they would be more familiar with the discourse environment and the inherent use of academic English.

The hypothesis in relation to the number and types of omissions was that all the sign language interpreters would make omissions in each category. I hypothesised that subjects dominant in using a free interpretation approach would use more conscious strategic omissions than those dominantly using a literal approach, as subjects using literal interpretation would concentrate more on the form of the message than on meaningful equivalents. I also predicted that interpreters in this study who had a university qualification and were more familiar with the lecture topic would make more conscious strategic omissions, because they would feel more comfortable about making strategic omissions based on their familiarity with academic English and subject-specific knowledge.

In relation to conscious intentional omissions, I expected that those who were not university educated, or not acquainted with the lecture topic, would make more omissions in this category due to lack of familiarity with the academic language register and subject-specific jargon. I assumed that all interpreters would unavoidably make conscious unintentional omissions due to cognitive overload. For conscious receptive omissions, however, the expectation was that those who had knowledge of the lecture topic would make less of this omission type than those without knowledge. Due to having frames of reference for the lecture content, I hypothesised that these interpreters would be able to predict what terminology they should expect to hear, and thus have less problems hearing and deciphering lexical items. Furthermore, I predicted that those without topic knowledge, but who were familiar with academic discourse environments, would be better equipped to infer meaning in what they heard, and consequently make less conscious receptive omissions. Finally, it was assumed that all the Auslan interpreters would make a small number of unconscious omissions.

I envisaged that the interpreters' dominant translation style would effect the number and types of omissions produced, and that all interpreters would use conscious strategic omissions as a linguistic coping strategy.

It can be asserted that the use of metacognitive strategies are intrinsic to the occurrence of conscious omissions, therefore I predicted that sign language interpreters would have a high level of metalinguistic awareness about types of omissions made while interpreting for the university lecture.

I suspected that the linguistic features of the source text would impact upon the translation style and occurrence and types of omissions produced by the interpreters, and that the interpreters would be most influenced by their level of familiarity with academic English and subject-specific terminology. I also expected that the interpreters would make more omissions in the most complex, that is, lexically dense, parts of the text. Consequently, I predicted that the interpreters would feel that their educational background effected their ability to interpret for the university lecture due to their comfort levels with the language use.

Finally, I predicted that Deaf university students would prefer interpreters to provide meaningful interpretations of university lectures, while appropriately providing access to English terminology. I also expected that they would not be comfortable with the idea of interpreters making conscious strategic omissions, and that it would be important for interpreters working in universities to have a good level of education, but that language and interpretation skills would be more important.

4.2 The interpreters

In order to select subjects to participate in the study, it was decided to focus on accredited interpreters only. Interpreters must have a minimum level of competence and sophistication in the language being analysed, for an effective analysis of linguistic coping strategies, and before they will be able to apply such strategies to their work.

Interpreters were selected from people who had responded to an earlier survey that collected information on interpreters' educational backgrounds and areas of work (Napier, 2001), and had expressed an interest in participating in further research. The recruitment process involved contacting 18 interpreters to ascertain their availability and willingness to participate, which meant sending a letter explaining what was to be involved in the data collection. Twelve agreed to participate, but due to unforeseen circumstances, data was only collected from ten interpreters. The ideal criteria required a representation of interpreters from those who were native signers and those who were not; those who had a university qualification or were studying towards a university qualification, and those who did not; and experience of interpreting in higher education. The final group of Interpreters included: seven native and three non-native signers; eight people with a university qualification and two without; and eight who had a lot of experience of university interpreting and two who had very little.

4.3 The source text

It was necessary to develop source material that would provide a text for the analysis of interpretation, which would be a university lecture of higher lexical density than typical spoken conversation. The source material was required to be presented in English, so that the interpreters involved in the study could interpret the message into Auslan.

Naturally, a real lecture was selected as the source text. A lecture entitled "Issues in sign language acquisition by young children", that was presented in English as part of a Masters degree program for teachers of the deaf, was recorded live on to videotape. The lecture was selected with confidence that analysis would show it to be lexically dense, due to the reputation of the lecturer, and my own previous experience of interpreting for this particular lecturer.[11]

At the time of presentation, the lecture was being simultaneously interpreted by an accredited interpreter into Auslan for a Deaf student, which authenticates the 'interpret-ability' of the lecture. In recording the data, however, the video camera was trained on the lecturer as he presented the material, and did not record any of the work of the interpreter present at the time of recording.

The whole lecture lasted for one hour and twenty minutes. It was decided for the purposes of this study, to focus on the first 30 minutes of the lecture. This section was chosen knowing that many of the participants who would interpret the piece would not be overly familiar with the subject, and therefore the first part of the lecture would contain some introduction to the area.

The chosen section of the lecture was transcribed using conventional orthography. Using the transcription, the 20-minute section of the lecture that the interpreters would actually translate was analysed for lexical density, adopting the method proposed by Ure (1971). The analysis took the form of counting the total number of words in the text, then dividing by the number of lexical items (content words) to work out the percentage of lexical rather than functional (grammatical) items used throughout the text. Lexical or content words are those with 'full' meaning, as opposed to grammatical or function words which are 'empty' of meaning (Crystal, 1995). The text was found to have slightly more content than grammatical words, giving a lexical density of 51%. Considering that typical spoken text has a lexical density of 33%, and an average lecture contains a lexical density of 39.6% (Ure, 1971), it was felt that the chosen lecture was more than suitable to use as the source material for the purposes of the study.

4.4 The task

The focus of this study was on what interpreters do well, rather than on what they do wrong, therefore in order to evaluate the skills of Auslan interpreters, it was decided to combine three different procedures. These procedures included: a 'tough-case analysis', that is, a tricky interpreting situation (Moser-Mercer, 1997); a task of 'process tracing',

120   whereby the subject runs through the task a second time (Moser-
Mercer, 1997); and a 'retrospective interview' (Hoffman, 1997). After
conducting several pilot studies to ensure that the methodology was
sound, the data collection took place over a period of two weeks.

It was decided that each interpreter participating in the study would
be given the task of interpreting the same twenty minute segment of the
chosen videotaped lecture, as this is the optimum period for interpreting before the qualitative output begins to suffer (CACDP, 1997). All
participants were made aware of the purpose of the data collection
when arrangements were being made for them to be involved in the
study. The notion of researching omissions as a positive linguistic
coping strategy, rather than a negative outcome was emphasised.

Whereas linguists researching spoken languages will often use tape
recorders to preserve data for future reference, in this instance it was
necessary to videotape each subject, due to the visual nature of signed
languages. In this way, a simultaneous recording could be made of
both the spoken English source message, and the signed target message, and the tape could be referred to by the researcher and participants "to elicit… explanations or spontaneous comments" (Stokoe &
Kuschel, 1979 p.19).

Each participant was recorded individually in a room with a
television and video camera, with the only other people in the room
being the researcher, and a Deaf person acting as a 'receiver' for the
interpretation[12]. The interpreter was positioned so he or she could be
filmed during the task, but still comfortably see the television screen.
The Deaf person sat next to the video camera facing the participant, and
the researcher sat in the corner of the room slightly outside the field of
vision of the interpreter.

Before commencing the task, each participant was given the same
instructions, with the researcher following a script to ensure consistency of information given. They were told the topic and source of the
lecture, but not given any further preparation in relation to content.
The participants were told that they would be permitted to watch the
first ten minutes of the lecture in order to familiarise themselves with
the topic and the pace of delivery, before interpreting the next twenty
minutes of videotape.

The subjects were informed that they would only be allowed one attempt at the exercise, whereby the videotape would be played all the way through without any pauses. It was acknowledged that in real life interpreting situations, it is common practice for interpreters to interrupt a speaker for clarification or repetition. However, for the purposes of this study, it was felt that it was not necessary to ensure accuracy, as the focus was on those omissions made as part of a conscious linguistic process and the translation style used. The participants were advised that if they did miss a piece of information, that they should stop, continue to listen and begin to interpret again as soon as they had picked up the thread of what was being said.

In order to prevent distractions or unnecessary confusion for the interpreters, each subject was given a list of names mentioned throughout the lecture before beginning the task. This procedure ensured they knew how to fingerspell the names, and would not be distracted from the point of the task by worrying about misspelling.

Throughout the task, I referred to a transcript of the lecture, and underlined any omissions that were made throughout the interpretation. Being an accredited interpreter myself, I was able to listen to the source language message and identify anything that was omitted from the target language output through the interpretation process. Omissions were noted according to the following definition that I developed based on a review of the literature: "When information transmitted in the source language with one or more lexical items does not appear in the target language, and therefore potentially alters the meaning".

On completion of the interpreting exercise, the interpreter and I performed a task review. The Deaf receiver was no longer in the room. The procedure of the task review involved myself and the participant watching a playback of the videoed interpreting task, and pausing the video when omissions were noted in the Auslan rendition of the English lecture. If omissions were noted, the participant was asked to explain why he or she thought the omission might have occurred, and whether he or she was aware of it at the time, that is, whether it was conscious or unconscious. The purpose of the review was to establish whether omissions were being made on a conscious or unconscious level. If subjects identified conscious omissions being made as a

122　linguistic strategy, they were asked to elaborate on why they had made the conscious decision to omit particular types of information. It was emphasised once again at this point, that the identified omissions did not necessarily indicate errors, but rather as potential strategic decisions. The feedback from the review gave an indication of the level of metalinguistic awareness that the interpreters had about their language use, cultural relevance of certain information and processing skills. Notes of his or her feedback were added to the transcript used by the researcher, at the same time that the whole review was videotaped.

A retrospective interview took place when the task review was completed. The notion of retrospective interview for the purposes of "knowledge elicitation" has been described favourably by Hoffman (1997). An interpreter interviewed in this way by Hoffman commented that "the process pulled out much of what [I] had thought, the difficulties [I] had encountered, and the ways [I] had managed [my] interpretation process" (p.205). The ultimate goal of the retrospective interview in this study was to elicit information from the subjects about their perceptions of the interpreting task.

The interview was conducted using pre-set focus questions, and was videotaped in order to provide evidence for inter-rater reliability checks at a later stage. The focus questions asked: how the interpreters felt about the overall piece of interpretation; whether there was anything they were particularly happy or not happy with; what they found most easy or difficult about the piece; whether they had any particular skills or knowledge which contributed to their ability to interpret for the lecture; and whether they thought there were any other skills or knowledge that they did not possess, which may have helped them to interpret the lecture more effectively. Finally, the interpreters were asked to comment on perceptions they had about their own educational background, and its effect or influence on their interpretation skills.

The goal of the retrospective interview was to ascertain whether the interpreters felt there was any relationship between their level of educational achievement, and their ability to interpret for a university lecture, alongside their ability to objectively reflect on their work and identify strengths and weaknesses.

In relation to the task, there is one issue that should be acknowledged and accounted for. In most circumstances, interpreters work
regularly with the same client when they attend university lectures.
Quite often an interpreter will be booked for a whole semester, and
therefore has the opportunity to get to know the client. This situation
means that interpreters also have the advantage of being able to
familiarise themselves with the content of lectures, and the pace and
delivery style of lecturers, and will develop specific ways of working
with a client to suit his or her needs.

Some might argue, therefore, that the scenario for this study was
unrealistic. However, an entire semester of a university course may not
be interpreted by the same interpreter throughout. For example,
interpreters fall ill, meaning that it is conceivable for interpreters to
provide cover for one-off occasions, and go into this type of assignment
without any preparation and without knowing the client. Chafin Seal
(1998) often referred to last minute 'substitute interpreting' in her
discussion of educational interpreting case studies. Another situation is
that interpreters may withdraw from the assignment if they feel they
cannot adequately understand the content to interpret effectively, or a
Deaf student may request that the interpreter be replaced if he or she
cannot follow their interpretations well enough to suit their needs. One
Deaf person revealed to me that during one semester at university, she
had eight different interpreters for one course, for exactly these reasons
(D. Thornton, personal communication, November 27, 2000). I would
argue, therefore, that the best way of testing interpreters' linguistic
coping strategies is by testing them in a new, possibly unprepared for,
situation, as it would seem that this is where their skills would be most
challenged.

4.5 The analysis

Once all the data had been collected, it was necessary to develop an
analysis tool, which could be appropriately applied to the data to elicit
the required information. At the conclusion of the analysis, the process
and results were checked for reliability. This was necessary to ascertain
that the data collected was sufficient in relation to the research questions, and that the subjects involved were appropriately tested.

124   The process of data analysis involved two stages. First, entering the number and types of omissions made by each subject into a database. Second, identifying the translation 'style' of each interpreter. The information was then cross-referenced in order to compare the output of each interpreter.

The database was set up to identify what patterns emerged in the use of certain types of omissions. The omission types were identified as: conscious strategic omissions; conscious intentional omissions; conscious unintentional omissions; receptive omissions; and unconscious omissions. The omission types were entered into a spreadsheet with the corresponding numbers for the lines of text where the omissions had occurred. There were a total of 176 lines counted in the source text. Using this system, it was possible to note whether an identifiable pattern of omission types emerged within particular pieces of text, for example, frequent conscious strategic omissions on line 22, and sporadic unconscious omissions on line 140. If an omission occurred across more than one line of text, it was counted on the first line that it appeared.

As well as distinguishing patterns of omissions in certain parts of the text, the purpose of the analysis was to determine the ratio of conscious and unconscious omissions made by each subject, and whether the types of omissions made were influenced by translation style. A final comparison was made with regard to the qualifications of each subject, and whether there was a relationship between the subjects' educational background and the types of omissions made.

In order to determine whether the number of omissions made per subject were influenced by translation style, it was necessary to develop a system for identifying the approach used by each interpreter. The aim was to distinguish between free and literal styles of interpretation. These styles were identified according to definitions put together from a literature search. The definitions are outlined with examples of a translated English sentence to illustrate how each method of translation might be applied.[13]

Free interpretation: "the linguistic structure of the source language is ignored, and an equivalent is found based on the meaning it conveys" (Crystal, 1987, p.344). In the context of discussing bilingual programs for

Deaf children, an example of a free interpretation of an English sentence
can be seen in Example 1.

EXAMPLE 1: FREE INTERPRETATION

'We should try and encourage families to support the first language
acquisition of their Deaf children.'

'ALL FAMILY HAVE DEAF CHILDREN.. WE SHOULD WHAT ENCOURAGE
           (point-arc)   *(q)*   *(point*

PARENTS LEARN SIGN LANGUAGE.. MEANS PARENTS AND CHILD HAVE
left-middle-right)   *(point-left point-right)*

SAME LANGUAGE.. MEANS CHILD CAN ACQUIRE SIGN FIRST LANGUAGE'
           (point-left)   *(their-left)*   *(hd)*

Literal interpretation: "the linguistic structure of the source text is
followed, but is normalised according to the rules of the target language" (Crystal, 1987, p.344). An example of a literal interpretation of
the same English sentence can be seen in Example 2.

EXAMPLE 2: LITERAL INTERPRETATION

'We should try and encourage families to support the first language
acquisition of their Deaf children'.

'WE SHOULD TRY WHAT ENCOURAGE FAMILY SUPPORT DEAF CHILDREN
                (q)   *(point-right)*   *(point-left)*

FIRST LANGUAGE ACQUISITION'
(their-left)   *(hd)*

In order to compare the translation styles of each subject, three sentences were chosen from the source text, one from the beginning, one
from the middle, and another from the end. Each sentence incorporated
one terminological word relevant to the subject, and was culturally
bound to the subject in terms of register and content.

The way that each of the ten subjects translated the sentences was
transcribed, and compared to the definitions and translation examples
given earlier in this section. The general translation style of each subject
was then judged from the transcriptions and the dominant style used. It
is generally difficult to compartmentalise and state categorically that

126 every interpreter only uses one method or another. Most of the interpreters tended to fluctuate depending on their level of comfort with the subject and the speed of delivery. Sometimes subjects could be seen to code-mix within one sentence, within one paragraph, or throughout a piece of text. It was noted, however, that the interpreters tended to be dominant in one approach, so although they might have code-mixed, and switched between approaches at certain parts of the text, they tended to have a certain style in terms of their general approach and how often they code-switched between translation styles. So for the purposes of this research, each subject was categorised as using either free or literal interpretation. It was decided that if a subject used a certain style for two or more of the three sentences selected for analysis, he or she would be judged to be dominant in that style. For example, subject one translated the first sentence freely, and the second and third literally, therefore she was deemed to dominantly use a literal interpretation approach. If, however, an interpreter used the same style for all three sentences, he or she would be judged to be extremely dominant in his or her use of a particular translation style.

This classification method was one of the unique aspects of this study, as it identified that although interpreters will be dominant in one translation style, some tend to switch style more than others, thus acknowledging that interpreters may switch translation style as a linguistic coping strategy to meet the needs of their client group within a particular discourse environment. Most literature tends to refer to interpreters adopting one particular style or another, with little recognition for the fact that interpreters can switch between translation styles, and therefore use more than one style in one scenario.

On completion of the analysis of the subjects' translation styles, it was necessary to ensure the reliability and validity of the findings. This was done by carrying out inter-rater reliability checks. Burns (1997) stated that "when data are obtained from a data gathering instrument or technique, we need to know what faith we can put in the data as truly indicating the person's performance or behaviour" (p.259). He asserted that the assessment instrument must be reliable and valid, and that extraneous factors, which might influence a subject's ability to perform, are controlled as much as possible. The key to determining whether a test is reliable, is whether it is dependable and can in fact be consistently emulated by other researchers. In relation to the assessment of sign language interpreters, Strong and Rudser (1992) noted that many techniques are subjective and rely on the opinion of just one person. Thus they condoned the checking of any test instrument for reliability, to eliminate any potential subjective decisions of the rater.

It was decided therefore, to administer a reliability check using the 'test-retest' method (Burns, 1997), whereby my scores were compared with results presented by the data analysis of another person. The reliability check incorporated the three stages of task analysis, as originally administered. The first, concentrating on the interpreting task itself, the second on the task review, and the third on the retrospective interview. The checks involved evaluating the data of three subjects, each collected at different stages of the data collection phase: the beginning, middle, and end.

An accredited interpreter was chosen to conduct the reliability checks, as she matched the criteria decided upon for the inter-rater. The criteria required the rater to be bilingual in English and Auslan, and have the ability to freely access each language (i.e., be able to listen to the English and watch the Auslan). It was also considered important for the rater to be a qualified interpreter with experience of analysing and critiquing interpretations of other interpreters.

The reliability check involved four stages: the rater watching the videotapes of the interpreting task and marking the omissions of each interpreter; the rater watching the videotapes of the task review and noting the specific omission types of each interpreter according to the omission taxonomy; the rater watching the videotapes of the retrospec-tive interview and noting the key points made by the interpreters about their perception of the interpreting task; and comparison of the rater's results with my own findings.

On analysis of the results the number of omissions noted by myself and the rater were found to be 90.8% reliable. With regards to reliability of the task review data, the types of identified omissions were found to be 86% reliable with those identified by myself. The retrospective interview check was found to have a reliability of 83%. Thus the methodology was judged reliable.

128   In order to validate the method developed for the classification of translation styles, and check for objective reliability, a different sign language researcher who is also an accredited interpreter was asked to emulate the translation style classification process. The rater was given the original style definitions and example sentences, and asked to check the written transcriptions of the three sentences for each subject, with the interpreted renditions on the videotapes. He was then asked whether he agreed with the style of translation for each sentence, and what he judged as the dominant translation style of each subject. This process resulted in a reliability score of 100%.

Notes

11. I am indebted to Dr Greg Leigh for agreeing to have his lecture videotaped and used for the purposes of the research study.

12. Interpreters often rely on feedback from their clients (in the form of facial expression, etc.) to gauge whether their interpretation is being understood, and whether they need to make any adaptations (Brennan & Brown, 1997). During this study, the interpreters were able to maintain eye contact with a 'real' Deaf person, thus making the interpretation process as authentic as possible. The Deaf person 'received' the interpreted lecture, and acted as a target for the interpreting output. Several writers have commented on the negative impact of not having a Deaf target audience when analysing the work of interpreters (such as Maroney & Singer, 1996; Napier, 1998b), therefore it was considered a necessary component of the data collection. It was important to have the same Deaf receiver for all participants, as lack of consistency may have skewed the interpreters' notions of their target audience. Therefore one Deaf person was hired as a research assistant for the duration of the data collection. He was present at every video recording, and his role was to just sit and watch the interpretation without giving any overt comments.

13. Transcription conventions can be found in Appendix A.

CHAPTER FIVE

Interpreters' use of linguistic coping strategies

5.0 Introduction

The aim of this chapter is to give a detailed breakdown of the results of the analysis of the linguistic coping strategies used by interpreters, namely translation style and omissions. Information is also presented on the final stage of the study, which involved discussion with a panel of Deaf people who regularly use interpreters in university lectures, to ascertain their expectations of interpreters in this discourse environment, and whether their expectations matched the findings of the study.

5.1 Translation style

Two particular styles were identified as key methods of translation: free interpretation and literal interpretation. The interpreters in the study were classified according to their dominant translation style, as described in the previous chapter.

Six of the interpreters were found to use a dominantly free interpretation approach, with two out of the six being extremely dominant, whereby they did not code-switch between free and literal interpretation methods. The other four subjects used a dominantly literal approach, with three of the four being extremely dominant. The classification of translation style was not a test of accuracy, merely a method to identify the interpretation approach of each subject. Examples of an extreme dominant approach and a dominant code-switching approach are shown in Examples 3 and 4.

Example 3 shows how the interpreter employed the method of free interpretation for all three sentences, demonstrating the features of free interpretation as identified in Appendix B, and thus was extremely dominant in her use of this interpretation method.

EXAMPLE 3: EXTREME DOMINANT APPROACH
(FREE INTERPRETATION)

Subject 9 sentence 1 (free):

'And what they did was contrast the acquisition of these these features

‘WELL THREE WRITE NOTE-DOWN WHAT THEY D-O WHAT WELL
(point-right)   (q)

with the acquisition of the same types of grammatical features in

COMPARE CHILDREN ACQUIRE SIGN LANGUAGE GROW-UP ACQUIRE
(left)   (right)

English, and came up with, as a result of this study, with what seemed

ENGLISH (STRUCTURE) G-R-A-M-M-A-R COMPARE+ FIND THEIR RE-
(hd)   (their-right)

to me some quite consistent patterns of grammatical acquisition

SEARCH SHOW HAVE+ SAME COMPARE+ CHILDREN ACQUIRE MANY

across the two languages.'

SAME HOW.'

Subject 9 sentence 2 (free):

'Er, any of you who're, er, particularly those of you that are interested
in early childhood education will be aware of the work in this area, the
work of people like John Piaget, who made a very very strong case

‘YOU AWARE
(point-middle)

KNOW WHAT J-O-H-N P-I-A-G-E-T WORK.. PERSON WRITE A-LOT-
(q)   (his-middle) (point-middle)

for... the, erm, for a binding relationship between early sensory-

OF-TEXT STRONG* TALK OVER WELL.. RELATIONSHIP WITH WHAT WHEN
(q)

motor development and early language acquisition.'

BABY CHILDREN GROW-UP THEIR HANDS EYES ARMS-MOVE EARLY MOVE
(their-right)

RELATE-TO EARLY ACQUIRE LANGUAGE.'
(point-right)

Subject 9 sentence 3 (free):

'If you look at the work of someone like Steve Krashen, even in second

‘DOESN'T-MATTER SECOND LANGUAGE

language research, his notion of, that we have to be at or just,
RESEARCH S-T-E-V-E K-R-A-S-H-E-N SECOND LANGUAGE RESEARCH
                            (point-right)   *(his-right)*
just above the language receptive capacities of the language learner,
AREA WELL THEIR LANGUAGE MUSTALMOST AHEAD ME ACQUIRE+
(point-right) *(their-right)* *(point-right)*
that if we're too far above it, then the capacity for the learner to
THEIR SPEAK+ T-O ME ME-UNDERSTAND LITTLE-BIT AHEAD WHAT MY
(their-right)
actually make use of language input is certainly diminished.'
UNDERSTAND ME CAN AHEAD IMPROVE WELL I-F FAR-AHEAD ME CAN'T
            (neg/hd)   *(point-right)*
ACQUIRE DAMAGE MY ACQUIRE T-O LEARN SECOND LANGUAGE.'
(neg)

Example 4, however, provides a transcription of the same three sentences from another subject, who code-switched between a free and a literal interpretation approach, and therefore was not as extreme in her dominance of translation style.

EXAMPLE 4: DOMINANT CODE-SWITCHING APPROACH
(FREE INTERPRETATION)

Subject 6 sentence 1 (free):
'And what they did was contrast the acquisition of these these features
           'WELL ACTUALLY COMPARE HOW PEOPLE
                                    (point-left)
with the acquisition of the same types of grammatical features in
LEARN F-E-A-T-U-R-E-S WITH HOW PEOPLE LEARN SAME G-R-A-M-M-A-R
English, and came up with, as a result of this study, with what seemed
F-E-A-T-U-R-E-S ENGLISH.. FROM.. FOUND SAME SAME HOW PEOPLE
                 (point-left-right) *(left)* *(right)*
to me some quite consistent patterns of grammatical acquisition
LEARN OR LEARN DOESN'T-MATTER WHICH LANGUAGE.'
(point left) *(point right)*   *(point both)*
across the two languages.'

Subject 6 sentence 2 (literal):

'Er, any of you who're, er, particularly those of you that are interested in early childhood education will be aware of the work in this area, the work of people like John Piaget, who made a very very strong case

'MAYBE YOU..

(point-arc)

for…the, erm, for a binding relationship between early sensory-motor
EXPERIENCE WITH WORK O-F J-E-A-N P-I-A-G-E-T HIMSELF REALLY
development and early language acquisition.'
BELIEVE.. VERY STRONG RELATIONSHIP B-I-N-D-I-N-G RELATIONSHIP
BETWEEN EARLY S-E-N-S-O-R-Y M-O-T-O-R DEVELOP AND EARLY
LANGUAGE ACQUISITION.'

Subject 6 sentence 3 (free):

'If you look at the work of someone like Steve Krashen, even in second language research, his notion of, that we have to be at or just, just above the language receptive capacities of the language

'I-F LOOK-AT WORK O-F S-T-E-

learner, that if we're too far above it, then the capacity for the learner
V-E SOMEONE RESEARCH.. ANOTHER PERSON HAVE-TO EQUAL-TO
    (their-right)   *(hd)*

to actually make use of language input is certainly diminished.'
SIMILAR T-O LANGUAGE LEARN I-F HIGH-ABOVE* SOPHISTICATED VERY
                                        (point-left)

DIFFICULT CAN'T-UNDERSTAND WHAT PERSON SAY.'
    (neg)   *(point-right)*

Table 1 provides a summary of the dominant translation style of each interpreter, plus information on their level of education. There did not seem to be any major relationship between the translation style and level of education of each interpreter. Four of the subjects who were dominant in their use of free interpretation held postgraduate qualifications, and two held undergraduate qualifications. Two of the subjects who were dominantly literal in their interpretation approach also held university qualifications. Only two of the 10 subjects had no postsecondary qualifications at all, and both of them used an extremely literal approach. Although I originally hypothesised that those with less education might rely more on literal translation if they were less comfortable with the academic discourse, this assumption was negated by the fact that one other subject with a postgraduate qualification also employed an extremely dominant literal approach.

TABLE 1: DOMINANT TRANSLATION STYLE AND
EDUCATIONAL BACKGROUND OF EACH SUBJECT

Subject	Translation style	Level of postsecondary qualification
2	Extreme dominant literal	None
3	Extreme dominant literal	None
10	Extreme dominant free	Undergraduate
7	Dominant free	Undergraduate
9	Extreme dominant free	Postgraduate
1	Dominant free	Postgraduate
4	Dominant free	Postgraduate
6	Dominant free	Postgraduate
8	Dominant free	Postgraduate
5	Extreme dominant literal	Postgraduate

It is possible to speculate on why these interpreters might have chosen to employ such a literal method, and the issues that informed their decision-making. For instance, the subjects who were university qualified may have made a decision to use literal interpretation as they felt it was the more appropriate method to use in a university context, rather than due to lack of understanding of the academic discourse. The two interpreters who were not university educated may have made their decision based on lack of familiarity with the discourse environ- ment. They could, however, just as easily have made their decision based on their understanding of university lectures and what they felt was the appropriate translation style to be used.

Although there does not seem to be a tangible link between transla- tion style and educational background, consistent patterns could, however, be identified between translation style and what Davis (1989, 1990a, 1990b) referred to as linguistic transference, in this case, fingerspelling.

5.1.1. *Translation style and linguistic transference*

Aside from fingerspelling of names, which would be the norm (Johnston, 1998), and the use of lexicalised fingerspelling where fingerspelled English words have been assimilated into Auslan (Schembri, 1996); certain lexical items were consistently fingerspelled by the majority of the subjects. The amount of fingerspelling used by the subjects was consistent with typical Auslan use, in that borrowing of English words into Auslan in the form of fingerspelling frequently occurs. Johnston (1998) stated that the manual alphabet is used in Auslan for the "fingerspelling of English words for which no direct sign equivalent exists or when there is a particular need to use an English word" (p.591). The same type of borrowing has also been observed in BSL (Brennan, 2001) and ASL (Lucas & Valli, 1992).

It can be argued that in a university context it would be important for a Deaf student to receive key English words, as the terminology would be central to the comprehension of the topic. This argument would be supported by Bremner and Housden (1996), who reported that Deaf postsecondary students preferred interpreters to fingerspell technical or subject-specific words that did not have an existing sign, rather than making up a sign.

Notwithstanding the appropriateness of fingerspelling in sign languages, it emerged that the interpreters used a different pattern of fingerspelling, depending on their translation style. Initially, it was thought that dominant literal interpretations incorporated more fingerspelling of a particular type. For example, it could be seen that one subject who was extremely dominant in using a free approach (i.e., did not code-switch at all) used far less fingerspelling when compared to another subject who was extremely dominant in a literal approach. Examples from subjects using a dominant free approach and dominant literal approach are shown in Examples 5 and 6.

EXAMPLE 5: DOMINANT FREE APPROACH

Subject 10

'And what they did was contrast the acquisition of these these features with the acquisition of the same types of grammatical features

in English, and came up with, as a result of this study, with what 135
'WHAT WHAT RESEARCH WHAT COMPARE WITH
(point arc) (q)
G-R-A-M-M-A-R LIST IN ENGLISH COMPARE WITH SIGN LANGUAGE HOW
seemed to me some quite consistent patterns of grammatical acquisi-
LIST COMPARE.. RESEARCH FOUND LIST ALMOST SAME LANGUAGE
(left)
tion across the two languages.'
ACQUISITION BOTH LANGUAGE ALMOST SAME.'
(their right) (their left) *(hd)*

Example 5 shows that the interpreter using a dominant free interpretation approach only employed the use of fingerspelling on one occasion,
whereas Example 6 shows an interpreter that used a dominant literal
approach, and incorporated the use of fingerspelling for eight different
words in the same sentence.

EXAMPLE 6: DOMINANT LITERAL APPROACH

Subject 2

'And what they did was contrast the acquisition of these these features
with the acquisition of the same types of grammatical features in
WHAT THEY.. RECEIVE
(point-right)
English, and came up with, as a result of this study, with what seemed
F-E-A-T-U-R-E WITH SAME TYPE O-F G-R-A-M-M-A-T-I-C-A-L F-E-A-T-U-R-
to me some quite consistent patterns of grammatical acquisition
E-S IN ENGLISH AND COME UP WITH.. BECAUSE O-F STUDY WHAT S-E-E-
M-E-D T-O B-E WHAT CONSISTENT P-A-T-T-E-R-N O-F G-R-A-M-M-A-T-I-
(q)
across the two languages.'
C-A-L ACQUISITION ACROSS AREA.'
(hd)

The number of times each subject fingerspelled a lexical item throughout the whole 20-minute piece of interpretation was counted, and it
was found that there was in fact no direct relationship between transla-

tion style and the amount of linguistic transference. Table 2 provides a breakdown of the number of fingerspelled lexical items produced by each subject.

On closer analysis, however, a distinct pattern could be seen in what lexical items the interpreters chose to fingerspell, according to their translation style. It is debateable why some subjects would incorporate more fingerspelling into their interpretations than others. First of all they may have made a conscious decision, as a linguistic strategy, to fingerspell key words which they identified as being important for the student to know. Alternatively, they might not have been aware of an existing equivalent sign for those words; or they may not have understood the meaning of the words in the context of the lecture, and therefore did not know what would be the most appropriate equivalent sign to use. The major difference noted, however, between those dominant in using a free or literal interpretation approach was in relation to the fingerspelling of lexical (content) or function (grammatical) words.

TABLE 2: NUMBER OF FINGERSPELLED
LEXICAL ITEMS PER SUBJECT.

Subject	Translation style	No. of fingerspelled lexical items	No. of aborted fingerspelling attempts
1	Dominant literal	100	2
2	Extreme dominant literal	271	5
3	Extreme dominant literal	93	5
4	Dominant free	114	2
5	Extreme dominant literal	141	3
6	Dominant free	172	1
7	Dominant free	83	2
8	Dominant free	115	1
9	Extreme dominant free	85	1
10	Extreme dominant free	78	2

Note. An aborted fingerspelling attempt was counted when an interpreter began to fingerspell a word then stopped, and either began fingerspelling a lexical item again, or chose to use a sign instead.

There was a corpus of lexical words that the researcher expected the
interpreters to fingerspell, regardless of translation style, that is, the
names of people or places. Regardless of the translation style, it would
be the norm for interpreters to fingerspell a name at least once when it is
first introduced. Their linguistic strategy could then involve either
establishing the person or place as a location in space, after which the
same location would be referred to every time the name was used, or
they could choose to fingerspell the name each time it is mentioned. In
relation to function words, it was confirmed by a sign language linguist
and a sign language teacher that various words are commonly
fingerspelled by deaf people. For example, fingerspelling of the words 'if'
and 'do' are considered appropriate as they are commonly recognised as
words that have been lexicalised into Auslan. Similarly, the word 'to' is
fingerspelled in specific contexts as a function word when it is not
automatically incorporated into a directional verb, such as 'give to'. For
example, in the context of the sentence 'a mother will adjust her language to meet the needs of…', it would be acceptable for the word to be
fingerspelled. With regards to the word 'so', this function word is
commonly used in Auslan as a discourse marker to signify the beginning
of a new topic, or for emphasis, and as no sign exists it is fingerspelled.

It was expected, therefore, that the interpreters would fingerspell the
lexical and function words described above, regardless of their translation style. The biggest difference noted was the way in which the
interpreters dominant in a free approach seemed to use linguistic
transference as a linguistic coping strategy, especially in relation to
lexical words. As mentioned earlier, all the interpreters tended to
fingerspell lexical words that could be classed as technical, subject-
specific terminology, such as *cognitive, modality, co-actional dueting*, and
motherese. It seemed, however, that the interpreters using a dominant
free approach strategically switched to literal borrowing from English
in order to convey information and enhance the meaning of the
message, while accounting for the needs of university students to access
academic English. It was noted that the interpreters in this group tended
to translate the concept into a meaningful visual Auslan rendition, plus
fingerspell the lexical item to introduce the English terminology. Those
interpreters dominant in a literal approach, however, only fingerspelled

138 the subject-specific lexical words, and did not translate the meaning. They also experienced more linguistic interference and fingerspelled English function words other than those identified above, which would not ordinarily be fingerspelled in Auslan, including: conjunctions such as if, so, or, then, that, than, but; prepositions such as, at, of, by; and auxiliary verbs such as be and did.

As a consequence of the findings outlined above, two points can be made: (1) Interpreters that dominantly used a free interpretation approach seemed to use linguistic transference as a linguistic coping strategy, and switched to a literal approach in order to complement paraphrasing with a fingerspelled lexical item and enhance the contextual force of a message, thus supporting the findings of Davis' (1990a) study of interpreters. (2) Free interpretation can be regarded as a method of interpretation appropriate for use in the context of a university lecture, if interpreters use code-switching between free and literal methods to provide access to English when appropriate.

The issue of translation style merits further discussion in relation to the other focus of this study, that is, the types of omissions produced by interpreters while interpreting for a university lecture, and the occurrence of omissions used as a linguistic coping strategy. Interpreting omissions were analysed on several levels taking a range of factors into consideration, including: the number and type of omissions made by each interpreter; the relationship between each interpreter's translation style, educational background and familiarity with the topic and the number and types of omissions made; the lexical density of the text and its impact on the number and type of omissions made; and the interpreters' level of metalinguistic awareness about omission occurrences, and their linguistic decision-making process.

5.2 Interpreting omissions

Hatim and Mason (1990) suggested that translators working on written texts use a process of selective reduction to decide which portions of source text should be omitted. They stated that translators "can and do take responsibility for omitting information which is deemed to be of insufficient relevance" (p.96). The same suggestion can be made for interpreters working between signed or spoken languages, yet it should be acknowledged that interpreters inevitably make some omissions that they do not necessarily make strategic decisions about, due to the more spontaneous nature of their work and the time constraints involved.

For the purposes of analysing interpreting omissions, a new omission taxonomy was defined, as described in chapter two. The taxonomy includes five key omission types, which incorporate omissions made during a process of selective reduction, as well as those made inadvertently: conscious strategic, conscious intentional, conscious unintentional, conscious receptive and unconscious omissions. A total of 341 omissions were made by all ten subjects, across all five categories, with an average of 34.1 omissions made per subject. The highest number of omissions made by one subject was 50, with the lowest number being 18. Table 3 provides a breakdown of the total number of omissions made from all ten subjects in each omission category.

TABLE 3: TOTAL OMISSIONS MADE BY ALL SUBJECTS
ACROSS ALL CATEGORIES

Omission categories	Number of omissions
Unconscious	92 (27%)
Conscious strategic	87 (26%)
Conscious intentional	61 (18%)
Conscious receptive	52 (15%)
Conscious unintentional	49 (14%)
Total	341 (100%)

From these figures, it can be seen that the most commonly occurring omissions were unconscious, closely followed by conscious strategic, conscious intentional, conscious receptive, with the least occurring omissions being conscious unintentional. Thus over half of the omissions made by the subjects were at opposite ends of the spectrum in terms of strategic use of omissions.

Analysis of the number and types of omissions made by individuals involved in the study shows a common thread, with minor exceptions, that unconscious and conscious strategic omissions are the most frequently occurring omission types. Table 4 provides information on

140   the number of omissions made by each subject in the different omission categories.

TABLE 4: TOTAL AND TYPES OF OMISSIONS PER SUBJECT

Subject	1	2	3	4	5	6	7	8	9	10
Conscious strategic	11	7	8	13	3	8	10	9	7	11
Conscious intentional	9	15	7	7	3	2	8	2	5	3
Conscious unintentional	5	5	4	8	5	5	4	5	4	4
Conscious receptive	1	11	9	5	4	6	4	3	4	5
Unconscious	8	12	16	8	3	9	7	10	9	10
Total	34	50	44	41	18	30	33	29	29	33

The figures demonstrate that interpreters do consciously employ the use of omissions as a linguistic coping strategy, and thus not all omissions should be counted as errors. The figures also demonstrate, however, that a large proportion of omissions made by interpreters are not intentional.

Focussing on the total number of omissions made by each interpreter, there is one important point to consider. The total number of omissions made by each interpreter is not the central issue, as the focus is on the types of omissions made. An evaluation of the total number of omissions may be misleading if judged on its own. Importance is placed on the proportion of those omissions that are strategic, intentional, unintentional, due to receptive difficulties, or are unconscious. Nevertheless, it is worth reflecting on the overall omission occurrences of each interpreter, as this evaluation can provide early indication of any patterns that may emerge during further analysis of individual omission types. Table 5 provides a ranking according to the total number of omissions per subject.

The most obvious pattern that emerges from evaluating the total number of omissions per subject, is the relationship between the number of omissions and the subjects' familiarity with the lecture topic. The total omission occurrence of those interpreters who were less familiar with the topic was higher than others with more familiarity, who made less than the average number of omissions (mean = 34.1). The two subjects who made the highest number of omissions also had no university qualifications (subjects 2 and 3), and therefore, one can assume, were less familiar with the academic discourse environment. Lack of qualifications is not necessarily linked to the total number of omissions, due to the fact that one subject with a postgraduate qualification also made a high number of omissions (subject 4). Nevertheless, apart from one anomaly, the majority of subjects with postgraduate qualifications made less than the average number of omissions, and all those with undergraduate qualifications also made less than the average number of omissions.

TABLE 5: TOTAL NUMBER OF OMISSIONS
AND BACKGROUND OF SUBJECT

Background information on each subject

Familiar with topic	N	N	N	N	N	Y	Y	Y	Y	Y
University qualification	NO	NO	PG	UG	UG	UG	PG	PG	PG	PG
Translation style	EL	EL	F	L	EF	F	F	F	EF	EL
Subject n°	2	3	4	1	10	7	6	8	9	5
Total omissions	50	44	41	34	33	33	30	29	29	18

key UG = Undergraduate, PG = Postgraduate; EL = Extremely literal approach; L = Dominant literal approach; EF = Extremely free approach; F = Dominant free approach.

It would seem, therefore, that there does seem to be some relationship between educational background and the total number of omissions made by each subject. In relation to the translation style of the interpreters, however, the figures do not show any distinct pattern. Thus an association cannot be made between the total number of omissions made and whether an interpreter was dominant in using a literal or free interpretation approach.

When studying the occurrence of the discrete omission types more closely, it can be seen that the patterns begin to shift, with different factors influencing the rate of particular omission occurrences with each subject. In proposing the concept of conscious strategic omissions, I would advocate that all interpreters use this omission type as a linguistic coping strategy, regardless of their translation style, educational background or familiarity with the topic. I originally hypoth-

142   esised, however, that the rate at which conscious strategic omissions are
used when interpreting for a university lecture would be effected by
these factors. I further hypothesised that subjects dominant in using a
free interpretation approach would be more likely to use more conscious strategic omissions than those dominantly using a literal
approach. The process of free interpretation necessitates the search for
linguistic and cultural equivalence, whereby interpreters judge what is
relevant and meaningful to their target audience. Thus interpreters
using a free approach would make conscious decisions to make
strategic omissions for the sake of clarity of a message. Alternatively, I
proposed that subjects using a more literal interpretation would make
less conscious strategic omissions, as they would concentrate on the
form of the message, and accuracy of the interpretation, rather than
meaningful equivalents. Further, I predicted that interpreters who had a
university qualification and were more familiar with the lecture topic
would make more conscious strategic omissions when interpreting for
a lexically dense university lecture, than those subjects with no
qualifications or lack of knowledge of the lecture topic. I assumed that
interpreters with more exposure to the general academic discourse
environment would feel more comfortable about making strategic
linguistic and cultural decisions with regards to making omissions,
especially if they had subject-specific knowledge and could thus judge
the importance of terminology used.

Table 6, however, demonstrates that these hypotheses were incorrect. There is no identifiable pattern between the rate of occurrence of
conscious strategic omissions and either the translation style, educational background or lecture topic familiarity of the interpreters. The
figures show that an average of 9.5 conscious strategic omissions were
made by each interpreter, with the highest number being 13, and the
lowest being three. The majority of those who made more than the
average number of conscious strategic omissions dominantly used a
free interpretation approach, but it can also be seen that subjects using
the same approach made less than the average number of this omission
type.

TABLE 6: OCCURRENCE OF CONSCIOUS STRATEGIC (CS) OMISSIONS

Background information on each subject

Familiar with topic	N	N	N	Y	Y	N	Y	N	Y	Y
University qualification	PG	UG	UG	UG	PG	NO	PG	NO	PG	PG
Translation style	F	L	EF	F	F	EL	F	EL	EF	EL
Subject n°	4	1	10	7	8	3	6	2	9	5
Total CS omissions	13	11	11	10	9	8	8	7	7	3

key UG = Undergraduate, PG = Postgraduate; EL = Extremely literal approach; L = Dominant literal approach; EF = Extremely free approach; F = Dominant free approach.

The two subjects with no qualifications (subjects 2 and 3) made less than the average number of this omission type, yet so did other subjects with postgraduate qualifications (subjects 5, 6 and 9), and surprisingly the three subjects who made the most conscious strategic omissions were less familiar with the lecture topic (subjects 1, 4 and 10). Thus it would appear that conscious strategic omissions are used as a linguistic coping strategy by all interpreters, and in the particular discourse environment of a university lecture, the translation style, educational background and topic familiarity of the interpreters does not influence the rate of occurrence of conscious strategic omissions.

The other four omission categories cannot be considered as strategic, even if the interpreters were conscious of making the omissions. Therefore, the fewer the number of omissions made intentionally, unintentionally, receptively or unconsciously, the better for a meaningful and accurate interpretation of the message. By identifying any patterns in relation to the occurrence of erroneous omissions, this information can be incorporated into education and training programs for sign language interpreters, to allow them to assess their strengths and weaknesses, and thus enhance the quality of their interpretation output.

Along with conscious strategic omissions, there also does not appear to be any particular pattern with the occurrence of conscious intentional omissions, as demonstrated in Table 7. On average, each

144   subject made this type of omission 6.1 times, with the highest number
at 15, and the lowest at two. It was hypothesised that those who were
not university educated, or not acquainted with the lecture topic, would
make more omissions in this category due to lack of familiarity with the
academic language register and subject-specific lexicon, yet this was not
the case. Although the subject who made the most omissions was not
university educated and not acquainted with the lecture topic (subject
2), and the two who made the least were educated to postgraduate level
with familiarity of the topic (subjects 6 & 8), there is not enough
consistency in the data to suggest that these factors influenced the
outcome; and translation style seemed to have no bearing at all.
Conscious intentional omissions were made by subjects who had
university qualifications and who were familiar with the subject area,
thus they still made omissions because they could not understand
lexical items or concepts, or did not know the meaningful equivalents
in the target language.

TABLE 7: OCCURRENCE OF
CONSCIOUS INTENTIONAL (CI) OMISSIONS

Background information on each subject

Familiar with topic	N	N	Y	N	N	Y	Y	N	Y	Y
University qualification	NO	UG	UG	PG	NO	PG	PG	UG	PG	PG
Translation style	EL	L	F	F	EL	EF	EL	EF	F	F
Subject n°	2	1	7	4	3	9	5	10	8	6
Total CI omissions	15	9	8	7	7	5	3	3	2	2

key   UG = Undergraduate, PG = Postgraduate; EL = Extremely literal approach; L =
Dominant literal approach; EF = Extremely free approach; F = Dominant free
approach.

Conscious unintentional omissions were made consistently by all
subjects, regardless of their translation style, educational background or
familiarity with the lecture topic. Almost all subjects made either four
or five conscious unintentional omissions, except for subject number
four who made eight omissions, giving rise to an average number of 4.9
conscious unintentional omissions per subject, as shown in Table 8.

TABLE 8: OCCURRENCE OF
CONSCIOUS UNINTENTIONAL (CU) OMISSIONS

Background information on each subject

Familiar with topic	N	N	N	Y	Y	Y	Y	N	Y	N
University qualification	PG	NO	UG	PG	PG	PG	UG	NO	PG	UG
Translation style	F	EL	L	EL	F	F	F	EL	EF	EF
Subject n°	4	2	1	5	8	6	7	3	9	10
Total CU omissions	8	5	5	5	5	5	4	4	4	4

key UG = Undergraduate, PG = Postgraduate; EL = Extremely literal approach; L = Dominant literal approach; EF = Extremely free approach; F = Dominant free approach.

This problem of unintentionally making omissions is a cognitive information processing issue, which could not necessarily be improved upon with better educational background or increased knowledge of the topic being interpreted, or be dependent on translation style. All the subjects in the study agreed that they had every intention of interpreting that particular piece of information, and had been trying to make a strategic decision in waiting for further contextual information, but the information somehow eluded them.

In relation to both conscious intentional and conscious unintentional omissions, Peterson (2000) suggested that metacognitive strategies can be used by interpreters as "tools for 'repairing' incomplete information or for compensating for messages that are not clearly comprehended" (p.136). Peterson argued that by having knowledge about how their cognitive processes function, interpreters can monitor their information processing, and thus be in a better position to process meaning and make inferences about meaning according to their linguistic and cultural knowledge.

An average of 5.2 conscious receptive omissions were made by each subject, with the highest being 11, and the lowest being 1, as seen in Table 9. Conscious receptive omissions occurred due to reported problems in hearing the source text, which some of the subjects attributed to the poor sound quality of the videotape used. It is worth

146   considering, however, the fact that the two interpreters who made well
above the average number of conscious receptive omissions had no
university qualifications and did not have any familiarity with the
lecture topic (subjects 2 & 3).

The three subjects who made an average number of conscious
receptive omissions were unfamiliar with the lecture topic, but had a
university education (subjects 4 & 10). All those who made less than the
average number of conscious receptive omissions had a university
education and were also familiar with the lecture content (subjects 5, 7,
8 & 9), apart from subject one who was unfamiliar with the lecture
topic (subject 1). There did not appear to be any relationship between
the number of receptive omissions and the translation style used.

TABLE 9: OCCURRENCE OF CONSCIOUS RECEPTIVE (CR) OMISSIONS

Background information on each subject

Familiar with topic	N	N	Y	N	N	Y	Y	Y	Y	N
University qualification	NO	NO	PG	UG	PG	PG	UG	PG	PG	UG
Translation style	EL	EL	F	EF	F	EL	F	EF	F	L
Subject n°	2	3	6	10	4	5	7	9	8	1
Total CR omissions	11	9	6	5	5	4	4	4	3	1

key UG = Undergraduate, PG = Postgraduate; EL = Extremely literal approach; L = Dominant literal approach; EF = Extremely free approach; F = Dominant free approach.

In applying the notion of frame theory to this process, it is possible to
assume that those who were more familiar with the discourse environment and lecture topic may have been better equipped to make predic-
tions about the information being presented, and 'second-guess' lexical
items that could not be heard properly, due to their contextual knowledge. Even those without familiarity of the topic, but an inherent
understanding of general academic discourse may have been able to infer
meaning and 'fill the gaps' of what they could not hear properly. Those
without the advantage of prior knowledge of the topic or familiarity with
the language register, however, would have been relying solely on what

they could hear, which is why it is understandable that an omission would be made if the lexical item could not be heard properly.

Finally, each subject made an average of 9.2 unconscious omissions, ranging from three to 16 omissions, which was a figure much higher than envisaged. Although it was hypothesised that the subjects would make a number of unconscious omissions, it was surprising to note that this type was as prevalent as the use of conscious strategic omissions. Table 10 shows that, again, the two interpreters with no university qualifications or lecture content knowledge made the most omissions in this category (subjects 2 & 3). Apart from these two subjects, however, the distribution of omission occurrences were not consistent with the level of qualification held or familiarity with the topic. The dominant translation style of the interpreters did not seem to effect the number of unconscious omissions made.

TABLE 10: OCCURRENCE OF
UNCONSCIOUS (U) OMISSIONS

Background information on each subject

Familiar with topic	N	N	N	Y	Y	Y	N	N	Y	Y
University qualification	NO	NO	UG	PG	PG	PG	PG	UG	UG	PG
Translation style	EL	EL	EF	F	EF	F	F	L	F	EL
Subject n°	3	2	10	8	9	6	4	1	7	5
Total U omissions	16	12	10	10	9	9	8	8	7	3

key   UG = Undergraduate, PG = Postgraduate; EL = Extremely literal approach; L = Dominant literal approach; EF = Extremely free approach; F = Dominant free approach.

It is generally accepted among interpreters and interpreter educators that it is not necessary to interpret every lexical item received, but rather the source language message should be 'chunked' into meaningful parts, and thus equivalent intent should be sought after in the target language (Winston & Monikowski, 2000). The notion, however, that interpreters are making omissions when interpreting a university lecture, because they do not even hear the information in the source language, regardless of their level of qualifications or subject knowledge, has implica-

148 tions for interpreter training and raising levels of awareness as to why this happens.

Thus far, the evaluation of omission occurrences has demonstrated that the translation style of an interpreter does not significantly influence the rate of omissions in any omission category. The educational background of interpreters is not a major factor on its own which effects the rate and type of omissions made, and the interpreters' previous knowledge of the lecture topic only seems to have a slight impact on the rate and type of omissions produced. When the two factors are combined, however, it is apparent that there is more likelihood of an increase in erroneous omissions, especially with conscious receptive and unconscious omissions. A combination, therefore, of interpreters' familiarity with the general academic discourse environment and the subject-specific content and terminology of a lecture, would appear to be the most consistent factor in effecting the rate of occurrence of omissions.

5.2.1 *Omission patterns and familiarity*

Closer examination of the relationship between omission patterns and familiarity revealed specific examples which demonstrated the link between the features of language use, which are bound both to the lecture topic and the discourse environment, and the occurrence of different omission types. Not surprisingly, a pattern emerged that specific features of language use elicited the occurrence of particular omissions, therefore implying that interpreters used their knowledge of language use to identify the significance of the message in the context of the university lecture, which impacted on the types of omissions they made. Figure 1 illustrates the pattern of omissions when aligned with the interpreters' familiarity with the lecture topic and their educational background.

In order to identify the specific language features it was decided to concentrate on key parts of the text that featured a high number of omissions, regardless of the omission type, and look for identifiable relationships with the number of omissions and the text itself. The printed version of the source text produced 176 lines of text, with only 32% of the lines producing no omissions at all from the ten subjects.

FIGURE 1: TOTAL AND TYPE OF OMISSIONS PER SUBJECT
(BY FAMILIARITY WITH TOPIC AND EDUCATION)

Number of
omissions

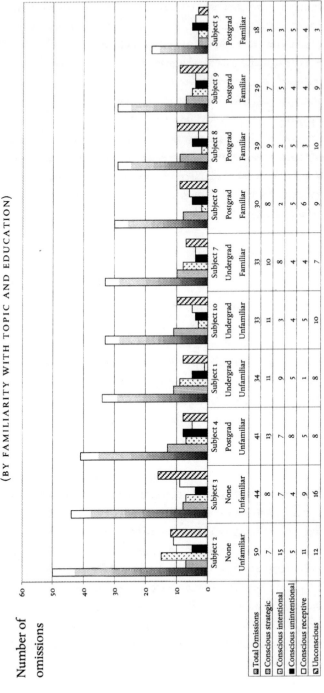

Background information on each subject

	Subject 2 None Unfamiliar	Subject 3 None Unfamiliar	Subject 4 Postgrad Unfamiliar	Subject 1 Undergrad Unfamiliar	Subject 10 Undergrad Unfamiliar	Subject 7 Undergrad Familiar	Subject 6 Postgrad Familiar	Subject 8 Postgrad Familiar	Subject 9 Postgrad Familiar	Subject 5 Postgrad Familiar
Total Omissions	50	44	41	34	33	33	30	29	29	18
Conscious strategic	7	8	13	11	11	10	8	9	7	3
Conscious intentional	15	7	7	9	3	8	2	2	5	3
Conscious unintentional	5	4	8	5	4	4	5	5	4	5
Conscious receptive	11	9	5	1	5	4	6	3	4	4
Unconscious	12	16	8	8	10	7	9	10	9	3

150 The number of omissions made by each subject in correspondence with each line of text were totalled to find which lines of text featured the most omissions. For example, subjects 4 and 6 both made an omission on line 4 of the text, meaning there were 2 omissions on that line of text. On line 79 of the text, subjects 2, 4, 8, 9 and 10 each made one omission, meaning that this line had 5 omissions. All the subjects made a total of 341 omissions, with an average of 1.95 omissions per line of text. The analysis showed that seven particular lines of text featured the highest proportion of omissions, with seven or more omissions per line. These seven lines of text (lines 59, 90, 104, 116, 117, 139 and 169) are outlined in Example 7 as follows, in the context of the sentence or paragraph that they were used.

EXAMPLE 7: LINES OF TEXT
FEATURING HIGHEST PROPORTION OF OMISSIONS

One

Line 57   The second issue I'd like to look at is, partly by way of
Line 58   exploding a myth, is the notion of early acquisition. What some people, or we can refer to
Line 59   as precocity or precociousness in, erm, sign language acquisition. There's very much a
Line 60   sort of an idea there in people's minds that children learning a sign language, acquire sign
Line 61   language earlier than children acquiring a spoken language…

Two

Line 87   Erm, as I said, we don't have time to go into it tonight, but some of the work on early sign
Line 88   language acquisition has, erm, made some interesting points in that regard and led a lot of
Line 89   researchers to challenge the notion that that's the necessary relationship in quite the, the
Line 90   lock-step way that Piaget and others were suggesting. And the last issue that, again, we
Line 91   won't have time to go into tonight is the… issue of nativisation and denativisation.

Three

Line 103   Where there's been a long tradition of oral education and

Line 104   very little El Salvador! El Salvador! And very little, er, use of sign language, and there's

Line 105   evidence on kids acquiring, sort of, linguistic or universal characteristics of sign language

Line 106   in the absence of good input, and then gradually as more and more exposure to a formal

Line 107   sign language occurs, denativising and moving towards that particular, erm, set of sign

Line 108   language rules and features.

Four and five

Line 114   Erm, and a number of authors over a long period of

Line 115   time have, and Snow, that we talked about last week, Catherine Snow? Who's been so

Line 116   vocal on the issue of erm, er… critical period hypothesis, thank you! (refers to student),

Line 117   has done an enormous amount of work on this. So, over to you for a minute. What do we

Line 118   know about the characteristics of caregiver input that makes it, that seems to be a critical Line 119: component of language acquisition?

Six

Line 137   But the actual nature of

Line 138   the features does seem to differ slightly across certain cultural groups. (student question)

Line 139   It was definitely a 60s thing, I'm not suggesting you were in the 60s, but there was a 60s/

Line 140   70s thing, a of, sort of, seeing pop psychology time, you know, making the child a genius

Line 141   type thing, which advocated a particular level of discourse with a child.

Seven

Line 167   Well you tell me, what are the features of mother/ child,

Line 168   motherese babytalk? (student comment) Repetition… (student comment) Erm, to a certain

Line 169   extent, imitation figures more highly in mother/ child,
                        you know, "say such and such" (babytalk intonation)
            Line 170   or "say daddy, say mummy" (babytalk intonation).

The types of omissions made by all subjects on each of these lines of
text were noted in order to identify any patterns between omission
categories and linguistic features of the text. Although a pattern could
be seen with omissions being made on certain lines, not all the omissions were the same, with the highest proportion of omissions being
conscious strategic or unconscious omissions. Twenty two per cent of
omissions on line 59 were conscious strategic and 78% were conscious
intentional. Line 90 had 28.5% conscious intentional omissions, 28.5%
conscious receptive omissions and 43% unconscious omissions. Line
104 had 40% conscious strategic omissions, 10% conscious unintentional omissions and 50% unconscious omissions. Line 116 had 28.5%
conscious receptive omissions and 71.5% unconscious omissions, and
line 117 had 14% conscious unintentional omissions and 86% unconscious omissions. The omissions on line 139 were 50% conscious
strategic, 12.5% conscious receptive and 37.5% unconscious; and on line
169 were 64% conscious strategic, 9% conscious unintentional, 18%
conscious receptive and 9% unconscious.

Table 11 provides information on the total number of omission
types made on each of the seven lines of text. The exact omission types
made by each subject can be seen in Appendix C. The highest number
of omissions occurred on lines of text with particular features of
language use: (1) unfamiliar (possibly academic English) or subject-
specific terms, for example, 'precocity' and 'precociousness' in line 59
and 'critical period hypothesis' in line 116; (2) idiomatic English, for
example, 'lock-step way' in line 90; (3) names of people or places, for
example, 'Piaget' in line 90 and 'El Salvador' in line 104; (4) repetition in
English, for example, 'it was a 60s thing, I'm not saying you were in the
60s, but it was a 60s/ 70s thing' in line 139; and (5) ambiguities in
English, for example, 'say such and such' in line 169.

TABLE 11: TOTAL NUMBER OF EACH
OMISSION TYPE ON KEY LINES OF TEXT

Line number

	59	90	104	116	117	139	169
Conscious strategic	2	0	4	0	0	4	8
Conscious intentional	7	2	0	0	0	0	1
Conscious unintentional	1	0	1	0	1	0	0
Conscious receptive	0	2	0	2	0	1	1
Unconscious	0	3	5	5	6	3	1
Total n° of omissions	10	7	10	7	7	8	11

Identifiable patterns of omissions can be seen on these lines of text according to the linguistic feature presented. For example, in relation to unfamiliar or subject-specific terms, line 59 featured the terms 'precocity' and 'precociousness', and the highest proportion of omissions on this line were in the conscious intentional category. It was reported by all the subjects who made this type of omission, that they either did not understand the use of the term in this context, or did not know how to find an equivalent sign in Auslan. Line 116 produced mostly conscious receptive or unconscious omissions, and the most commonly omitted lexical item was the academic term 'hypothesis'. Most subjects explained that because the concept was unfamiliar to them, they had focussed on the preceding two words, which they considered to be important ('critical' and 'period') and did not hear the word 'hypothesis' following on; or they were unfamiliar with the term 'hypothesis' and could not hear it clearly enough to decipher.

All but one of the omissions that appeared on line 117 were unconscious, and occurred with the phrase 'So, over to you for a minute…'. All the respondents remarked that they probably had not heard this phrase because they were still concentrating on the difficult interpretation of the previous sentence in line 116, and therefore experienced cognitive overload.

With regards to repetition in English, lines 104 and 139 both predominantly featured unconscious omissions or conscious strategic omissions, meaning therefore, that subjects either did not hear the

154   repetition of the words/concept, or heard it and chose to delete it. All subjects who had made a strategic omission reported that the repetition was redundant, and thus had made a conscious decision to omit as it would not detract from the message.

In relation to ambiguities in English, line 169 featured the phrase 'say such and such', and the majority of omissions were conscious strategic. Subjects unanimously commented that it was impossible to interpret such a phrase into Auslan as it was too abstract, so they opted to omit this information in favour of the subsequent phrase 'say mummy, say daddy', which presented concrete information that could be clearly interpreted into Auslan.

Finally, although line 90 did not present any consistency in the omission types that occurred, it did demonstrate a pattern when compared with the other lines of text. Several omission types occurred due to the fact that some subjects omitted the term 'lock-step way', whereas others omitted the name 'Piaget'. The conscious receptive omissions were made because they were not familiar with the name Piaget, and could not hear it pronounced clearly enough, whereas the term 'lock-step way' was either not heard at all, or was omitted consciously and intentionally because the subjects were not familiar with this idiomatic expression, and were unsure how to represent it in Auslan.

It was predicted that the type of patterning discussed thus far would also feature in other lines of text that had fewer omissions. Therefore other lines were chosen at random from those with less than seven, but above the average, number of omissions (mean = 1.95). As envisaged, the number of omissions were higher on lines using subject-specific or unfamiliar terms, such as 'pronouns' (line 6), 'denativising' (line 99) and 'motherese' (line 143). Omissions were also present on lines using English idioms, such as 'photocopy powers that be' (line 10) and 'in a nutshell' (line 12); as well as in lines using names, such as Reilly, McIntire and Bellugi (lines 15 and 16), and Caselli and Volterra (line 66). Omissions were found on lines featuring repetition, for example in line 166: 'there's that principle in, in mother/child, or caregiver/ child interaction'. The same was found with redundant repetition, where two different words that were perceived by the interpreters to mean the same thing, were used one after the other, for example, 'what happens to kids when they have incomplete or inadequate input in their first language' (line 95). English words such as 'saliency' (line 151) and 'consumable' (line 166), which were regarded by the interpreters as being ambiguous in this context, also featured in lines with above the average number of omissions.

It can be stated, therefore, that one explanation for the pattern of omission occurrence in this text is in relation to interpreters' familiarity with the features of language use, which are bound both to the lecture topic and the academic English used in the university discourse environment. Although their familiarity of the discourse environment alone did not necessarily effect the number of omissions they produced, it certainly seemed to effect the types of omissions that occurred in different parts of the text in relation to the linguistic features presented.

Another linguistic feature of the discourse environment that was thought to have influenced the prevalence and types of omissions occurring in different parts of the text, is that of lexical density.

5.2.2 Omission patterns and lexical density

Lexical density refers to the complexity of language (Halliday, 1985), and is a concept that can be used to measure the difficulty of a piece of text (Richards, Platt and Platt, 1992). I hypothesised that more omissions would be made on the most lexically dense parts of the text, and if this was the case, that more omissions would therefore be made in the most complex parts of the text. In order to validate this assumption, it was necessary to calculate the average lexical density of a line of text and compare the number of omissions on an average line of text, with the number of omissions present on those lines with higher than average lexical density. I expected that a relationship would be found between the number of omissions and the lexical density of a line of text.

The overall lexical density of the university lecture text was calculated (adopting the method proposed by Ure (1971)), at 51%. Using the same calculation method, the average lexical density for a random line of text was calculated at 47.6%. This figure was reached by adding up the total number of words on the first line of each page of text, then dividing each total by the number of lexical items on that line to arrive at a percentage. Of the eight lines of text selected at random, three were

156 of average lexical density, two were above and three were below the average. Table 12 presents the number of functional and lexical words, and the lexical density for each line of text analysed in order to arrive at an average figure.

TABLE 12: LEXICAL DENSITY PER RANDOM LINE OF TEXT

Line number	N° of lexical (content) words	N° of function (grammatical) words	Lexical density
1	5	10	33%
44	6	10	37.5%
21	7	8	46%
67	9	10	47%
136	9	10	47%
113	7	7	50%
159	9	7	56%
90	10	6	62.5%
Average lexical density of text			47.6%

In order to test the relationship between the number of omissions and lexical density of text, the seven lines of text highlighted as those with the highest number of omissions were also calculated for lexical density, as seen in Table 13. It was found that, apart from one anomaly, all the lines of text with the highest number of omissions had a lexical density higher than the average line of text.

TABLE 13: LEXICAL DENSITY OF LINES OF TEXT
WITH HIGHEST NUMBER OF OMISSIONS

Line number	N° of lexical (content) words	N° of function (grammatical) words	Lexical density
117	4	15	21%
139	10	10	50%
116	8	6	57%
59	10	6	62.5%
90	10	6	62.5%
104	12	5	71%
169	11	3	78.5%

In order to identify whether those lines of text with a lower percentage of lexical density produced a smaller number of omissions, all the lines of text featured in Tables 12 and 13 were compared for lexical density and omission rates, as seen in Table 14.

TABLE 14: NUMBER OF OMISSIONS
COMPARED WITH LEXICAL DENSITY OF TEXT

Line number	N° of omissions	Lexical density
117	7	21%
1	0	33%
4	1	37.5%
21	2	46%
67	0	47%
136	1	47%
113	1	50%
139	8	50%
159	0	56%
116	7	57%
59	10	62.5%
90	7	62.5%
104	10	71%
169	11	78.5%

Apart from anomalies in lines 117 and 139, Table 14 shows that the lexical density of the text does seem to influence the number of omissions. It can be seen that the issue is not whether the text is higher than the average lexical density, but rather the extent to which it is higher than the average. The lines of text of average lexical density (lines 67 & 136) or below (lines 1, 21 & 44), presented between 0–2 omissions. The increased relationship between omissions and density begins when the lexical density of a line of text reaches 57%, almost 10% above the average, with an almost exponential increase in the number of omissions in relation to an increase in lexical density. Interestingly, those lines with the highest lexical density (104 & 169) were those that featured the highest number of conscious strategic omissions in proportion to the total number of omissions on that line.

From this superficial analysis it can be seen, therefore, that the lexical density of text does seem to influence the occurrence and types of omissions produced by Auslan interpreters to some extent. If, as stated by Halliday (1978), university lectures are typically presented in lexically dense text, the results of this study illustrate that it is inevitable that sign language interpreters will make omissions, some of which will be strategic.

It is arguable, however, that it is not the lexical density alone that influences the rate and type of omissions, but the lexical items them-selves, as demonstrated with regards to familiarity with academic discourse and subject-specific terminology. If interpreters are familiar with content words being used in lexically dense parts of text, they are less likely to erroneously omit the meaning of those particular lexical items, but might choose to strategically omit them as part of the linguistic decision-making process. Interpreters may, however, gener-ally experience difficulties in interpreting lexically dense text, dependent on the presentation style and whether the text is read out or spontane-ous. In order to establish the extent to which the lexical density of a text effects the rate and occurrence of omissions, it would be necessary to analyse the omissions made by interpreters when interpreting for a lexically dense piece of prepared text that is read out, or when interpret-ing for different texts with alternative percentages of lexical density. These preliminary findings do suggest, however, that the lexical density of the source text has a bearing on the omissions made by interpreters.

Thus far it has been established that the lexical density of source text, and familiarity with the source text, effects the number of omis-sions made by interpreters. Findings show that the discourse environ-ment influences the number and types of omissions made by sign language interpreters. It has been demonstrated that interpreters make different types of omissions based on their conscious monitoring of the discourse, and the application of their knowledge of the discourse environment and the linguistic and cultural expectations of the dis-course participants.

5.3 Metalinguistic awareness during the interpreting process

The concept of metalinguistic awareness refers to the ability to monitor and change language use, and it has been suggested that interpreters need to apply their metalinguistic knowledge and use 'meta-strategies' (Hoffman, 1997) or 'metacognitive strategies' (Peterson, 2000; Smith, 2000) while interpreting, to monitor the linguistic choices they make during the interpretation process.

The very nature of this study has demonstrated the fact that the subjects involved had a level of metalinguistic awareness while performing the interpreting task. This awareness is evident in the categories developed for defining the types of omissions identified, which referred to whether the omissions were conscious or unconscious. The categories were developed as a consequence of reviewing the interpreting tasks with the subjects, and asking them whether they remembered making certain omissions. Through discussion of the interpreting task, it was possible to ascertain the interpreters' level of consciousness about the linguistic choices they were making, and thus the extent of their metalinguistic awareness.

It can be noted that all the subjects involved in the study were highly cognisant of their linguistic choices, and were particularly conscious of omissions being made and why they were being made. In fact, because of their level of metalinguistic awareness, I was able to explore why omissions were being made. If the subjects had not been so metalinguistically aware, it would not have been possible to develop the categories of omissions in the first place. All the subjects referred to an internalised self-critical commentary in their head that accompanied the interpreting process, whereby they were constantly re-evaluating and commenting on their linguistic decision-making during the process. The results of the study imply that the subjects were engaged in using metacognitive strategies as a linguistic coping strategy to monitor and enhance the effectiveness of their interpreting output, as they were able to engage in the task review and refer to the commentary in their head about the linguistic choices they made. Additionally, it can be stated that the interpreters must have been applying their metalinguistic awareness to the interpreting process in order to consciously make the

160   decisions to use strategic omissions, due to the fact that conscious strategic omissions comprise a larger percentage of the total omissions made by the subjects.

Nonetheless, it is interesting to reflect on some of the comments made by the interpreters with regards to their own level of metalinguistic awareness. One subject commented that she became more conscious of the process of making omissions during the task review, and stated that she might therefore have been more conscious during the study than she would normally be when interpreting elsewhere. It could be argued, however, that although the process of review may have heightened the interpreters' awareness, all interpreters were able to reflect on their thought processes during the interpretations, and whether they were conscious of omissions they had made. This ability would imply that this is a process they are comfortable with, and probably consistently engage in while interpreting, but perhaps on a less conscious level.

Another of the subjects also felt that her metalinguistic awareness was heightened due to being able to watch the video of herself interpreting. She stated that the knowledge that she would be able to review her work prompted her to remember how she felt and what she was thinking during the interpreting task, and that it may have been more difficult to reflect on the experience without the visual prompt of the recorded interpretation.

All interpreters involved in the study expressed an interest in the types of omissions made, their level of awareness at the time of making the omissions, and their ability to reflect on their interpreting decisions. A few of the subjects expressed amazement at the extent to which they relied on the commentary going on in their head while they were interpreting, and that participating in this study made them realise for the first time. Although the extent of metalinguistic awareness is difficult to measure, the comments made by some of the subjects are worthwhile considering for any future study on interpreting. Comments made by the study subjects in relation to their educational backgrounds are also worth considering.

5.4 Sociolinguistic and sociocultural influences on interpreters: Education

The ten subjects involved in the study had diverse educational backgrounds, some held undergraduate or postgraduate qualifications, while others had not studied since they left school. In the retrospective interview, the interpreters were asked to comment on their educational backgrounds, and how their ability to interpret for the university lecture segment was effected by that background. I hypothesised that the subjects would comment on how their comfort and confidence during the interpreting task was predominantly effected by their level of familiarity with the language used, and the lecture topic itself. This prediction was substantiated, as comments revealed unanimous agreement that their educational backgrounds did influence their ability to interpret for the lecture. Examples of some comments made by subjects are shown in Example 8.

EXAMPLE 8: SUBJECTS' COMMENTS REGARDING
EDUCATIONAL BACKGROUND

a. 'I was hindered by my lack of higher education... I haven't studied since I was fifteen. I found this task hard because of the academic language used in universities. I didn't have enough knowledge of the subject matter, the English language or the terminology used.'

b. 'I am not familiar with university language and jargon, especially subject-specific words... I don't have a strong educational background... I didn't understand the language sufficiently enough to "freely" interpret, I think I could have gone for the meaning more.'

c. 'I've had a university education and that contributes greatly. But I'm not overly familiar with academic language as I don't work much in universities, so that threw me a little... My English skills would need to be improved to the register of university level language.'

d. 'Knowledge about the subject helped a lot... and having been to university myself helped me to deal with the language register... It helps the more familiar you are with the topic... I think a lot of interpreters are under-qualified to interpret. In an ideal world interpreters would be matched with situations or subjects they have studied or are familiar with… [For university interpreting] I think you need either a university education yourself, or plenty of experience interpreting in university settings—you can't do justice to difficult concepts if you don't understand them.'

e. 'I have a university education… so I am familiar with the language use and with university situations, so I wasn't intimated by that, but the ideal is to have knowledge of the content. I was comfortable with the level of language because I have interpreted this type of lecture lots of times before… Plus my educational background helped me to deal with the level of language—I'm used to the university environment and the language use.'

f. 'My education supports me in what I do… I couldn't have coped without a university education background.'

g. 'My ability to interpret has improved dramatically since studying at H.E level… I have a greater understanding of language and how culture and language are linked. I have more familiarity with university level discourse and a better understanding of how someone can use a creative lexicon.'

It can be seen from the comments shown in Example 8 that the subjects involved in this study felt that their educational backgrounds made a difference to their ability to interpret for the university lecture segment. It can be stated therefore, that a university education, plus knowledge of the subject, meant that the subjects felt more able to cope with the linguistic demands of the interpreting task. Even without subject-specific knowledge, it is apparent that subjects with a general university education were less perturbed by the linguistic pressures of the task, due to their familiarity and comfort with the university discourse environment. Although the subjects felt that their educational background influenced their ability to interpret the lecture, the results of this study have not shown that educational background on its own is a major factor. Larger numbers of subjects would need to be tested in order to determine the extent that educational background effects the quality of interpretation of a university lecture. Nevertheless, the reporting of the subjects involved in the study is valid, and provides insight into interpreters' self-perceptions of the relationship between education and interpreting skills.

5.5 Expectations of interpreting service consumers

In order to validate the findings of this study for discussion of wider implications, it was important to ensure that the perspective of Deaf university students was taken into consideration. Various European and North American studies have assessed the expectations of consumers of interpreting services. Moser (1996) found that users of spoken language interpreters at conferences had different qualitative expectations of the interpreting service, dependent on their experience of attending conferences and using interpreters, and the type of conference they were attending. Viera and Stauffer (2000) found that Deaf people using interpreters in professional arenas had very particular preferences in relation to the translation style used by interpreters, so that they could access English terminology. Locker (1990) found that American Deaf students had similar expectations of interpreters they used in university settings, with regards to the type of errors made and translation style used. It can be assumed, therefore, that Australian Deaf people would have particular expectations in terms of the interpreting service they would expect to receive in a university context.

University lectures and conference presentations are both situations that offer potentially complex information, in which the audience chooses to participate. If participants choose to attend a conference presentation or a university lecture, it can be assumed that they will have a clear idea of how they would like to access the information. Consequently, a panel of Deaf university students were brought together to discuss the issues mooted during this study.

The panel comprised four Deaf people from different backgrounds, in order to provide a representative sample of the Deaf community. The people involved were: two native signers and two non-native signers; two had been educated using some form of signed communication in a deaf unit within a mainstream school, and the other two educated orally in a mainstream school; three of the panel members were studying towards undergraduate degrees at the time the research took place, and the other had completed both undergraduate and postgraduate study,

164   and was still studying towards another university qualification. Two of the participants were familiar with the subject of language acquisition, which was the lecture topic in the interpreting task.

The panel was shown two extracts of interpreting taken from the data collected as part of this study. First, an example of an interpreter using an extremely dominant free interpretation approach, and second, an interpreter using an extremely dominant literal interpretation approach. They were asked to discuss the different interpretation methods, their preferences, and reasons for those preferences. A series of questions were developed, with reference to questions addressed by Moser (1996) and Locker (1990), in order to prompt discussion in relation to the issues of translation style, interpreting omissions, educational background of interpreters and expectations in university settings.

When asked which interpretation approach they preferred out of the two clips they were shown, the panel concurred that they liked both approaches, but each was more appropriate in different contexts. They stated that the extremely dominant free interpretation approach would be fine for more general interpreting situations, but that the literal approach would be more suitable for interpreting in university lecture situations. The reasons posited were that a literal approach incorporated more use of fingerspelling, thus allowing the students to access technical vocabulary and academic English. The panel members also trusted that they were receiving more information from the interpreter using the extremely dominant literal approach, as she seemed to be keeping up with the pace of the lecturer, and pausing less, thus conveying that she was confident to interpret the information.

One person stated that it was important for key concepts to be interpreted using a more free approach, but that terminology should be fingerspelled (i.e., the interpreter should switch to a more literal interpretation at key points of the text). The general consensus seemed to be that the extracts they had been shown were both too extreme, and that they would prefer to receive information in conceptually accurate Auslan, with the use of fingerspelling and English mouth patterns when appropriate, for conveying terminology and academic terms (i.e., a dominant free interpretation approach, with occasional code-switching into a literal approach).

The panel members were asked to consider a university lecture, and to discuss in more depth whether interpreters should be more free or literal in their interpretation approach. It was during discussion of this point that many contradictions seemed to occur. One member, who had previously stated a preference for a literal approach, proceeded to say that concepts should be freely interpreted because it made it easier to absorb more complex information. Another member pointed out that a free interpretation approach was sometimes more appropriate, but that it made taking notes difficult as Deaf students would have to re-interpret the information into written English. In relation to this point, the other three panel members agreed, and asserted therefore that a mixture of free and literal interpretation approaches were required. Two people went on to explain that the appropriate mix should fit the needs of the student, and interpreters could work towards this by building a close relationship with their clients.

The panel was then asked to consider the same issue in relation to interpretation of university tutorials, and whether a free or literal approach was desired. One person remarked that an interpreter needed to be extremely fluent in Auslan to cope with the demands of a tutorial, and that an interpreter who worked effectively in a lecture was not necessarily the best choice for a tutorial.

When asked how much they understood when following an interpreted university lecture, one panel member said she felt she got about 80% of lecture material, whereas another said he accessed between 50–70% of a lecture and had to follow up what he has missed in his own timethrough additional reading and study. Another person claimed to understand 80 - 90% of her lectures, which she was happy with. The first person who said she followed 80% stated that she was very satisfied with what interpreting provides, and that the 20% she missed was mostly due to her own inattention. Another person commented that the brain could only take in a limited amount of information anyway, and that how much you understand of the lecture can depend on yourself, and not just the interpreter's skills.

Although the panelists stated that they followed a high percentage of university lectures through sign language interpretation, their comments were subjective and based only on reported, rather than

166   definitive, understanding. Murphy (1978) stated that sign language can effectively convey the content of university lectures, yet a Deaf person's actual level of comprehension may contradict his or her reported understanding. Steiner (1998), for example, conducted a study of Deaf viewers' understanding of sign language production on television in the UK, and found that the expressed preference of Deaf viewers in relation to signing style did not always correspond with their actual level of comprehesion. The comprehension of sign language on television will invariably be influenced by different factors than the comprehension of a university lecture, due to the fact that the medium of television provides less clarity of depth, which is crucial to the effective articulation of sign language (through use of signing space, location, etc.). Nonetheless, the key issue is the fact that the respondents in Steiner's study contradicted themselves in terms of how much they understood, and how accurately they received information from their preferred signing style. Livingston, Singer and Abramson (1994) studied North American Deaf postsecondary students' understanding of a lecture, and found similar results. Further empirical study would be needed, therefore, to ascertain the actual extent of comprehension of Australian Deaf students in university lectures.

In relation to the Deaf students' reported level of understanding, all of the panel conceded that they never accessed 100% of a university lecture, thus raising questions about their perspective on interpreting omissions.

The responses from the panel members were varied when asked what they felt about various kinds of omissions that may occur during interpretation of a university lecture. One panel member stated that occasional omissions do not matter, but that she was not comfortable with the idea that interpreters might choose to omit something, as she was afraid she might miss out on information. Two other panel members felt that less omissions would occur if the interpreter was familiar with the subject, and that it was more important to have an understanding of the lecture content, rather than the interpreter conveying every single piece of information.

Opinions differed in relation to the concept of conscious strategic omissions, and whether it was appropriate for interpreters to consciously omit information. One panel member felt that some omissions were linguistically and culturally appropriate, whereas the other three were not convinced. One of these three admitted it was appropriate if an interpreter chose to omit "trivia"; and everybody was in agreement that it would be difficult to interpret everything in a lecture anyway. The question was not really answered, however, as three of the panel members seemed uncomfortable with the idea that interpreters might make judgments about what information should be imparted, and thus make omissions accordingly.

With regards to the occurrence of omissions, the panelists in this study seemed reluctant to comment, probably because they assumed that omissions would always be erroneous, in the same way that the Deaf students involved in Locker's (1990) study also regarded omissions negatively. Interestingly, the one panel member in this study who acknowledged that omissions could be used strategically was studying for a degree in linguistics, and therefore was likely to have had a better understanding of the linguistic processes involved in interpreting. Although reluctant to comment with regards to interpreting omissions, the panel members had very clear opinions about the education of interpreters, and their expectations of interpreters working in university settings.

The issue as to whether interpreters should have some knowledge of the subject matter they are interpreting provoked varied responses. One person claimed that subject knowledge definitely helps in a lecturing situation, but perhaps is less necessary in a tutorial situation. Another person complained that she has had many different interpreters over several years as a part-time student, and even had eight different interpreters for one subject. Yet she has never hesitated to reject interpreters who did not have adequate background knowledge to be able to cope with the subject matter of her studies. One panel member explained that, in an ideal world, students would be able to choose the interpreter most suited to their needs from a whole "army" of different interpreters. It was recognised that this is not the current reality, however, and that the mismatch between supply and demand must be acknowledged. The other members expressed the view that regardless of the reality, it is best to aspire to have an interpreter with the appropriate subject knowledge, although it was not the only criteria.

168 In response to the question whether interpreters should have a university qualification before being allowed to interpret in universities, the panel unanimously agreed that it was necessary, although one panel member admitted that perhaps knowledge and skills equivalent to having a university qualification were also appropriate. Two people pointed out that a high school certificate should be the minimum requirement. Another three panel members re-asserted their opinion that interpreters really ought to have a university background themselves if they aimed to work in that environment. One person gave an example of an experience, in which a non-university educated interpreter could not recognise a word that was fingerspelled, and was even unable to pronounce it.

This discussion was followed with a debate about whether interpreters should have a university qualification to interpret in general, again with differing perspectives. One person agreed that all interpreters should have a university education, stating that it was especially important if interpreters were going to work in medical and legal settings. Another person added that for working in linguistically demanding interpreting situations, interpreters must be university educated. The other two panel members were unsure. One person felt that, as a university educated professional, she would prefer to have an interpreter with a similar background in a range of interpreting situations so that his or her language skills can reflect her skills and education to her colleagues and work mates. Another person argued that the reverse of this problem was, however, that some over-qualified interpreters misrepresented the language skills of grassroots Deaf people by interpreting their limited signing into a formal and sophisticated variety of English, giving the impression that they were more educated than they actually were.

In relation to the educational background of interpreters, there was general agreement that interpreters should have a university education, especially if they are going to interpret in university contexts, and that familiarity with the subject they were interpreting was preferable, although not mandatory. This finding is comparable to that of Locker (1990), who stated the ideal that interpreters should be familiar with content of lectures they interpret; and also to that of Bremner and

Housden (1996), who reported that Deaf students felt that subject-specific knowledge would be an advantage to educational interpreters, and they should be encouraged to 'specialise' in interpreting for subjects they have studied.

Ultimately, the panel agreed that there were fundamental prerequisite skills an interpreter needed to work in a university context. The panel recognised the importance of context of situation, however, by stating that ideal skills would be prioritised differently according to whether the interpretation happened in a lecture or tutorial situation.

In summary, the panel described the ideal skills of interpreters working in university lectures. All members of the panel generally agreed that interpreters should have a good university education, and good skills in both languages, especially in fingerspelling. They should be able to code-switch between free and literal interpretation as the situation, consumer and content of the message required, using clear mouth patterns and fingerspelling when appropriate. They should be expressive, confident, and assertive. They needed to be able to develop a good rapport with the Deaf student, and have a reasonable knowledge of the subject.

In evaluating the outcome of the discussion panel, it would seem that Australian Deaf university students have differing expectations depending on their experience and the university setting they are in, much like users of conference interpreters (Moser, 1996). The participants in this panel agreed with the Deaf students in Locker's (1996) study, that information should be interpreted conceptually into sign language for ease of understanding, yet they also agreed with respondents in Bremner and Housden's (1996) study, which found that Deaf students also wanted access to English terms. It would seem, therefore, that the university students involved in this study would endorse the notion of interpreters utilising a dominant free interpretation approach, and switching into a literal approach as a linguistic coping strategy, to deal with the complexity of the information received, and the demands of the context of situation. The students would also advocate for interpreters to have a university qualification in general, especially if they are working in a university context.

170   With regards to the use of conscious strategic omissions, it can be
stated that more time would be needed to explain the concept properly,
in order for Deaf people to make an informed decision about their
perspective on the use of omissions as a linguistic coping strategy. A
possible explanation, however, as to why the Deaf university students
were reluctant to accept that interpreters might use omissions strategically, is in relation to the issue of trust. It is understandable that Deaf
students would want to ensure that they are receiving all the information presented in a university lecture, as they rely solely on interpreters
for access to information in this type of environment. It is also understandable that Deaf people might not trust an interpreter's decision to
omit information, due to the historic relationship between the Deaf
community and hearing 'helpers' who have made decisions on their
behalf.

Issues to consider

6.0 Summation

The aim of this research was to study particular linguistic coping strategies of sign language interpreters working in lexically dense university lectures, with a view to highlighting issues in relation to working practices of sign language interpreters in higher education settings, and also in relation to the training and education of sign language interpreters in general. Some of the results of the study have not been particularly surprising, and have corroborated findings of other studies of sign language interpreter working practices. Other results, however, have yielded new information with regards to interpreters' use of translation style, types of omissions produced, and metacognitive strategies used while interpreting. This chapter seeks to further explore and summarise the results presented in chapter five, leading to a discussion of the relevance of this study to Deaf consumers and sign language interpreter education and training.

6.1 Linguistic coping strategies: Discussion

Chapter two introduced the notion of linguistic coping strategies as those linguistic processes used by interpreters as a pro-active measure to cope with the interpreting task at hand. It was suggested that linguistic coping strategies are consciously used by interpreters to cope with the sociolinguistic and sociocultural influences on any communicative event. One of the linguistic coping strategies discussed was the use of translation style, and how linguistic transference could be used in combination with code-switching between free and literal interpretation approaches in order to meet the needs of Deaf students in university lectures. It has been established that interpreters should recognise that a free interpretation approach is probably the most effective translation style for interpreting information with cultural sensitivity. Yet interpreters should also recognise that use of a literal approach is just as valid, especially when interpreters code-switch between the two

172 translation styles to ensure the interpreted message achieves its meaning potential.

The concept of omissions being used by interpreters as a conscious linguistic coping strategy has been one of the main threads throughout the book. It has been determined that in order to effectively work as linguistic and cultural mediators using an interactive model of interpreting, interpreters employ the use of *conscious strategic omissions* in deciding what information is translatable and relevant to each language and culture. The level of metalinguistic awareness that interpreters have about their use of omissions has been another thread throughout the book, with particular focus on their level of awareness about the types of omissions made and why they were made. It has been established that in order to make strategic decisions based on linguistic and cultural knowledge, interpreters must engage in metalinguistic processing in order to monitor the source language they are receiving and their target language output, to make conscious strategic omissions appropriately.

The results of this study revealed that sign language interpreters do use linguistic coping strategies while interpreting for a university lecture. The extent to which they used these strategies varied dependent on their level of familiarity with the subject and university lectures as a discourse environment.

6.1.1 Translation style and translational contact

The results of the analysis showed that the interpreters involved in the study had a dominant interpretation approach, using either a free or literal interpretation method, even if they code-switched between approaches during the interpretation. A spectrum was identified which demonstrated that the interpreters were either extremely literal or extremely free, or code-switched between literal and free, but were still dominant in one style or the other. Of the ten subjects involved in the study, one subject was dominant in using a literal approach, three were extremely dominant in using a literal approach, four were dominant in using a free approach, and two subjects were extremely dominant in using a free approach.

The majority of recent literature on spoken and sign language interpreting advocates for a free, equivalence-based, approach to interpreting, as this allows interpreters to make linguistic and cultural decisions based on their knowledge of the communities with whom they work. It can be argued, however, that sign language interpreting in university settings may require a more flexible approach due to the sociolinguistic and sociocultural factors within the discourse environment. This study has advocated that it might be more appropriate, in a university context, for both free and literal interpretation methods to be used in combination. By switching between free and literal methods as a linguistic coping strategy, it has been suggested that interpreters can provide conceptually accurate interpretations of lecture content, as well as giving access to academic jargon or subject-specific terminology, as Johnston (1996) would agree.

This suggestion was corroborated with discussion on the issue of language contact in relation to sign language. Arguments have been presented from several authors (Davis, 1989, 1990a, 1990b; Fontana, 1999; Lucas & Valli, 1989, 1990) that code-mixing or linguistic transference often occurs in sign language use in more formal situations, leading to use of more mouth patterns and fingerspelling than would be expected, for example, in conversational use of sign language. Davis' (1989, 1990a, 1990b) research showed that interpreters used linguistic transference appropriately to the formality of the interpreting context. Therefore, in relation to this study, it could be argued that those subjects who incorporated use of fingerspelling (i.e., linguistic transference) for key lexical items of the text were using the most appropriate translation style for a university lecture. Given the fact that university lectures will often utilise subject-specific terminology which is central to the understanding of the subject matter, it is imperative that Deaf university students are given access to terminology in the form in which it is delivered. It is also essential, however, that Deaf students receive information in semantically and syntactically correct sign language structure. Therefore an interpretation approach that introduces subject-specific lexicon through the use of fingerspelling, incorporating patterning as appropriate to the formality of the situation, would be an effective way of transmitting this information.

Pollitt (2000b) discussed the appropriateness of switching between use of an interactive interpretation model (free) and conduit interpreta-

174 tion model (literal) according to the context of the interpreting situation, and cited university settings as one context where it would be appropriate to employ both literal and free interpretation approaches, depending on the content, for example, whether it was a lecture or tutorial. Rather than proscribe the use of one translation style in the university context, I would agree with Pollitt and suggest that interpreters should switch between different styles as a linguistic strategy for coping with the context of situation. This study has found that interpreters using a dominant free interpretation approach switched to a more literal style at key points of the message, in order to borrow English lexical items, as well as interpreting the concept visually into Auslan. For example, idiomatic English such as the term 'in a nutshell' was fingerspelled, followed by a conceptually accurate translation of the meaning of the term. The same process also occurred with the interpretation of subject-specific vocabulary, such as the term 'critical period hypothesis'. This linguistic transference allowed the interpreters to provide a meaningful rendition of the message in Auslan, as well as providing access to the discourse-specific lexicon. It would seem, therefore, that it is appropriate for interpreters to use a free interpretation approach in the context of a university lecture, as long as they employ the linguistic coping strategy of switching to a more literal technique when they judge that it is suitable to do so. According to Bremner and Housden (1996), it is this kind of translation style that Deaf university students prefer, as they want interpretation into "an Auslan framework with English terms" (p.13). I would interpret Bremner and Housden's statement to mean interpretation using a free translation style with code-switching into a more literal style for the introduction of English terms.

As a consequence of this study, it has transpired that it may not be appropriate to discuss translation styles as distinct entities, but rather interpretation approaches should be considered within a continuum. I would favour a free interpretation approach as the most effective method for translation, but I recognise that a literal approach can also be effective and may in fact be preferred by some Deaf consumers. Although extreme forms of free and literal interpretation may be appropriate for some contexts of situation, I would suggest that for

university lectures, a combination of the two approaches is the most
appropriate. In giving consideration to language contact between
signed and spoken languages, and the notion of a continuum of sign
language use, I propose a translation style continuum, as seen in Figure
2. I would posit that the use of code-switching between translation
styles should be used particularly in contexts presenting features of
language contact in formal discourse environments, such as university
lectures. A suggested term for this type of code-switching is that of
translational contact (Napier, 2001, 2002b).

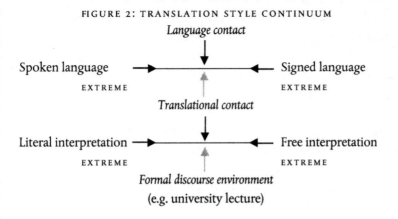

FIGURE 2: TRANSLATION STYLE CONTINUUM

Steiner (1998) goes some way towards acknowledging the need for
translational contact in his 'five pronged model on motivational
strategies'. He proposed ways of presenting information to meet the
needs of a target audience through *purist, empowerment, education, conglomerate* or *holistic* attitudes towards the Deaf community and sign language.
Steiner described the purist perspective as one that is driven to preserve
language in its purest form, without any interference from other
languages, therefore in the example of Auslan, ASL or BSL, the borrowing of English would be reduced to a minimum, and the use of visualisa-
tion would be maximised. This suggestion seems somewhat idealistic as
it is debateable whether 'pure' forms of language exist. The empowerment aspect, however, is explained by Steiner as one used by people
that understand "the linguistic struggles of the Deaf community and
their needs within wider society" (p.108). Steiner suggested that people

176   using an empowerment approach produce language that benefits the community "beyond the production of the message itself" (p.108), by explaining concepts believed not to have been accessed by the Deaf community to the same extent as the hearing majority, through the use of paraphrasing, anecdotes or simplification. Alternatively, the educational aspect is used by somebody who is aware that the Deaf community cannot acquire English in the same way that hearing people do, but recognises that they do have exposure to English, and therefore allows a Deaf audience to acquire new English vocabulary through a visual medium. This is done by "shadowing the source language or selecting specific lexical items that will need to be borrowed into the target language" (p.108), that is, the use of linguistic transference. The conglomerate belief incorporates understanding of both the empowerment and educational needs of the Deaf community, which is reflected in the language production dependent on the context of the situation, whereby code-mixing may occur between, for example, Auslan and English. Finally, the holistic belief means that a person is aware of all four of the categories outlined and attempts to produce a language that best reflects all categories.

By taking the essence of the categories outlined by Steiner (1998) and applying them to sign language interpreting, it is possible to identify approaches that would meet the needs of interpreting in different contexts. It is possible to equate the 'empowerment' aspect with the use of an extremely free interpretation, and the 'educational' aspect with a dominant free interpretation approach that incorporates code-switching into a literal style in order to introduce fingerspelling. The conglomerate strategy suggested by Steiner can be thought of as a succinct way of describing the linguistic coping strategy used by interpreters in deciding when to switch between the empowerment and educational approaches, or the free or literal interpretation models, depending on the content and intent of the message. Thus the aspects suggested by Steiner can be considered within a translation style continuum, in order to account for the issue of translational contact.

In recognising that sign language interpreters can use different interpretation approaches and adapt their translation style to meet the needs of Deaf consumers in different contexts, it is possible to accept that they are continuously making linguistic decisions based on the sociolinguistic and sociocultural influences on the interpreting situation. With the acceptance that interpreters can use translation style as a linguistic coping strategy, it is also possible to acknowledge that interpreters consciously utilise other linguistic coping strategies, such as the use of omissions. Steiner (1998) reinforces this point:

> The 'Educational Aspect' and 'Empowerment Aspect' would certainly influence a signer to make informed omissions or additions to a translated presentation. Cultural, social, and educational notions about the D/deaf community are used to modify approaches to the interpretation or translation (Steiner, 1998, p.109).

By conceding that omissions may be used as a linguistic coping strategy, it is important to discuss the use of conscious strategic omissions within a specific interpreting context.

6.1.2 *Interpreting omissions and omission potential*

The concept of omissions being made by interpreters has been discussed in detail, with consideration given to omissions produced as errors, and those produced strategically as part of the linguistic process to find meaningful equivalence for the target audience. This study has, for the first time, determined interpreters' levels of consciousness while producing omissions, within a context of omission types.

It has been acknowledged that although interpreters might use omissions as a conscious linguistic strategy, it was inevitable that they would make other omissions for different reasons. Through a process of conducting an immediate task review with the interpreters involved in this study, it was possible to categorise the different types of omissions made during the interpreting task. During the study, it became obvious that the interpreters were conscious of various omissions they made, but only one omission type could be considered as a productive linguistic coping strategy.

It was found that all of the interpreters made omissions in each category, with the highest number of total omissions being made by subjects that had no university education and were unfamiliar with the lecture topic. The most common omissions made were unconscious

178   omissions (27%) and conscious strategic omissions (26%). Conscious strategic omissions were used as a linguistic coping strategy by all the subjects, regardless of their educational background, familiarity with the topic or translation style. The prevalence of unconscious omissions was noted with astonishment, by both myself and the subjects, as it was not foreseen that such a large proportion of omissions would be unconscious. This level of unconscious omission production reinforces the notion that an interpretation can never convey 100% of the information imparted in a message, as there will always be a level of information loss, of which even the interpreter is unaware. It was surprising, however, to find that as much information is lost unconsciously, as is selectively omitted as part of a conscious linguistic process.

Overall, there were no obvious patterns of omission occurrences in relation to influencing factors, although the results showed that the most erroneous omissions tended to be made by subjects with no university education and no knowledge of the lecture topic. It would seem, therefore, that the most influential factor is a combination of familiarities, that is, familiarity with the discourse environment and familiarity with the topic itself.

The results of the empirical study demonstrate the importance of considering omissions within a context of omission types. It can be seen that interpreters do use omissions pro-actively, making conscious decisions as a linguistic coping strategy, as an inherent part of the interpreting process. Conscious omissions can be used effectively by interpreters to manage the communication event, and therefore in this context, the use of omissions is something that interpreters can do well. Nevertheless, it must still be recognised that interpreters also make other omissions, conscious or unconscious, intentional or unintentional. The fact that omissions can be used strategically does not negate the fact that erroneous omissions do occur, some of which interpreters are aware of, and others not. This study corroborates that within the framework of an interpretation, erroneous omissions do occur. The key issue to note, however, is that a high percentage of the omissions made by interpreters in this study were conscious strategic omissions—the second most frequent category. When considering interpreting omissions, it should therefore be recognised that for every item of information mistakenly

excluded, there are several which are omitted consciously and strategically to enhance the equivalence of the message.

In accounting for the occurrence of omissions within a context of
omission types, I suggest that omissions should be considered within a
framework of *omission potential*, as seen in Figure 3. By doing so, it is
possible for interpreters to recognise the sociolinguistic and sociocultural factors that may influence their production of different omission
types. The framework allows for recognition of the fact that omissions
can be used strategically to achieve the meaning potential of an utterance, but that there is also the potential to make erroneous omissions,
which may skew the contextual force of the message.

FIGURE 3: OMISSION POTENTIAL FRAMEWORK

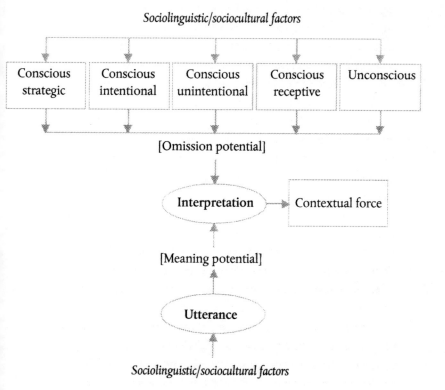

180 Another major issue to take into account when evaluating the prevalence of interpreting omissions is the context of situation, and in the
case of this study, the context of a lexically dense university lecture. It
was noted in the results that the highest number of omissions tended to
occur on higher than average lexically dense lines of text, that is, the
most grammatically complex parts of the text (mean lexical density of
line of text = 47.6%); and on lines of text featuring subject-specific
terminology or academic terms, that is, the most unfamiliar parts of the
text. Seven lines of text featured seven or more omissions on each line.
This finding is not particularly surprising, as any interpreting scholar
would expect interpreters to struggle when dealing with factors
contributing to 'cognitive overload' (Moser-Mercer, Kunzli & Korac,
1998). What is a revelation, however, is the fact that some interpreters in
this study seemed to use conscious strategic omissions to cope linguistically with the density and complexity of information featured on
particular lines of text. For example, line 169 of the text had a lexical
density of 78.5% and featured 11 omissions in total. Nearly 73% of these
omissions were conscious strategic.

   Although the interpreters in this study did produce more omissions
on lexically dense lines of text, consideration needs to be given to the
actual lexical items omitted before making any concrete conclusions
with regards to lexical density. The highest number of omissions occurred on higher than average lexically dense lines of text that featured
English terms that were unfamiliar to the interpreters. Therefore it
would seem that lexical density may only have a bearing on the number
and types of omissions in combination with interpreters' familiarity
with the text. If interpreters were assessed on their production of
omissions when interpreting non-lexically dense text, it would be
possible to evaluate the extent to which density influences omission
occurrence.

   Nonetheless, it can be seen that the linguistic features of the source
text do have an impact on the use of omissions. Thus in order to make
better use of omissions as a conscious linguistic strategy while interpreting for a university lecture, an interpreter needs to be familiar with
academic discourse, and preferably with specific subjects, before
interpreting in a university context. It can be reasonably assumed,

therefore, that interpreters will make more use of conscious strategic omissions, and produce less erroneous omissions, the more familiar they are with the context of situation and the characteristics of the discourse environment, whether they are working in educational, legal, medical, political or other arenas.

It has been established that the interpreters involved in this study had a high level of metalinguistic awareness in relation to the omissions they produced and why. Although the interpreters did not discuss their level of metalinguistic awareness in relation to the translation style they chose to use at any given time, the level of awareness exhibited while discussing their interpreting omissions would imply a similarly high level of awareness with respect to choice of translation style. This assumption would need to be verified, however, with further study.

Now that the linguistic coping strategies of interpreters working in a lexically dense university lecture have been discussed, it is possible to reflect on one of the key issues raised in this study, that of the educational background of interpreters.

6.2 Socio-educational influences: Discussion

Earlier discussion raised the question about how interpreters would cope linguistically in a university setting, if they had not studied at university themselves. This study sought to answer this question by comparing the interpretations of the interpreters involved, as well as interviewing the interpreters, to ascertain the impact of their educational backgrounds on their ability to cope linguistically with the lecture segment.

Throughout this book it has been asserted that a postsecondary qualification should be requisite for all sign language interpreters, especially if they work in higher education (Chafin Seal, 1998; Eighinger, 2000; Patrie, 1993; Roy, 2000b; Sanderson, Siple & Lyons, 1999). It has been suggested that studying at university would enable interpreters to attain a level of cognitive and academic linguistic proficiency, which would provide the range of linguistic sophistication needed to work effectively as an interpreter.

It can be considered, therefore, a necessity for interpreters to have a university level education in order to be able to cope linguistically with

182   the various situations they encounter in their interpreting work (as
stated by Locker, 1990). If it is deemed necessary for interpreters to have
a university qualification to be linguistically better equipped to do their
job, it can be stated that the requirement of interpreters to have a
university qualification before working in university settings is of
paramount importance, and "should be preferred, if not required"
(Stuckless, Avery & Hurwitz, 1989, p.12). This point is reinforced in the
World Federation of the Deaf policy statement on the education of Deaf
people:

> Ensure that Deaf students in mainstream educational settings (particu-
> larly secondary schools and universities) have access to the services of
> sign language interpreters who are: (a) fully trained and qualified as
> sign language interpreters; and (b) *have themselves attained a level of
> education appropriate to the situation in which they are interpreting* (Aquiline,
> 2000; emphasis added).

The results of a survey of Auslan interpreters (Napier, 2001) found that
only 48% of the 125 interpreters surveyed had completed, or were
studying towards, a university qualification. Of those respondents who
confirmed that they accepted interpreting work in higher education,
only 59% had a university qualification. Harrington and Traynor (1999)
surveyed 142 BSL interpreters, and found that 43% of the respondents
had postsecondary qualifications.

Almost 20 years ago, Cokely (1981) surveyed 160 working ASL
interpreters participating in a convention of the Registry of Interpreters
for the Deaf. He found 60.6% had completed four or more years at
college or university. Later figures showed that things had improved,
but not dramatically. Humphrey and Alcorn (1996) stated that the
majority of qualified sign language interpreters in the USA are university graduates, with 32% holding a Bachelor's degree, 25% holding a
Masters degree, and 2% holding a Doctorate. Stewart, et al (1998) cited
similar numbers, referring to a survey of the 1991 - 1992 membership of
the Registry of Interpreters for the Deaf. They stated that 8.4% of ASL
interpreters had studied for less than two years at college, 16.0% had
completed an Associate degree, 26.1% a Bachelor degree, 24.1% Masters
degree and 2.7% had attained a Doctorate.

More specifically to those sign language interpreters working only in
education, Hayes (1992) conducted a survey of 52 educational interpreters working in primary and secondary schools in Western Pennsylva-
nia. All respondents had at least a high school diploma and over 65%
had completed some type of college or university degree, ten of which
(31.2%) were Associate degrees. Jones, Clark and Soltz (1997) also
surveyed educational interpreters working in primary or secondary
schools, but collected data from interpreters throughout the USA. They
reported that 17% of the respondents to their survey had a high school
diploma or vocational certificate, 36% had studied at college but had not
completed a degree, 21% had a community college Associate degree,
21% had a Bachelors degree, and 5% had a Masters degree.

McIntire (1990) conducted an informal survey on the work and
education of sign language interpreters from various countries. She
surveyed 45 interpreters from 11 countries, including Canada, Denmark,
Finland, Germany, Greece, Italy, New Zealand, Norway, Sweden,
Switzerland and the UK. McIntire emphasised that the results of her
survey do not necessarily represent an accurate sample, as she con-
tacted interpreter colleagues, rather than carrying out an empirical
study based on random selection. McIntire questioned the respondents
about their highest level of formal education completed, and found that
31% had studied for one to two years beyond national minimum of their
country, 60% had studied at university, 9% had attended a vocational or
technical school, and 13% had completed a non-degree education.
Although this survey gives an interesting picture of the educational
qualifications held by sign language interpreters worldwide, as McIntire
herself stated, the figures are not based on empirical data collection, and
therefore do not necessarily accurately reflect the sign language
interpreting profession.

Drawing on overall figures from Cokely (1981), Hayes (1992) and
McIntire (1990) it would seem that on average, 60–65% of sign language
interpreters hold, or are studying towards, a postsecondary qualification
equivalent to that of an undergraduate university degree or above.

The empirical study of ten Auslan interpreters translating a segment
of a lexically dense university lecture found that familiarity with the
topic, combined with educational background (i.e., familiarity with the

184   discourse environment) did in fact influence the linguistic coping strategies used, that is, the translation style and the rate and number of omission occurrences. It should be remembered, however, that these results only give an indication of the possible influence of educational background, as only two of the subjects did not have a university qualification. Further study would be needed with a balanced number of subjects representing people with and without qualifications, before any definitive conclusions can be made with regards to educational background.

Nevertheless, those subjects who were familiar with the topic of language acquisition presented in the university lecture commented that it helped them a great deal in processing the information. As a consequence, they felt that their knowledge of the area made their interpretation more effective. This study emphasises, however, that familiarity plays an important part in the success of an interpreted event, as interpreters are better able to not only understand the message, but also evaluate the significance of the message in the relation to the context of situation and the target audience. Seleskovitch (1978) stated that interpreters must have generalist knowledge, in that they must understand everything, but not necessarily to the same extent as specialists. By having generalist knowledge, they will be familiar with language use and content, but will not necessarily be experts in the area. Thus in relation to interpreting in university contexts, it is imperative that interpreters have studied at university themselves, to give them generalist knowledge in academic discourse. Additionally, they should ideally interpret for lectures in subjects that they have studied themselves, giving them more than a generalist understanding of the context in which they are interpreting.

A level of generalist knowledge and familiarity can also be gleaned through having studied generally, whether at university or at technical college. Having completed coursework and written assignments or oral presentations, interpreters will be able to broaden their understanding of academic language use in tertiary education in general. Interpreters will also have frames of reference for discourse expectations within such a learning environment, and be able to apply their knowledge accordingly.

In relation to interpreters' perceptions about own their educational background, however, it can be seen that the majority of subjects involved in the empirical phase of this study felt that their level of education impacted upon their ability to interpret for the university lecture. The general comments amounted to the fact that if they were university educated, they felt more comfortable with the register of language, as they were familiar with university discourse. For those that were not university educated, they said that they struggled with the formality of the language, and especially with some of the lexical items used. The data analysis supports the views of these interpreters in particular, as it was the two subjects with no university education that made the most omissions.

The importance of education was expressly stated by two subjects, who recognised that their interpreting skills began to improve when they began to study at university. They felt that their understanding, knowledge and use of the English language was expanding. Thus they had more mastery in English, and could therefore focus more on meaning and searching for semantic equivalence in Auslan when interpreting from English. This acknowledgment reinforces the need for interpreters to be generally educated to university standard as it will allow them to expand their vocabulary, their familiarity with various registers of language use, and their interpretation of language.

The notion of sign language interpreters needing a tertiary education to effectively work as interpreters is certainly not a new one. The results of this study have demonstrated how interpretation of a university lecture, and the use of linguistic coping strategies, can be particularly influenced by interpreters' familiarity with English and familiarity with subject-specific language use. The results have also shown that the occurrence of omissions can be effected by the educational experience of interpreters, with regards to the exposure they have had to different subject areas and the inherent terminology. The interpreters' familiarity with language use in academic settings also seemed to influence their use of translation style. These findings not only endorse the necessity for interpreters to be university educated before being permitted to interpret in university settings, but also to have completed tertiary level study as a

186   general requirement, in order to be better prepared for the range of
linguistic demands presented in different interpreting scenarios.

Discussion of the results thus far has highlighted an important issue
with respect to interpreters' familiarity with discourse environment,
familiarity with linguistic features of source text, and familiarity with
subject-specific terminology. This issue reinforces the relationship
between familiarity and interpreters' need for preparation.

6.2.1 Familiarity and preparation

Preparatory techniques can be used as coping strategies by interpreters
to deal with environmental and other extra-linguistic factors that may
influence their ability to effectively interpret a communication event.
The results and discussion of this study have emphasised the need for
interpreters to familiarise themselves not only with the logistics of
working in a particular discourse environment, but also to familiarise
themselves with linguistic aspects of the discourse environment,
particularly if working in university settings.

Although it has been suggested that the best way for interpreters to
familiarise themselves with academic discourse and subject-specific
terminology is to study at tertiary level, it should be acknowledged that
additional preparation is always advisable. It is widely recognised in the
literature that preparation contributes to the effectiveness of any
interpretation (Frishberg, 1990; Humphrey & Alcorn, 1996; Mackenzie,
1998; Napier, 1996; Neumann Solow, 2000; Stewart, Schein &
Cartwright, 1998). Regardless of interpreters' educational background or
acquaintance with topics they are expected to interpret, however, they
should strive to prepare specifically for assignments in order to familiarise themselves with idiosyncratic language use within the context of
situation. This particular study concentrated on the linguistic coping
strategies of interpreters working unprepared in order to reflect
situations in which interpreters often find themselves. It should never
be assumed, however, that a general university education guarantees
interpreters the level of familiarity necessary for dealing with the
linguistic aspects of the university discourse environment, or any other
discourse environment. Similarly, interpreters should not presume that
because they are familiar with particular topics, that they can predict

what subject-specific terminology will be used. The ideal situation should always require interpreters to carry out preparation before any type of interpreting assignment, to ensure they are prepared for all contingencies, linguistic or otherwise.

6.3 Conclusions

Thus far, the issues of translation style, interpreting omissions, educational background and familiarity have been discussed within the context of linguistic coping strategies used by sign language interpreters when interpreting for a university lecture. In relation to the research questions originally proposed, the findings of this study have concluded the following:

1. The interpreters involved in the study were dominant or extremely dominant in using either a free or literal interpretation approach. During interpretation of the university lecture, those who were dominant in using free interpretation used their translation style as a linguistic coping strategy, by switching to a more literal interpretation at key points of the text, in order to borrow English lexical items and thus provide access to subject-specific terms, academic or idiomatic English.

2. The interpreters made five different types of omissions while interpreting for a lexically dense university lecture segment— conscious strategic, conscious intentional, conscious unintentional, conscious receptive and unconscious. They made a total of 341 omissions across all five categories of omission type. Of these identifiable omissions, 26% were conscious strategic omissions, 18% were conscious intentional omissions, 14% were conscious unintentional omissions, 15% conscious receptive omissions, and 27% unconscious omissions.

3. The translation style of interpreters does not stand alone as a factor that effects the rate and type of omissions made.

4. The study results indicate that interpreters do use conscious strategic omissions as a linguistic coping strategy in order to deal with the linguistic features of a university lecture.

5. The interpreters demonstrated a high level of metalinguistic aware-

ness about the types of omissions they made while interpreting for the lexically dense university lecture segment.

6. The linguistic features of the university lecture source text did influence the use of translation style and the rate and occurrence of omissions. Translation style was affected by familiarity with academic English and subject-specific terminology. The lexical density of the source text, combined with the interpreters' familiarity with the discourse environment and the subject-specific terminology, influenced the rate and types of omissions produced by the interpreters.

7. The sign language interpreters in this study felt that their educational background impacted upon their ability to interpret for the university lecture, whereby those with a university education felt better able to cope with the linguistic demands of the lecture, due to their familiarity with university level discourse. Those interpreters that had previously studied the lecture topic felt that their familiarity with the subject also contributed to their ability to effectively interpret the university lecture.

8. The expectations of Deaf university students with regards to sign language interpreters varies, but generally there was agreement that interpreters should be fluent, and should provide interpretations freely, while occasionally switching to a more literal approach. There was general consensus that interpreters should be educated to equivalent standard to interpret in university settings, and that there was suspicion about interpreters making any kinds of omissions while interpreting.

6.4 Implications: Interpreter education and training

The findings of this study have significant implications for the education and training of interpreters, in relation to the linguistic coping strategies used by interpreters, as well as the education of interpreters. In accordance with the statement that "graduates of university programs with bachelors' and more especially masters' degrees are prepared for most interpreting tasks" (Frishberg & Wilcox, 1994, p.18), it has been the general finding of this study that the interpreters felt that they coped better with interpreting for a university lecture when they had completed a university education themselves. Deaf university students also reported that interpreters work more effectively in university lectures if they are familiar with the discourse environment. The educational background of the interpreters in the study also had some impact on the linguistic coping strategies that were used, which implies that the level of education achieved by interpreters is of significance.

In many countries there is no requirement for sign language interpreters to have completed a university degree, and there are no university programs available in sign language interpreting. Patrie (1994) stated that interpreter education and training are two different experiences that should provide entry to the profession at two different levels. The interpreter training and education system in both Australia and America allows people to enter postsecondary, non-university, interpreter training and achieve recognition as interpreters. This system corroborates a suggestion from Patrie (1994), that community college interpreter training is sufficient for entry to the profession at a 'Technical' level. Patrie also suggested, however, that for entry to the profession at a 'Professional' level, interpreter education at a minimum level of undergraduate study should be a requirement. Education at this level would provide interpreters with a deeper and broader base of knowledge, analysis and application. In the UK and USA it is possible to study sign language interpreting at undergraduate level, where as postgraduate study of sign language interpreting is available in the UK, USA, and Australia.

The field of sign language interpreting has recognised that highly skilled interpreters must be highly educated, but has also recognised that entry to the profession at a technical level is appropriate, if graduates restrict their work to particular areas for which they have been trained (Stauffer, 1994). The infrastructure for two levels of entry already exists in Australia, with paraprofessional interpreters being assessed on their ability to interpret for one-to-one communication events, and professional interpreters being assessed for their skills in interpreting for more complex and linguistically sophisticated situations (NAATI, 1999). A similar system has been proposed in the UK, with National Vocational Qualifications for BSL interpreters suggested at different levels of competence and expertise (CACDP). However, by establishing

190   more university interpreter education programs more practitioners can enter the field at the professional level, and thus have the necessary skills to provide interpreting services in highly demanding discourse environments, such as university lectures.

It has also been recognised that as well as being essential for working in a university context, a university education also better enables interpreters to cope linguistically with the varied situations they face in their everyday interpreting work. Thus another consideration of this study is that all interpreters should complete a general university undergraduate degree before they attend an interpreter education or training program. In doing so, they will have a wider linguistic repertoire with which to enter their interpreter education or training. The ideal situation would be for interpreters to have studied either a related subject at undergraduate level (such as Deaf Studies or Linguistics), or have had a broader liberal arts undergraduate education (for example in the Social Sciences) before then going on to train in a technical program, or be educated as interpreters at postgraduate level.

Another implication of this study is in relation to the content of interpreter education and training programs. The study has demonstrated that interpreters use translation style to different ends, with some interpreters switching between free and literal interpretation approaches as a linguistic coping strategy to deal with the complexity of the message, and the needs of their Deaf consumers. Discussion with Deaf university students found that they prefer to receive information in a university context through a process of free interpretation, with interpreters switching to a more literal approach in order to borrow English terminology and academic terms when appropriate. It was recognised that the use of more fingerspelling and mouth patterns would be acceptable in the formal situation of a university lecture, but that a more interactive cultural approach would be necessary in university tutorials. This study reinforces, therefore, the notion that interpretation does not have "context-independent rules" (Moser-Mercer, 1997 p.3).

I have previously suggested that sign language interpreters be educated on the theoretical standpoints of free interpretation (Napier, 2000). I would now suggest, however, that interpreters be educated in both free and literal interpretation theory and techniques, and be taught how to switch between these two methods as a linguistic coping strategy, depending on the context of situation and the consumers with whom they are working. This approach is endorsed by various writers (Davis, 2000; Ingram, 2000; Metger, 2000; Pollitt, 2000a; Roy, 2000c; Winston & Monikowski, 2000), who advocate for interpreter education to treat interpreting as a discourse process. They suggest that interpreter education should incorporate theoretical and practical discourse analysis to better enable interpreters to understand, and develop strategies for coping with, the various discourse environments they will encounter in their everyday work. In doing so, interpreters can adopt an interactive model of interpreting and thus make informed linguistic and cultural decisions about which interpretation approach to use in order to ensure the successful outcome of a communication event.

This study has also highlighted the fact that interpreters make different types of omissions while interpreting, of which one type is used as a conscious linguistic coping strategy. It was found that the rate and type of omission occurrences were influenced by the complexity of, and familiarity with, the source text. This finding highlights the need for interpreters to be educated about the types of omissions they make, and why they make them. In having a better understanding of various omission types, and the sociolinguistic and sociocultural influences on their occurrence, interpreters will be enabled to use certain omissions pro-actively as a linguistic coping strategy, while having heightened awareness about the possibilities of erroneous omissions.

With regards to heightened awareness, this study has demonstrated that although the interpreters applied their metalinguistic awareness of their language use to monitor their interpretation output, this application only became conscious through the interpreting task review. Sign language interpreter education and training should therefore incorporate activities to enhance the metalinguistic processes involved in interpreting. Peterson (2000) and Smith (2000) assert that by allowing interpreting students to explore and develop metacognitive strategies, they will be better equipped to evaluate their interpretation output, and the linguistic and cultural decisions made within the context of the discourse environment.

6.5 Wider implications: Interpreting in different contexts

The focus of this study has been on the linguistic coping strategies of sign language interpreters working in university lectures. It should be emphasised, however, that the findings can be extrapolated to interpreters working in other languages and in other contexts. It can be assumed that interpreters can use translation style as a linguistic coping strategy in contexts other than university settings, and it can also be assumed that interpreters can potentially make five types of omissions, regardless of the interpreting situation in which they are working. This study has demonstrated that the interpreters involved had high levels of metalin-guistic awareness while interpreting, and there is no reason to doubt this would not be the case for other interpreters in different contexts.

It should be recognised that an interpreter's ability to use translation style as a linguistic coping strategy may well be affected by several sociolinguistic issues, such as the context of situation, her familiarity with the discourse environment, her knowledge of the topic being discussed, and her familiarity with the Deaf and hearing interaction participants. These same sociolinguistic factors could also impact upon the rate and types of omission occurrences, regardless of whether the interpreting was taking place in a medical, legal or political arena, or the signed or spoken languages with which the interpreter was working.

In recognising the wider implications for this research, and the fact that the findings can be applied in other areas of interpreting, it is possible to recognise a limitation of the study, which consequently generates suggestions for further research that would expand on the ideas presented in this book.

6.6 Future research

The major limitation of the study is that the findings of the empirical research are presented with the assumption that the linguistic coping strategies adopted by interpreters, in the forms of translation style and conscious omissions, are appropriate according to interpreting theory presented in the literature. The interpretations in this study were not analysed for accuracy, and were not tested for comprehensibility. To date, there have been very few studies on Deaf people's comprehension of information received through sign language interpreting, some of which were discussed (Jacobs, 1976; Livingston, Singer & Abramson, 1994; Llewellyn Jones, 1981; Steiner, 1998). It is recognised that the ideal study would have incorporated testing of comprehensibility of Deaf university students, before reporting the effectiveness of sign language interpreters in using linguistic coping strategies, such as use of translation style and conscious strategic omissions. Due to time constraints, however, it was only possible to interview Deaf university students about their expectations of interpreters working in university settings, and their opinions on the use of omissions, the translation style and educational background of interpreters. Although the perspective of Deaf university students is valid, the information does not provide empirical evidence about interpreters' effectiveness at using linguistic coping strategies appropriately in university lectures. Thus the presentation of the research findings are done so with faith that the interpreting theory is correct, but with the hope that one day further studies may be carried out on comprehension, to verify the efficacy of the interpretations presented in this study.

Similar studies could be carried out in different ways to analyse and cross-reference the issues raised in this study, to gain a better understanding of working practices of interpreters in a range of situations. Discussion of the research findings has flagged key issues that require further analysis, as well as tangential issues of relevant interest.

One of the most important issues raised that necessitates further research, is that of comprehensibility. Although this study incorporated the perspective of Deaf people in terms of their expectations and preferences, in order to verify whether interpreters are using linguistic coping strategies appropriately, it would be necessary to test Deaf people's comprehension levels. In this way, it would be possible to determine whether sign language interpreters are meeting the communicative needs of Deaf university students, in addition to how well they conform to theoretical perceptions of what effective interpreting means. A study of this kind would also provide insight into whether Deaf people's preferred translation style actually provides them with adequate access to information in a university lecture.

194   Another suggestion is that the panel discussion that took place with Deaf university students in this study could be extended to include debate about the expectations of Deaf consumers in a variety of different settings. Representatives of Deaf people from a range of backgrounds could be brought together to discuss the translation style they prefer interpreters to use in diverse contexts, and the reasons for citing different preferences. Further comprehensibility studies could be conducted, asking Deaf people to rate their understanding of different interpreters interpreting in a range of scenarios. Information derived from this data could then be transferred into interpreter training and education programs, to better prepare student interpreters for the level of flexibility required to meet the needs of Deaf people in various discourse environments.

One suggestion to resolve the Deaf students' misunderstanding in this study about interpreters' coping strategies, would be to engage Deaf people in a similar interpreting task and task review. By asking Deaf people to interpret a source text received in a signed language into another signed or written language, or to re-tell the text in the same signed language, it would be possible to identify any omissions made, reflecting the task review of the interpreters involved in this study. In so doing, it is possible to assume that the Deaf people would discover that they had made linguistic decisions about what information to omit based on their knowledge and understanding of the source text, the context of situation, and the linguistic and cultural relevance and meaning potential of the text to the target audience. Experiencing this process for themselves would better enable them to understand, and comment on, interpreters' use of omissions as a linguistic coping strategy.

In relation to the context of situation examined in this study, it would be interesting to conduct a study of interpreters working in a lecture that was not lexically dense, but in a similar situation. For example, interpretation of a conference keynote presentation could be compared with the lecture interpretation in this study, to highlight similarities and differences in use of translation style and omissions as linguistic coping strategies. Alternatively, a comparative study of omissions made by interpreters interpreting for a lecture read out verbatim from a prepared text, meaning that the text would be even more lexically dense than the one used in this study, and thus more complex to interpret.

Another comparative study could involve interpretations of the same university lecture, but allowing the interpreters more preparation and time to clarify terminology, or academic terms. This altered methodology would provide interesting contrastive data, as it would be possible to ascertain exactly how the use of linguistic coping strategies changed, and to what extent.

In terms of studying interpreting in different contexts, it would be valuable to replicate this study, and analyse the rate and prevalence of conscious strategic, conscious intentional, conscious unintentional, conscious receptive and unconscious omissions in other interpreting scenarios. This would create a picture of the different factors that impact on the use of conscious strategic omissions and the production of erroneous omissions, for example, in a medical appointment, a job interview, a conference paper, a board meeting, or a university tutorial. The research could then be taken one step further, contrasting interpreters working in identical situations that had received more preparation. The same replication could offer opportunity to analyse the strategic use of free and literal interpretation approaches in different contexts.

The superficial identification of lexical borrowing, or linguistic transference, in this study provides a foundation for further research in relation to the degree of fingerspelling used strategically by interpreters, and the sociolinguistic factors that influence the incidence of fingerspelling. References have been made to the amount of fingerspelling typical of Auslan and BSL use and the extent to which Auslan and BSL interpreters reflect the language use of the Deaf community with whom they work (Napier & Adam, 2002). As far as I know, however, there has been no empirical research into the amount of fingerspelling used by Deaf people in Australia and the UK. Thus a study recording and analysing spontaneous sign language production of Deaf people in various discourse environments would provide a picture of any fingerspelling patterns in different contexts. It would then be possible, therefore, to investigate interpreters' use of fingerspelling in comparison with the original Deaf corpus group.

196   Although not an exhaustive list, these few suggestions for future research are offered with the goal of discovering more about interpreters and interpreting and broadening our understanding of the various linguistic processes and factors involved. Any future research should endeavour to develop a better understanding of the relationship between interpreters, consumers, and the discourse environments in which they participate in interactive events. Additional research will allow interpreters, interpreter educators and interpreter researchers to further explore the linguistic coping strategies of interpreters, and the sociolinguistic and sociocultural factors that influence the outcome of an interpreted communicative event. Rather than thinking about whether interpreters succeed or fail, research enables us to consider the strategies employed, and interpreters' contributions to the outcomes of such events:

> …there are no absolute criteria for defining "good" interpretations. Different discourse events with different goals and needs and different participants require changing actions on the part of the interpreter (Roy, 2000a, p.126).

Transcription conventions

know	conventional orthography represents spoken English words
KNOW	English representation (gloss) of an Auslan sign
I-ASK-YOU	when more than one English word is needed to gloss an Auslan sign, the English words are separated by a hyphen
T-R-U-E	when an English word is fingerspelled, the letters in the word are separated by a hyphen
WHAT*	the asterisk indicates the sign is emphasised
KNOCK+	the plus symbol indicates that the sign is repeated
(VERY)	the signer has started to execute a particular sign but has stopped and moved on to another sign
LIMIT (1) LIMIT (2)	numbers indicate that two different signs are used for the same gloss, one directly after another
point-left	the signer has pointed to aspecific location with
point-right	reference to an location or established entity or entities, e.g. FAMILY point-left/ FAMILY or FAMILY FAMILY point-arc
left/ right	indicates placement of sign by either left or right side of signer's body, e.g, ACQUIRE-left ACQUIRE-right
their-left/right	indicates placement of possessive his/her-left/right pronoun

Non-manual grammatical markers

..	noticeable pause (equivalent to use of comma in orthographic English)
q	the facial expression and head movements used indicate a question is being asked (often rhetorical)
hd	indicates affirmation through head nod
neg	indicates negation through head shake

Adapted and developed from Baker and Cokely (1980), Harrington (2000), Roy (1992) and Sutton-Spence and Woll (1998).

Characteristics of translation styles

Example English sentence: *'We should try and encourage families to support the first language acquisition of their Deaf children'.*

b.1 Free interpretation

Free interpretation is "the process by which concepts and meanings are translated from one language into another, by incorporating cultural norms and values; assumed knowledge about these values; and the search for linguistic and cultural equivalents (Napier, 1998b, p.36), whereby "the linguistic structure of the source language is ignored, and an equivalent is found based on the meaning it conveys" (Crystal, 1987, p.344).

Linguistic markers: Use of possessive pronouns, placement and corresponding spatial reference, exploitation of visual metaphor, use of rhetorical questioning and non-manual features. Elaboration on meaning. Interpretation provides equivalency of meaning, not necessarily equivalency of each lexical item. Use of fingerspelling typically limited to glosses already lexicalised in Auslan. Grammatically appropriate use of lip pattern. Possible translation of example sentence:

'We should try and encourage families to support the first language

       'ALL FAMILY HAVE DEAF CHILDREN.. WE SHOULD WHAT

       (point-arc)   *(q)*

acquisition of their Deaf children.'

ENCOURAGE PARENTS LEARN SIGN LANGUAGE.. MEANS PARENTS AND CHILD

  (point left-middle-right)   *(point-left point-right)*

HAVE SAME LANGUAGE.. MEANS CHILD CAN ACQUIRE SIGN FIRST

              (point-left)   *(their-left)*

LANGUAGE.'

    (hd)

Literal interpretation means that "the linguistic structure of the source text is followed, but is normalised according to the rules of the target language" (Crystal, 1987: 344).

Linguistic markers: Use of rhetorical questioning, possessive pronouns, spatial reference and non-manual features. Less exploitation of visual metaphor, and little meaningful elaboration. Equivalency based on lexical gloss, with higher proportion of borrowing from English in terms of fingerspelling. Use of lip patterns articulating English words especially noticeable when fingerspelling. Possible translation of example sentence:

'We should try and encourage families to support the first language

'WE SHOULD TRY WHAT ENCOURAGE FAMILY

(q)

acquisition of their Deaf children.'

HAVE DEAF CHILDREN SUPPORT CHILD FIRST LANGUAGE ACQUISITION.'

  (point-left-middle-right)   (point-left)   (their-left)

b.3 Sentences transcribed from original source data

Sentence 1: *'And what they did was contrast the acquisition of these features with the acquisition of the same types of grammatical features in English, and came up with, as a result of this study, with what seemed to be some quite consistent patterns of grammatical acquisition across the two languages'.*

Sentence 2: *'Any of you who are aware of the work in this area, the work of people like Jean Piaget, who made a very very strong case for a binding relationship between early sensory-motor development and early language acquisition'.*

Sentence 3: *'If you look at the work of someone like Steve Krashen, even in second language research, his notion of, that we have to be at or just above the language receptive capacities of the language learner, that if we are too far above it then the capacity for the learner to actually make use of language input is certainly diminished'.*

b.4 Transcriptions of three sentences for each subject

Subject 1 sentence 1

'And what they did was contrast the acquisition of these features with

    'WHAT D-I-D LOOK A-T COMPARE ACQUISITION ACQUISITION
               (point-left)   *(left)*   *(right)*

the acquisition of the same types of grammatical features in English,

SAME TYPE O-F G-R-A-M-M-A-R THING IN ENGLISH.. SHOW COMPARE
                                  (point-right)

and came up with, as a result of this study, with what seemed to be

FROM RESULT RESEARCH RESEARCH WHAT LOOK LIKE REALLY SAME*
        (left)   *(right)*

some quite consistent patterns of grammatical acquisition across the

PARALLEL HOW G-R-A-M-M-A-R ACQUIRE SAME SAME.'
                                    (left) (right)

two languages.'

Subject 1 sentence 2

'Any of you who are aware of the work in this area, the work of people

        'AWARE THAT AREA PEOPLE LIKE J-O-H-N G-O-U-G-E-R MAKE
        (point-left) *(point-left)*

like Jean Piaget, who made a very very strong case for a binding

VERY GOOD PROOF PRESENT FOR FOR.. (BECAUSE) BETWEEN EARLY CHILD
 (point-left)

relationship between early sensory-motor development and early

S-E-N-S-O-R-Y M-O-T-O-R AND EARLY LANGUAGE ACQUISITION.'
language acquisition.'

Subject 1 sentence 3

'If you look at the work of someone like Steve Krashen, even in second

        'LOOK-AT S-T-E-V-E K-R-A-S-H-E IN SECOND* LANGUAGE
language research, his notion of, that we have to be at or just above the
ACQUISITION RESEARCH YOU HAVE-TO A-T O-R JUST SLIGHTLY-ABOVE
language receptive capacities of the language learner, that if we are too
LANGUAGE ABILITY ACQUIRE CAN'T TOO-FAR-ABOVE ABILITY LEARN OR
                                         (point-left)

far above it then the capacity for the learner to actually make use of
USE LANGUAGE.. (RECEPTIVE DIFFICULTY).'
   (neg)
language input is certainly diminished.'

Subject 2 sentence 1

'And what they did was contrast the acquisition of these features with
  'WHAT THEY.. RECEIVE F-E-A-T-U-R-E WITH SAME TYPE O-F G-R-
     (point-right)
the acquisition of the same types of grammatical features in English,
A-M-M-A-T-I-C-A-L F-E-A-T-U-R-E-S IN ENGLISH AND COME UP WITH..
and came up with, as a result of this study, with what seemed to be
BECAUSE O-F STUDY WHAT S-E-E-M-E-D T-O B-E WHAT CONSISTENT P-A-
        (q)
some quite consistent patterns of grammatical acquisition across the
T-T-E-R-N O-F G-R-A-M-M-A-T-I-C-A-L ACQUISITION ACROSS AREA.'
    (hd)
two languages.'

Subject 2 sentence 2

'Any of you who are aware of the work in this area, the work of people
   'AWARE O-F WORK AREA.. PEOPLE LIKE P-I-A-G-E-T HE MAKE
    (point-right)   (point-right)
like Jean Piaget, who made a very very strong case for a binding
VERY STRONG C-A-S-E FOR..TALK-ABOUT.. WORD SOMETHING RELATION-
relationship between early sensory-motor development and early
SHIP BETWEEN EARLY S-E-N-S-O-R-Y M-O-T-O-R DEVELOP AND EARLY
    (hd)
language acquisition.'
LANGUAGE ACQUISITION.'

Subject 2 sentence 3

'If you look at the work of someone like Steve Krashen, even in second
   'S-T-E-V-E K-R-A-S-H-E-N IN RESEARCH WE HAVE-TO T-O
    (his-right)
language research, his notion of, that we have to be at or just above the

J-U-S-T LANGUAGE MUST SLIGHTLY-ABOVE RECEPTIVE LANGUAGE TOO-
language receptive capacities of the language learner, that if we are too
FAR-ABOVE LANGUAGE LEVEL MUST LEARN MAKE U-S-E LANGUAGE
      (neg)   *(point-right)*
far above it then the capacity for the learner to actually make use of
ACQUISITION LITTLE-BIT DIFFICULT.'
language input is certainly diminished.'

Subject 3 sentence 1

'And what they did was contrast the acquisition of these features with
   'WHAT THEY D-I-D LOOK DIFFERENT HOW THEY ACQUIRE FACIAL-
      (point-right)   *(point-left)*
the acquisition of the same types of grammatical features in English,
EXPRESSION -F- ENGLISH OCCUR FROM STUDY LOOK LIKE CONSISTENT
    (point-right) (point-right)
and came up with, as a result of this study, with what seemed to be
VARY P-A-T-T-E-R-N G-R-A-M- M-A-R ACQUIRE+ IN(ENGLISH) AL
some quite consistent patterns of grammatical acquisition across the
LANGUAGES.'
two languages.'

Subject 3 sentence 2

'Any of you who are aware of the work in this area, the work of people
   'THEY KNOW WORK IN THIS AREA (VERY) MAKE VERY
   (point-right) (point-right)   *(point-right)*
like Jean Piaget, who made a very very strong case for a binding
STRONG EXPLAIN C-A-S-E FOR LIKE CONNECT RELATIONSHIP EARLY GROW
relationship between early sensory-motor development and early
CONNECT PLUS LANGUAGE ACQUIRE.'
language acquisition.'

Subject 3 sentence 3

'If you look at the work of someone like Steve Krashen, even in second
   'IDEA HAVE-TO B-E THERE O-R LITTLE-BIT SLIGHLTY-ABOVE
   (point-right)   *(point-middle)*
language research, his notion of, that we have to be at or just above the

ABILITY T-O ACQUIRE I-F TOO-MUCH HIGH-ABOVE* (CAN'T) ABILITY FOR
(their-middle)   *(point-right-middle)*

language receptive capacities of the language learner, that if we are too

THEM UNDERSTAND ACQUIRE.. HAVE LIMIT(1) LIMIT(2).'
(point-middle)

far above it then the capacity for the learner to actually make use of
language input is certainly diminished.'

Subject 4 sentence 1

'And what they did was contrast the acquisition of these features with

'THEIR WORK WHAT COMPARE HOW ACQUIRE THOSE DIFFERENT
     (their-left)   *(q)*   *(point-right)*

the acquisition of the same types of grammatical features in English,

G-R-A-M-M-A-T-I-C-A-L STRUCTURE INCLUDE+ COMPARE WITH SAME IN

and came up with, as a result of this study, with what seemed to be

ENGLISH OR NOT.. S-O WHEN COMPARE UNTIL HAVE SAME+ SIGN AND
               (q)

some quite consistent patterns of grammatical acquisition across the

ENGLISH A-S-L.'
(hd) (their-right)

two languages.'

Subject 4 sentence 2

'Any of you who are aware of the work in this area, the work of people

'IF YOU INTEREST CHILDREN EDUCATION MAYBE YOU
             (q)

like Jean Piaget, who made a very very strong case for a binding

INTEREST PEOPLE LIKE P-I-A-G-E-T MAKE STRONG-FIGHT* TALK OVER

relationship between early sensory-motor development and early

RELATIONSHIP BETWEEN (QUOTATION MARKS) S-E-N-S-O-R-Y MOTOR M-
         (point-right)

language acquisition.'

O-T-O-R IMPROVE AND EARLY LANGUAGE ACQUISITION.'
(right)   *(left)*

Subject 4 sentence 3

'If you look at the work of someone like Steve Krashen, even in second
language research, his notion of, that we have to be at or just above the

LOOK A-T S-T-E-V-E

language receptive capacities of the language learner, that if we are too
K-R-A-S-H OVER SECOND LANGUAGE RESEARCH FOUND.. HAVE WE CAN

(point-right)

far above it then the capacity for the learner to actually make use of
MUST MATCH LANGUAGE LEVEL WHEN DISCUSS I-F TOO-MUCH HIGH-
    (their-right)

language input is certainly diminished.'
ABOVE CAN'T (ACQUIRE) NOT FULL UNDERSTAND LIMIT THEIR .. FULL
(point-right)   (neg)   (their-right)
COMMUNICATION.'

Subject 5 sentence 1

'And what they did was contrast the acquisition of these features with
    'PEOPLE WHAT COMPARE ACQUISITION LIST WITH COMPARE
    (point-arc)   (q)

the acquisition of the same types of grammatical features in English,
SAME* TYPE G-R-A-M-M-A-T-I-C-A-L LIST IN ENGLISH FOUND WHAT FOR

(q)

and came up with, as a result of this study, with what seemed to be
STUDY HAPPEN WHAT LOOK LIKE VERY CONSISTENT P-A-T-T-E-R-N-S G-R-
        (q)

some quite consistent patterns of grammatical acquisition across the
A-M-M-A-T-I-C-A-L ACQUISITION OVER TWO LANGUAGE

(left)

two languages.'
LANGUAGE.'
(right)   (their-left-right)

Subject 5 sentence 2

'Any of you who are aware of the work in this area, the work of people
    'YOU KNOW WORK WRITE LIKE J-E-A-N P-I-A-G-E-T
    (point-right) (hd)   (point-left)

like Jean Piaget, who made a very very strong case for a binding
VERY+ STRONG* FAVOUR OVER B-I-N-D-I-N-G RELATIONSHIP WITH EARLY
relationship between early sensory-motor development and early
S-E-N-S-O-R-Y MO-T-E-R M-O-T-O-R DEVEOP AND EARLY LANGUAGE
language acquisition.'
ACQUISITION.'

Subject 5 sentence 3

'If you look at the work of someone like Steve Krashen, even in second
    'LIKE LOOK-AT S-T-E-V-E C-R-A-S-H-E-N IN HIS SECOND
                                (his-right)

language research, his notion of, that we have to be at or just above the
LANGUAGE RESEARCH HIS IDEA WE HAVE-TO LITTLE-BIT SLIGHTLY-
                  (his-right)

language receptive capacities of the language learner, that if we are too
ABOVE LANGUAGE ACQUIRE ABILITY O-F LANGUAGE LEARNER I-F TOO-
far above it then the capacity for the learner to actually make use of
MUCH HIGH-ABOVE* CAN -T- FOR LEARNER T-O MAKE USE O-F LAN
language input is certainly diminished.'
GUAGE INPUT WILL REDUCE-DRASTICALLY.'

Subject 6 sentence 1

'And what they did was contrast the acquisition of these features with
       WELL ACTUALLY COMPARE HOW PEOPLE LEARN F-E-A-T-U-R-
                          (point-left)

the acquisition of the same types of grammatical features in English,
E-S WITH HOW PEOPLE LEARN SAME G-R-A-M-M-A-R F-E-A-T-U-R-E-S
and came up with, as a result of this study, with what seemed to be
ENGLISH.. FROM.. FOUND SAME SAME HOW PEOPLE LEARN OR
           (point-left-right)(left) (right)

some quite consistent patterns of grammatical acquisition across the
LEARN DOESN'T-MATTER WHICH LANGUAGE.'
(point-left) (point-right)   (point both)
two languages.'

Subject 6 sentence 2

'Any of you who are aware of the work in this area, the work of people
'MAYBE YOU.. EXPERIENCE WITH WORK O-F J-E-A-N P-I-A-
(point-arc)

like Jean Piaget, who made a very very strong case for a binding
G-E-T HIMSELF REALLY BELIEVE.. VERY STRONG RELATIONSHIP B-I-N-D-I-

relationship between early sensory-motor development and early
N-G RELATIONSHIP BETWEEN EARLY S-E-N-S-O-R-Y M-O-T-O-R DEVELOP

language acquisition.'
AND EARLY LANGUAGE ACQUISITION.'

Subject 6 sentence 3

'If you look at the work of someone like Steve Krashen, even in second
I-F LOOK-AT WORK O-F S-T-E-V-E SOMEONE RESEARCH..
(their-right)

language research, his notion of, that we have to be at or just above the
ANOTHER PERSON HAVE-TO EQUAL-TO SIMILAR T-O LANGUAGE LEARN
(hd)

language receptive capacities of the language learner, that if we are too
I-F HIGH-ABOVE* SOPHISTICATED VERY DIFFICULT CAN'T-UNDERSTAND
(point-left) *(neg)*

far above it then the capacity for the learner to actually make use of
WHAT PERSON SAY.'
(point-right)

language input is certainly diminished.'

Subject 7 sentence 1

'And what they did was contrast the acquisition of these features with
'REALLY COMPARE HAVE ACQUIRE+ LIST F-E-A-T-U-R-E-S
(their-left)

the acquisition of the same types of grammatical features in English,
AND OTHER HAVE G-R-A-M-M-A-R ENGLISH PUT+ COMPARE.. LOOK-AT..

and came up with, as a result of this study, with what seemed to be
HAPPEN FOUND HAVE ALMOST SAME+ PARALLEL P-A-T-T-E-R-N F-O-R

some quite consistent patterns of grammatical acquisition across the

 (left) *(right)*
two languages.'

Subject 7 sentence 2

'Any of you who are aware of the work in this area, the work of people
'WHO J-O-H-N P-I-A-R-G-E.. STRONG SUPPORT+ (RECEPTIVE
(q) *(point-arc)* *(hd)*
like Jean Piaget, who made a very very strong case for a binding
DIFFICULTY) EARLY THINK+M-O-T-O-R PROCESS COMPARE WITH EARLY
relationship between early sensory-motor development and early
LANGUAGE ACQUISITION.'
language acquisition.'

Subject 7 sentence 3

'If you look at the work of someone like Steve Krashen, even in second
'SOMEONE RESEARCH S-T-E-V-E K-R-A-S-H-I-N-G SECOND
(their-right) *(their-right)*
language research, his notion of, that we have to be at or just above the
LANGUAGE RESEARCH MUST..WHAT ABILITY ACQUIRE-FROM-ME LITTLE-
(their-left)
language receptive capacities of the language learner, that if we are too
BIT SLIGHTLY-ABOVE THAN WHAT THINK CAN TOO-MUCH HIGH-ABOVE
far above it then the capacity for the learner to actually make use of
CAN'T ACQUIRE.'
(neg)
language input is certainly diminished.'

Subject 8 sentence 1

'And what they did was contrast the acquisition of these features with
'SO HOW THEY COMPARE ACQUISITION F-E-A-T-U-R-E-S ACQUISITION
(point-left) *(point-left)*
the acquisition of the same types of grammatical features in English,
SAME K-I-N-D F-E-A-T-U-R-E-S IN ENGLISH WELL.. FINISH STUDY RESEARCH
and came up with, as a result of this study, with what seemed to be
FOUND SAME P-A-T-T-E-R-N-S G-R-A-M-M-A-T-I-C-A-L ACQUISITION BOTH

some quite consistent patterns of grammatical acquisition across the
LANGUAGE SAME.'
two languages.'

Subject 8 sentence 2

'Any of you who are aware of the work in this area, the work of people
    'YOU SHOULD KNOW OVER P-I-A-G-E.. P-I-A-G-E-T MAKE
                                            (hd) (point-middle)
like Jean Piaget, who made a very very strong case for a binding
STRONG* SUPPORT THEORY BELIEVE STRONG RELATIONSHIP S-E-N-S-O-R-
       (his-middle)   (hd)
relationship between early sensory-motor development and early
Y M-O-T-O-R MOVEMENT-OF-ARMS-AND- BODY WALK EVERYTHING AND
language acquisition.'
LANGUAGE ACQUISITION.'

Subject 8 sentence 3

'If you look at the work of someone like Steve Krashen, even in second
    'SOMEONE LIKE S-T-E-V-E K-R-A-S-H-E-N HE SAY (IDEA)
                                      (point-middle)
language research, his notion of, that we have to be at or just above the
SECOND* LANGUAGE RESEARCH BUT MUST TALK SLIGHTLY-ABOVE MY
(point-middle)
language receptive capacities of the language learner, that if we are too
TALK HIGH LEARNER LOWER TOO-FAR- ABOVE ACQUIRE-FROM-ME CAN'T
      (their-middle)   (point-middle)   (neg)   (neg)
far above it then the capacity for the learner to actually make use of
SLIGHTLY-ABOVE SAME-LEVEL LEARN NOTHING SLIGHTLY-ABOVE NEED
                                                      (hd)
language input is certainly diminished.'
THAT PHILOSOPHY.'

Subject 9 sentence 1

'And what they did was contrast the acquisition of these features with
    'WELL THREE WRITE NOTE-DOWN WHAT THEY D-O WHAT
    (point-right)   (q)

the acquisition of the same types of grammatical features in English,
WELL COMPARE CHILDREN ACQUIRE SIGN LANGUAGE GROW-UP ACQUIRE
           (left)   *(right)*
and came up with, as a result of this study, with what seemed to be
ENGLISH (STRUCTURE) G-R-A-M-M-A-R COMPARE+FIND THEIR RESEARCH
                      (hd)   *(their-right)*
some quite consistent patterns of grammatical acquisition across the
SHOW HAVE+ SAME COMPARE+ CHILDREN ACQUIRE MANY SAME HOW.'
two languages.'

Subject 9 sentence 2

'Any of you who are aware of the work in this area, the work of people
     'YOU AWARE KNOW WHAT J-O-H-N P-I-A-G-E-T WORK..
     (point-middle)   *(q)*   *(his-middle)*
like Jean Piaget, who made a very very strong case for a binding
PERSON WRITE A-LOT-OF-TEXT STRONG* TALK OVER WELL.. RELATION-
(point-middle)
relationship between early sensory-motor development and early
SHIP WITH WHAT WHEN BABY CHILDREN GROW-UP THEIR HANDS EYES
        (q)   *(their-right)*
language acquisition.'
ARMS-MOVE EARLY MOVE RELATE-TO EARLY ACQUIRE LANGUAGE.'

Subject 9 sentence 3

'If you look at the work of someone like Steve Krashen, even in second
     'DOESN'T-MATTER SECOND LANGUAGE RESEARCH S-T-E-V-E
language research, his notion of, that we have to be at or just above the
K-R-A-S-H-E-N SECOND LANGUAGE RESEARCH AREA WELL THEIR LAN-
    (point-right) (his-right)   *(point-right) (their-right)*
language receptive capacities of the language learner, that if we are too
GUAGE MUSTALMOST AHEAD ME ACQUIRE+ THEIR SPEAK+ T-O ME ME-
     (point-right)   *(their-right)*
far above it then the capacity for the learner to actually make use of
UNDERSTAND LITTLE-BIT AHEAD WHAT MY UNDERSTAND ME CAN AHEAD
                                 (neg/hd)

language input is certainly diminished.'

IMPROVE WELL I-F FAR-AHEAD ME CAN'T ACQUIRE DAMAGE MY ACQUIRE
        (point-right)   (neg)
T-O LEARN SECOND.'

Subject 10 sentence 1

'And what they did was contrast the acquisition of these features with

'WHAT WHAT RESEARCH WHAT COMPARE WITH G-R-A-M-
        (point arc)   (q)

the acquisition of the same types of grammatical features in English,

M-A-R LIST IN ENGLISH COMPARE WITH SIGN LANGUAGE HOW LIST
                                                (left)

and came up with, as a result of this study, with what seemed to be

COMPARE.. RESEARCH FOUND LIST ALMOST SAME LANGUAGE ACQUISI-

some quite consistent patterns of grammatical acquisition across the

TION BOTH LANGUAGE ALMOST SAME.'
        (their right)   (their left)   (hd)

two languages.'

Subject 10 sentence 2

'Any of you who are aware of the work in this area, the work of people

'SHOULD WORK AREA SOME PEOPLE STRONG EXPLAIN*
        (point-left)   (point+ left)

like Jean Piaget, who made a very very strong case for a binding

TRUE STRONG RELATIONSHIP EARLY DEVELOP FOR EYES EARS ACQUIRE+

relationship between early sensory-motor development and early

PLUS LANGUAGE ACQUISITION.. HOW CONNECT
                                (point-left-right-left)

language acquisition.'

Subject 10 sentence 3

'If you look at the work of someone like Steve Krashen, even in second

'ANOTHER S-T-E-V-E K-R-A-S-H-E-N-E-W.. SAY (WHO) WHAT PERSON CAN
                                        (point-left)

language research, his notion of, that we have to be at or just above the

ACQUIRE I-F SPEAK*+ HIGH-ABOVE WILL GO-OVER-HEAD MAKE LITTLE-BIT

language receptive capacities of the language learner, that if we are too
SLIGHTLY-ABOVE WATCH WILL LEARN MORE.'
     (point-left)
far above it then the capacity for the learner to actually make use of
language input is certainly diminished.'

Omission types made by subjects on key lines of text

Subject   *Line number*

	59	90	104	116	117	139	169
1	CS	CI	CS	U	–	U	CS
2	CI	CR	U	U	U	CS	CI
3	CI	CI	CU	R	U	U	CS
4	CU	U	CS	U	U	CS	CS
5	CI	–	CS	U	U	–	CS
6	CS	–	U	–	–	–	CS
7	CI	U	CS	U	U	CS	CS
8	CI	–	U	–	CU	U	CR & CS
9	CI	U	U	CR	–	R	U
10	CI	R	U	–	U	CS	CS

Total n° of omissions per line

	59	90	104	116	117	139	169
	10	7	10	7	7	8	11

key   CS = Conscious strategic omissions; CI = Conscious intentional omissions; CU = Conscious unintentional omissions; CR = Conscious receptive omissions; U = Unconscious omissions.

References

A confluence of diverse relationships: Proceedings of the 13th National Convention of the Registry of Interpreters for the Deaf (1995). Silver Spring, MD: RID Publications.

Altman, H. J. (1989). Error analysis in the teaching of simultaneous interpretation: A pilot study. Fremdsprachen, 33(3), 177–183.

Anderson, B. (1978). Interpreter roles and interpretation situations: Cross-cutting typologies. In D. Gerver, & H. W. Sinaiko (Eds.), Language interpretation and communication (pp. 217–230). New York: Plenum Press.

Aquiline, C. (2000, July). World Federation of the Deaf: Towards a policy on Deaf education. Paper presented to the International Congress of Educators of the Deaf, Sydney, Australia.

Astington, J., Harris, P.L., & Olsen, D.R. (Eds.) (1988). Developing theories of mind. Cambridge: Cambridge University Press.

Atwood, A. (1985). Environmental distractions in interpreting. Journal of Interpretation, 2, 94–98.

Atwood, A., & Gray, D. (1986). Interpreting: The Culture of Artful Mediation. In M. McIntire (Ed.), Interpreting: The art of cross-cultural mediation. (pp. 80–85). Silver Spring, MD: RID Publications.

Baetens Beardsmore, H. (1986). Bilingualism: Basic principles (2nd ed.). Clevedon: Multilingual Matters Ltd.

Baker, C., & Cokely, D. (1980). American Sign Language: A teacher's resource text on grammar and culture. Maryland, TJ: Publishers Inc.

Baker, M. (1992). In other words: A coursebook on translation. London: Routledge.

Baker-Shenk, C. (1986). Characteristics of oppressed and oppressor peoples. In M. McIntire (Ed.), Interpreting: The art of cross-cultural mediation (pp.43–53). Silver Spring, MD: RID Publications.

Barik, H. A. (1975). Simultaneous interpretation: qualitative and linguistic data. Language and Speech , 18, 272–297.

Beaman, K. (1984). Co-ordination and subordination revisited: Syntactic complexity in spoken and written narrative discourse. In D. Tannen (Ed.), Coherence in spoken and written discourse (pp. 45–80). Norwood, NJ:

214   Ablex Publishing.

Beylard-Ozeroff, A., Králová, J., & Moser-Mercer, B. (Eds.) (1998). *Translators' strategies and creativity: Selected papers from the Ninth International Conference on Translating and Interpreting.* Philadelphia: John Benjamins.

Bialystok, E., & Ryan, E. B. (1985a). Toward a definition of metalinguistic skill. *Merrill-Palmer Quarterly, 31,* 229–251.

Bialystok E., & Ryan, E. B. (1985b). The metacognitive framework for the development of first and second language skills. In D. L. Forrest-Pressley, G. E. Mackinnon, & T. G. Waller (Eds.), *Metacognition, cognition and human performance.* New York: Academic Press.

Bialystok, E. (1991a). Metalinguistic dimensions of bilingual proficiency. In E. Bialystok (Ed.), *Language processing in bilingual children* (pp.113–140). Cambridge: Cambridge University Press.

——(Ed.) (1991b). *Language processing in bilingual children.* Cambridge: Cambridge University Press.

——(1993). Metalinguistic awareness: The development of children's representations of language. In C. Pratt, & A.F. Garton (Eds.), *Systems of representation in children: Development and use.* Chichester: Wiley.

Bienvenu, M.J. (1987). Third culture: Working together. *Journal of Interpretation, 4,* 1–12.

Blewett, J. (1985). *Problem solving in interpreting.* Milperra, NSW: Macarthur Institute of Higher Education.

Bowen, M. (1980). Bilingualism as a factor in the training of interpreters. In J. E. Alatis (Ed.), *Georgetown University round table on languages and linguistics, 1980: Current issues in bilingual education* (pp. 201–207). Washington, D.C: Georgetown University Press.

Bowman, J., & Hyde, M. (1993). Manual communication as support for deaf students in the regular classroom. *Australian Teacher of the Deaf, 33,* 32–46.

Brasel, B. (1975). The effects of fatigue on the competence of interpreters for the deaf. In H. J. Murphy (Ed.), *Selected readings in the integration of deaf students at CSUN* (pp. 19–22). Northridge, CA: California State University.

Bremner, A., & Housden, T. (1996). *Issues in educational settings for deaf students and interpreters.* http://www.deakin.edu.au/extern/rdlu/

deafstud.html.

Brennan, M. (1992). The visual world of BSL: An introduction. In D. Brien (Ed.), *Dictionary of British Sign Language/ English* (pp. 1–133). London: Faber & Faber.

Brennan, M. (2001). Making borrowings work in British Sign Language. In D. Brentari (Ed.), *Foreign vocabulary in sign languages* (pp.49–86). Mahwah, NJ: Lawrence Erlbaum.

Brennan, M., & Brown, R. (1997). *Equality before the law: Deaf people's access to justice.* Durham: Deaf Studies Research Unit, University of Durham.

Brien, D. (Ed.) (1992). *Dictionary of British Sign Language/ English.* London: Faber & Faber.

Brislin, R. (Ed.) (1976). *Translation: Applications and research.* New York: Gardner Press.

Brown, P., & Fraser, C. (1979). Speech as a marker of situation. In K. Scherer, & H. Giles (Eds.), *Social markers in speech* (pp. 33–62). Cambridge: Cambridge University Press.

Brown, L. (1993). *The new shorter Oxford English dictionary.* Oxford: Clarendon Press.

Burns, R. B. (1997). *Introduction to research methods.* Melbourne: Addison Wesley Longman.

Burns, S., Matthews, P., & Nolan-Conroy, E. (2001). Language attitudes. In C. Lucas (Ed.), *The sociolinguistics of sign languages* (pp.181–216). Cambridge: Cambridge University.

CACDP (1997). *Directory 1997/98.* Durham: Council for the Advancement of Communication with Deaf People.

Carter, S. M., & Lauritsen, R. R. (1974). Interpreter recruitment, selection and training. *Journal of Rehabilitation of the Deaf, 7* (3).

Cavell, J. L., & Wells, M. (1986). The interpreter as cross-cultural mediator: How does a student learn to do it? In M. McIntire (Ed.), *Interpreting: The art of cross-cultural mediation* (pp.95–110). Silver Spring, MD: RID Publications.

Cerney, B. (2000). The ten C's of effective target texts. *Journal of Interpretation, 131–150.

Chafe, W. (1980). *The pear stories: Cognitive, cultural and linguistic aspects of narrative production.* Norwood, NJ: Ablex.

216   Chafin Seal, B. (1998). *Best practices in educational interpreting*. Needham Heights, MA: Allyn & Bacon.

Christie, K., Wilkins, D. M., Hicks McDonald, B., & Neuroth-Gimbrone, C. (1999). GET-TO-THE-POINT: Academic bilingualism and discourse in American Sign Language and written English. In E. Winston (Ed.), *Storytelling and conversation: Discourse in Deaf communities* (pp.162–189). Washington, D.C: Gallaudet University Press.

CIT at 21: Celebrating excellence, celebrating partnership. Proceedings of the 13th National Convention of the Conference of Interpreter Trainers (2000). Silver Spring, MD: RID Publications.

Clark, E. V. (1978). Awareness of language: Some evidence from what children say and do. In A. Sinclair, R. J. Jarvella, & W. J. M. Levelt (Eds.), *The child's conception of language*. Berlin: Springer–Verlag.

Cokely, D. (1981). Sign Language Interpreters: A demographic survey. *Sign Language Studies, 32,* 261–286.

——(1983a). Metanotative qualities: How accurately are they conveyed by interpreters? *The Reflector, 5,* 16–22.

——(1983b). When is pidgin not a pidgin? An alternate analysis on the ASL-English contact situation. *Sign Language Studies, 38,* 1–24.

——(1985). *Towards a sociolinguistic model of the interpreting process: Focus on ASL and English.* Unpublished doctoral dissertation, Georgetown University.

——(1992a). *Interpretation: A sociolinguistic model.* Burtonsville, MD: Linstok Press.

——(1992b). Effects of Lag Time on Interpreter Errors. In D. Cokely (Ed.), *Sign Language Interpreters and Interpreting* (pp.39-69). Burtonsville, MD: Linstok Press.

——(Ed.)(1992c). *Sign Language Interpreters and Interpreting.* Burtonsville, MD, MD: Linstok Press.

——(1995, September). *When worlds collide: Reflections on interpreting differing cultural realities.* Keynote paper presented to the Issues in Interpreting 2 conference, University of Durham.

——(2001). Interpreting culturally rich realities: Research implications for successful interpretation. *Journal of Interpretation,* 1–46.

Compton, M., & Shroyer, E. (1997). Educational interpreter preparation and liberal education. *Journal of Interpretation, 7*(1), 49–61.

Cooper, C. L., Davies, R., & Tung, R. L. (1982). Interpreting stress: Sources of job stress amongst conference interpreters. *Multilingua,* 1(2), 97–107.

Corfmat, P. (1990). *Please sign here: Insights into the world of the deaf.* Worthing, UK: Churchman Publishing.

Corker, M. (1997). Deaf people and interpreting—The struggle in language. *Deaf Worlds, 13*(3), 13–20.

Crystal, D., & Davey, D. (1969). *Investigating English style.* Bloomington: Indiana University Press.

Crystal, D. (1984). *Who cares about usage?* New York: Penguin.

——(1987). *The Cambridge encyclopedia of language.* Cambridge: Cambridge University Press.

——(1995). *The Cambridge Encyclopedia of the English language.* Cambridge: Cambridge University Press.

Cummins, J. (1980). The cross-lingual dimensions of language proficiency: implications for bilingual education and the optimal age issue. *TESOL Quarterly, 14,* 175–188.

Dahl, C., & Wilcox, S. (1990). Preparing the educational interpreter: A survey of sign language interpreter training programs. *American Annals for the Deaf, 135*(4), 275–279.

Darò, V. (1994). Non-linguistic factors influencing simultaneous interpretation. In S. Lambert, & B. Moser-Mercer (Ed.), *Bridging the gap: Empirical research in simultaneous interpretation* (pp.249–271). Philadelphia: John Benjamins.

Darò, V., Lambert, S., & Fabbro, F. (1996). Conscious monitoring of attention during simultaneous interpretation. *Interpreting, 1*(1), 101–124.

Davis, J. (1989). Distinguishing language contact phenomena in ASL. In C. Lucas (Ed.), *The sociolinguistics of the Deaf community* (pp.85–102). California: Academic Press.

——(1990a). *Interpreting in a language contact situation: The case of English-to-ASL interpretation.* Unpublished doctoral dissertation, University of New Mexico.

——(1990b). Linguistic transference and interference: Interpreting between English and ASL. In C. Lucas (Ed.), *Sign language research: Theoretical issues* (pp.308–321). Washington, D.C: Gallaudet University

218   Press.

———(2000). Translation techniques in interpreter education. In C. Roy (Ed.), *Innovative practices for teaching sign language interpreters* (pp.109-131). Washington,, D.C: Gallaudet University Press.

Dean, R., & Pollard, R. Q. (2001). The application of demand-control theory to sign language interpreting: Implications for stress and interpreter training. *Journal of Deaf Studies and Deaf Education, 6*(1), 1–14.

Demanez, S. (1987). Secondary education for hearing and adolescent deaf people. Two years experience of interpreting in French Sign Language. In J. Alegria et al (Eds.), *Deaf life. Today... and tomorrow? Pedagogy and deafness* (Volume 4) (pp.113–122). Bruxelles: Mecaprint.

Deuchar, M. (1979). *Diglossia in British Sign Language*. Unpublished doctoral dissertation, Stanford University.

———(1984). *British Sign Language*. London: Routledge & Kegan Paul.

Dicker, L. (1976). Intensive interpreter training. *American Annals of the Deaf, 121.*

Domingue, R., & Ingram, B. (1978). Sign language interpretation: The state of the art. In D. Gerver, & H. W. Sinaiko (Ed.), *Language interpretation and communication* (pp.81–86). New York: Plenum Press.

Donath, P. (1987). Interpreting for deaf people: A first stocktake. In *Das Zeichen 1*(1), 62–63.

Eighinger, L. (2000). *Re: Literate interpreters*. IEPFAC email discussion list, 26 February 2000. listserv@admin.humberc.on.ca.

Emmorey, K., & Lane, H. (Eds.) (2000). *The signs of language revisited: An anthology to Ursula Bellugi and Edward Klima*. Mahwah, NJ: Erlbaum.

Enkvist, N. E. (1973). Should we count errors or measure success? In J. Svartvik (Ed.), *Errata* (pp.16–23). Lund: CWK Gleerup.

Erting, C. (1994). Introduction. In C. Erting, R. Johnson, D. Smith and B. Snider (Eds.), *The Deaf way* (pp.xxiii-xxxi). Washington, D.C: Gallaudet University Press.

Erting, C., Johnson, R., Smith, D., & Snider, B. (Eds.) (1994). *The Deaf way: Perspectives from the international conference on Deaf culture*. Washington, D.C: Gallaudet University Press.

Fenton, S. (1993). Interpreting in New Zealand: An emerging profession. *Journal of Interpretation, 6,* 155–166.

Finegan, E., Besnier, N., Blair, D., & Collins, P. (1992). *Language: It's structure and use.* Sydney: Harcourt Brace Jovanich Publishers.

Fischer, T. (1993). Team interpreting: The team approach. *Journal of Interpretation, 6*(1), 167–174.

Fleischer, L. (1975). *Sign language interpretation under four conditions.* Unpublished doctoral dissertation, Brigham Young University, Provo, UT.

Flores d'Arcais, G. B. (1978). The contribution of cognitive psychology to the study of interpretation. In D. Gerver, & H. W. Sinaiko (Eds.), *Language interpretation and communication* (pp.385–402). New York: Plenum Press.

Fontana, S. (1999). Italian Sign Language and spoken Italian in contact: An analysis of interactions between Deaf parents and hearing children. In E. Winston (Ed.), *Storytelling and conversation: Discourse in Deaf communities* (pp.149–161). Washington, D.C: Gallaudet University Press.

Ford, L. (1981). *The interpreter as a communication specialist.* Paper presented to the Third International Symposium on Interpretation of Sign Languages, Bristol.

Foster, S. B., & Walter, G. G. (Eds.) (1992). *Deaf students in postsecondary education.* London: Routledge.

Fox, G. (Ed.) (1988). *Collins Cobuild essential English dictionary.* Glasgow: William Collins Sons & Co.

Freedle, R. (Ed.) (1979). *New Directions in Discourse Processing (Advances in Discourse Processes, Vol. 2).* Norwood, NJ: Ablex.

Frishberg, N. (1990). *Interpreting: An introduction* (2nd ed.). Silver Spring, MD: RID Publications.

——(2000). An interpreter creates the space. In K. Emmorey, & H. Lane (Eds.), *The signs of language revisited: An anthology to Ursula Bellugi and Edward Klima* (pp.169–192). Mahwah, NJ: Erlbaum.

Frishberg, N., & Wilcox, S. (1994). Issue paper: Differentiating training from education, technical and professional. In E. Winston (Ed.), *Mapping our course: A collaborative venture, Proceedings of the 10th National Convention of the Conference of Interpreter Trainers* (pp.15–20). USA: CIT.

Fromkin, V., Rodman, R., Collins, P., & Blair, D. (1990). *An introduction to language* (2nd Australian ed.). Sydney: Holt, Rinehart & Winston.

Garton, A., & Pratt, C. (1998). *Learning to be literate: The development of spoken and written language.* Oxford: Blackwell Publishers.

220   Gentile, A., Ozolins, U., & Vasilakakos, M. (1996). *Liaison interpreting: A handbook*. Melbourne: Melbourne University Press.

Gerot, L., & Wignell, P. (1995). *Making sense of functional grammar*. Cammeray, NSW: Antipodean Educational Enterprises.

Gerver, D. (1969). *The effects of source language presentation rate on the performance of simultaneous conference interpreters*. Louisville, KY: University of Louisville,

——(1974). The effects of noise on the performance of simultaneous interpreters: Accuracy of performance. *Acta Psychologica, 38,* 159-167.

Gerver, D., & Sinaiko, H. W. (Eds.) (1978). *Language interpretation and communication*. New York: Plenum Press.

Gile, D. (1995). *Basic concepts and models for interpreter and translator training*. Philadelphia: John Benjamins.

Goffman, E. (1974). *Frame analysis*. New York: Harper & Row.

——(1981). *Forms of talk*. Oxford: Basil Blackwell.

Goldman-Gisler, F. (1978). Segmentation of input in simultaneous translation. *Journal of Psycholinguistic Research, 1(2),* 127–140.

Goldman-Gisler, F., & Cohen, M. (1974). An experimental study of interference between receptive and productive processes relating to simultaneous translation. *Language and Speech, 17.*

Gran, L. (1998). Developing translation/ interpretation strategies and creativity. In-training development of interpreting strategies and creativity. In A. Beylard-Ozeroff, J. Králová, & B. Moser-Mercer (Eds.), *Translators' strategies and creativity*. Philadelphia: John Benjamins.

Greenhaw, D. (1985). Postsecondary education survey of interpreter services: A statistical study. *Journal of Interpretation, 2,* 40–57.

Gregory, S., & Hartley, G. (Eds.) (1992). *Constructing deafness*. Milton Keynes: Open University Press.

Grosjean, F. (1982). *Life with two languages: An introduction to bilingualism*. Cambridge, MA: Harvard University Press.

——(1997). The bilingual individual. *Interpreting, 2(2),* 163–188.

Gumperz, J. (Ed.) (1982). *Discourse strategies*. Cambridge: Cambridge University Press.

Gumperz, J., & Hymes, D. (Eds.) (1972). *Directions in sociolinguistics: The ethnography of communication*. New York: Holt, Rinehart & Winston.

Halliday, M. A. K. (1978). *Language as a social semiotic: The social interpreta-*

tion of language and meaning. London: Edward Arnold.

——(1979). Differences between spoken and written language: Some implications for literacy teaching. In G. Page, J. Elkins, & B. O'Connor (Eds.), *Communication through reading: Proceedings of the 4th Australian Reading Conference* (pp.37–52). Adelaide, SA: Australian Reading Association.

——(1985). *Spoken and written language.* Burwood, VIC: Deakin University Press.

Halliday, M. A. K. & Hasan, R. (1985). *Language, context and text: Aspects of language in a social semiotic perspective.* Burwood, VIC: Deakin University Press.

Hansen, B. (1991). Sign language interpreting in Scandinavia. In World Federation of the Deaf (Ed.), *Equality and self-reliance. Proceedings of the XI World Congress of the World Federation of the Deaf. Tokyo, Japan, 2–11 July 1991*(pp.887–894). Tokyo: Japanese Association of the Deaf.

Harrington, F. (2000). Sign language interpreters and access for Deaf students to university curricula: The ideal and the reality. In R. Roberts, S. A. Carr, D. Abraham, & A. Dufour (Eds.), *The critical link 2: Interpreters in the community. Selected papers from the 2nd International Conference on Interpreting in legal, health and social service settings, Vancouver, BC, Canada, 19–23 May 1998.* Philadelphia: John Benjamins.

——(2001a). Deaf students and the interpreted classroom: The effect of translation on education? In F. Harrington, & G. H. Turner (Eds.), *Interpreting interpreting: Studies and reflections on sign language interpreting* (pp. 74–88). Gloucestershire: Douglas McLean.

——(2001b). The rise, fall and re-invention of the communicator: Redefining roles and responsibilities in educational interpreting. In F. Harrington, & G. H. Turner (Eds.), *Interpreting interpreting: Studies and reflections on sign language interpreting* (pp. 89–102). Gloucestershire: Douglas McLean.

Harrington, F., & Traynor, N. (1999, July). *Second-hand learning: Experiences of Deaf students in higher education.* Paper presented at the Pathways to Policy: Deaf Nation 2 conference, University of Central Lancashire, Preston, UK.

Harrington, F., & Turner, G. H. (Eds.)(2001). *Interpreting interpreting: Studies and reflections on sign language interpreting.* Gloucestershire: Douglas

222　McLean.

Hassinen, L. & Lehtomaki, E. (1986). *Interpreting services for the deaf and deaf-blind and deafened people in Finland.* Helsinki: Finnish Association of the Deaf.

Hatim, B., & Mason, I. (1990). *Discourse and the translator.* London: Longman.

Hayes, L. (1992). Educational interpreters for deaf students: Their responsibilities, problems and concerns. *Journal of Interpretation, 5*(1), 5–24.

Herbert, J. (1978). How conference interpretation grew. In D. Gerver, & H. W. Sinaiko (Eds.), *Language interpretation and communication* (pp.5–10). New York: Plenum Press.

Higgins, P. (1980). *Outsiders in a hearing world: A sociology of deafness.* London: Sage Publications.

Hoffman, C. (1991). *An introduction to bilingualism.* London: Longman.

Hoffman, R. (1997). The cognitive psychology of expertise and the domain of interpreting. *Interpreting, 2*(2), 189–230.

Hough, J. (1981). *Court interpreting... who are we interpreting for?* Paper presented at the 3rd International Symposium on Sign Language Interpreting, Bristol.

Humphrey, J. (2000). Portfolios: One answer to the challenge of assessment and the "readiness to work" gap In C. Roy (Ed.), *Innovative practices for teaching sign language interpreters* (pp.153–176). Washington DC: Gallaudet University Press.

Humphrey, J., & Alcorn, B. (1996). *So you want to be an interpreter? An introduction to sign language interpreting.* Amarillo, Texas: H & H Publishers.

Hymes, D. (1967). Models of the interaction of language and social setting, *Journal of Social Issues, 23.*

——(1972). Models of the interaction of language and social life. In J. Gumperz, & D. Hymes (Eds.), *Directions in sociolinguistics: The ethnography of communication* (pp.35–71). New York: Holt, Rinehart & Winston.

Ingram, R. (1974). A communication model of the interpreting process. *Journal of Rehabilitation of the Deaf, 7,* 3–9.

——(1978). Sign language interpretation and general theories of language interpretation and communication. In D. Gerver, & H. W.

Sinaiko (Eds.), *Language interpretation and communication* (pp.109–118) .
New York: Plenum Press.

——(1985). Simultaneous interpretation of sign languages: Semiotic and psycholinguistic perspectives. *Multilingua*, 4(2), 91–102.

——(2000). *Why discourse matters.* in C. Roy (Ed.), Innovative practices for teaching sign language interpreters. Washington D.C: Gallaudet University Press.

Isham, W. (1986). The role of message analysis in interpretation. In M. McIntire (Ed.), *Interpreting: The art of cross-cultural mediation* (pp.111–122). Silver Spring, MD: RID Publications.

——(1994). Memory for sentence form after simultaneous interpretation: Evidence both for and against deverbalisation. In S. Lambert, & B. Moser-Mercer (Eds.), *Bridging the gap: Empirical research in simultaneous interpretation* (pp.191–211). Philadelphia: John Benjamins.

Isham, W., & Lane, H. (1993). Simultaneous interpretation and the recall of source language sentences. *Language and Cognitive Processes, 8*(3), 241–264.

——(1994). A common conceptual code in bilinguals: Evidence from simultaneous interpretation. *Sign Language Studies, 23*, 291–317.

Ivir, V. (1998). Linguistic and communicative constraints on borrowing and literal translation. In A. Beylard-Ozeroff, J. Králová, & B. Moser-Mercer (Eds.), *Translators' strategies and creativity* (pp.137–144). Philadelphia: John Benjamins.

Jacobs, L. R. (1976). *The efficiency of sign language interpretation to convey lecture information to deaf students.* Unpublished doctoral dissertation, University of Arizona.

Johnson, K. (1991). Miscommunication in interpreted classroom interaction. *Sign Language Studies, 70*, 1–34.

Johnston, T. (1989). *Auslan dictionary: A dictionary of the sign language of the Australian Deaf community.* Maryborough, VIC: Deafness Resources Australia.

——(1996). *The representation of English in a native sign language: Implications for deaf bilingualism and English literacy.* Paper presented to the 12th National Workshop on Communication Development for Deaf Students, Griffith University, Brisbane, July 1996.

——(Ed.) (1998). *Signs of Australia: A new dictionary of Auslan.* North

224   Rocks, NSW: North Rocks Press.

Jones, B. E., Clark, G., & Soltz, D. (1997). Characteristics and practices of sign language interpreters in inclusive education programs. *Exceptional Children, 63*(2), 257–268.

Jones, D. M. (Ed.) (1996). *Assessing our work: Assessing our worth, Proceedings of the 11th National Convention of the Conference of Interpreter Trainers, October 1996.* USA: CIT.

Joos, M. (1967). *The five clocks.* New York: Harbinger Books.

Kamata, K. et al (1989). A basic study of Japanese Sign Language translation. In *Proceedings of the Japanese Society of Sign Language Studies, 10* (pp.15–29). Tokyo: Japanese Society of Sign Language Studies.

Kannapell, B. (1989). An examination of Deaf college students' attitudes toward ASL and English. In C. Lucas (Ed.), *The sociolinguistics of the Deaf community* (pp.191–210). New York: Academic Press.

Karmiloff-Smith, A. (1986). From meta-processes to conscious access: Evidence from children's metalinguistic and repair data. *Cognition, 23,* 95–147.

Kluwin, T. (1985). The acquisition of content from a signed lecture. *Sign Language Studies, 48,* 269–286.

Kopczynski, A. (1980). *Conference interpreting: Some linguistic and communicative problems.* Poznan: Adam Mickiewicz Press.

———(1994). Quality in conference interpreting: Some pragmatic problems. In S. Lambert, & B. Moser-Mercer (Eds.), *Bridging the gap: Empirical research in simultaneous interpretation* (pp.87–99). Philadelphia: John Benjamins.

Kummer, K. (Ed.) (1987). *Proceedings of the 28th annual conference of the American Translators Association.* Alburquerque, NM: Learned Information Inc.

Kurz, I. (1993). Conference interpretation: Expectations of different user groups. *The Interpreters' Newsletter, 5,* 13–21.

Kyle, J., & Woll, B. (1985). *The study of deaf people and their language.* Cambridge: Cambridge University Press.

Labath, J. E. (1998). Independent study techniques: Using videotapes of American Sign Language models. In *Celebrating the vision: RID in the 21st century. Proceedings of the 15th National Convention of the Registry of Interpreters for the Deaf, August 1997* (pp.59–69). Silver Spring, MD: RID

Publications.

Ladd, P. (2002). *Understanding Deaf culture: In search of Deafhood.* Clevedon: Multilingual matters.

Lambert, S., & Moser-Mercer, B. (Eds.) (1994). *Bridging the gap: Empirical research in simultaneous interpretation.* Philadelphia: John Benjamins.

Lane, H. (1993). *The mask of benevolence: Disabling the Deaf community.* New York: Vintage Books.

Lane, H., Hoffmeister, R., & Bahan, B. (1996). *A journey into the DEAF-WORLD.* USA: DawnSign Press.

Lawrence, R. (1987). Specialised preparation in educational interpreting. *Journal of Interpretation, 4,* 87–90.

Lawson, L. (1981). The role of sign in the structure of the Deaf community. In B. Woll, J.G. Kyle, & M. Deuchar (Eds.), *Perspectives on British Sign Language and deafness.* London: Croom Helm.

Le Ny, J. (1978). Psychosemantics and simultaneous interpretation. In D. Gerver, & H. W. Sinaiko (Eds.), *Language interpretation and communication* (pp.289–298). New York: Plenum Press.

Lee, D. (1982). Are there really signs of diglossia? Re-examining the situation. *Sign Language Studies, 35,* 127–152.

Lee, R. (1997). Roles, models and world views: A view from the States. *Deaf Worlds, 13*(3), 40–44.

Livingston, S., Singer, B., & Abramson, T. (1994). Effectiveness compared: ASL interpretation versus transliteration. *Sign Language Studies, 82,* 1–54.

Llewellyn Jones, P. (1981a). *Target language styles and source language processing in conference sign language interpreting.* Paper presented at the 3rd International Symposium on Sign Language Interpreting, Bristol.

——(1981b). Simultaneous Interpreting. In B. Woll Kyle, J. & Deuchar, M. (Eds.), *Perspectives on British Sign Language and Deafness.* London: Croom Helm.

Llewellyn Jones, P., Kyle, J., & Woll, B. (1979). *Sign language communication.* Paper presented at the International Conference on Social Psychology & Language, Bristol.

Locker, R. (1990). Lexical equivalence in transliterating for deaf students in the university classroom: Two perspectives. *Issues in Applied Linguistics, 1*(2), 167–195.

226 Longacre, R. (1983). *The grammar of discourse*. New York: Plenum Press.

Lörscher, W. (1996). A psycholinguistic analysis of translation processes. *Meta, 41*(1), 26–32.

Lucas, C. (Ed.) (1989). *The sociolinguistics of the Deaf community*. New York: Academic Press.

——(Ed.) (1990). *Sign language research theoretical issues*. Washington, D.C: Gallaudet University Press.

——(Ed.) (2001). *The sociolinguistics of sign languages*. Cambridge: Cambridge University.

Lucas, C., & Valli, C. (1989). Language contact in the American Deaf community. In C. Lucas (Ed.), *The sociolinguistics of the Deaf community* (pp.11–40). Washington, D.C: Gallaudet University Press.

——(1990). ASL, English and contact signing. In C. Lucas (Ed.), *Sign language research: Theoretical issues* (pp.288–307). Washington, D.C: Gallaudet University Press.

——(1992). *Language contact in the American deaf community*. San Diego: Academic Press.

Lucas, Bayley, Valli, Roser & Wulf (2001). Sociolinguistic variation. In C. Lucas (Ed.), *The sociolinguistics of sign languages*. Cambridge: Cambridge University.

Mackenzie, R. (1998). Creative problem solving and translator training. In A. Beylard-Ozeroff, J. Králová, & B. Moser-Mercer (Eds.), *Translators' strategies and creativity* (pp.201–206). Philadelphia: John Benjamins.

Madden, M. (2001). *The incidence and impact of occupational overuse syndrome on sign language interpreters in Australia*. Unpublished doctoral dissertation, Griffith University.

Malakoff, M., & Hakuta, K. (1991). Translation skill and metalinguistic awareness in bilinguals. In E. Bialystok (Ed.), *Language processing in bilingual children* (pp.141–165). Cambridge: Cambridge University Press.

Maroney, E., & Singer, B. (1996). Educational interpreter assessment: The development of a tool. In D. Jones (Ed.), *Assessing our work: Assessing our worth, Proceedings of the 11th National Convention of the Conference of Interpreter Trainers, October 1996* (pp.93–148). USA: CIT.

Massaro, D. W. (1978). An information processing model of understand-

ing speech. In D. Gerver, & H. W. Sinaiko (Eds.), *Language interpreta-*
tion and communication (pp.299–314). New York: Plenum Press.

McDade, R. (1995). *What can interpreters learn from professional footballers?*
Paper presented to the Issues in Interpreting 2 conference, University
of Durham, September 1995.

McIntire, M. (Ed.) (1986). *Interpreting: The Art of cross cultural mediation,*
Proceedings of the 9th National Convention of the Registry of Interpreters for
the Deaf, July 1985. Silver Spring, MD: RID Publications.

——(Ed.) (1987). *New dimensions in interpreter education: Curriculum and*
instruction, Proceedings of the 6th National Convention of the Conference of
Interpreter Trainers. Silver Spring, MD: RID Publications.

——(1990). The Work and education of sign language interpreters. In S.
Prillwitz, & T. Vollhaber (Eds.), *Sign language research and application*
(pp.263–273). Hamburg: Signum Press.

McIntire, M., & Sanderson, G. (1993). Bye-Bye! Bi-Bi! Questions of
empowerment and role. In *A confluence of diverse relationships: Proceed-*
ings of the 13th National Convention of the Registry of Interpreters for the Deaf
(pp.94–118). Silver Spring, MD: RID Publications.

McKee, R. L. (1996). Identifying difficulty factors in interpreting assignments. *Deaf Worlds, 12*(2), 16–24.

Meadow, K. (1977). Name signs as identity symbols in the deaf community. *Sign Language Studies, 16,* 237–246.

Meadow-Orlans, C. P. (1990). Research on developmental aspects of
deafness. In D. F. Moores, & C. P. Meadow-Orlans (Eds.), *Educational*
and developmental aspects of deafness. Washington, D.C: Gallaudet
University Press.

Messina, A. (1998). The reading aloud of English language texts in
simultaneously interpreted conferences. *Interpreting, 3*(2), 147–161.

Metzger, M. (1995). *The paradox of neutrality: A comparison of interpreters goals*
with the reality of interactive discourse. Unpublished doctoral dissertation,
Georgetown University.

——(1999). *Sign language interpreting: Deconstructing the myth of neutrality.*
Washington, D.C: Gallaudet University Press.

——(2000). Interactive role-plays as a teaching strategy. In C. Roy (Ed.),
Innovative practices for teaching sign language interpreters (pp.83–108).
Washington,, D.C: Gallaudet University Press.

228   Mindess, A. (1990). What name signs can tell us about deaf culture. *Sign Language Studies, 66*, 1–24.

Moser, B. (1978). Simultaneous interpretation: A hypothetical model and its practical application. In D. Gerver, & H. W. Sinaiko (Eds.), *Language interpretation and communication* (pp.353–368). New York: Plenum Press.

Moser, P. (1996). Expectations of users of conference interpretation. *Interpreting, 1*(2), 145–178.

Moser-Mercer, B. (1997). Methodological issues in interpreting research: An introduction to the Ascona workshops. *Interpreting, 2*(1), 1–12.

Moser-Mercer, B., Kunzli, A., & Korac, M. (1998). Prolonged turns in interpreting: Effects on quality, physiological and psychological stress (Pilot study). *Interpreting, 3*(1), 47–64.

Murphy, H. J. (Ed.) (1975). *Selected readings in the integration of deaf students at CSUN.* Northridge, CA: California State University.

———(1978). Research in sign language interpreting at California State University, Northridge. In D. Gerver, & H. W. Sinaiko (Eds.), *Language interpretation and communication* (pp.87–98). New York: Plenum Press.

NAATI. (1999). *Directory of accredited and recognised practitioners of interpreting and translation.* National Accreditation Authority of Translators and Interpreters. http://www.naati.com.au.

Napier, J. (1996). Interpreter support: An ambiguous concept? *CACDP Standard.* Durham: Council for the Advancement of Communication with Deaf People.

———(1998a, November). *What makes an ideal interpreter?* Paper presented to the inaugural conference of the Australian Sign Language Interpreters Association (Victoria), Melbourne.

———(1998b). *An analytical study of free interpretation and its use by British Sign Language interpreters.* Unpublished masters dissertation, University of Durham.

———(1998c). Free Your Mind—The Rest Will Follow. *Deaf Worlds, 14*(3), 15–22.

———(2000). Free interpretation: What is it and does it translate into training? In A. Schembri, J. Napier, R. Beattie, & G. Leigh (Eds.), *Deaf studies, Sydney 1998: Selected papers from the Australasian Deaf studies research symposium, Renwick College, Sydney, August 22–23 1998, Renwick College Monograph No. 4* (pp.21–33). North Rocks, NSW: North Rocks Press.

——(2001). *Linguistic coping strategies of sign language interpreters.* Unpublished doctoral dissertation, Macquarie University.

——(2002a). The D/ deaf–H/ hearing debate. *Sign Language Studies, 2*(2), 141–149.

——(2002b). University interpreting: Linguistic issues for consideration. *Journal of Deaf Studies and Deaf Education, 7*(4), 281–301.

Napier, J., & Adam, R. (2002). A comparative linguistics analysis of BSL and Auslan interpreting. *Deaf Worlds, 18*(1), 22–28.

Neumann Solow, S. (1981). *Sign language interpreting: A basic resource book.* Silver Spring, MD: National Association of the Deaf.

——(2000). *Sign language interpreting: A basic resource book* (Rev. ed.). Burtonsville, MD: Linstok Press.

Nida, E. (1998). Translators' creativity versus sociolinguistic constraints. In A. Beylard-Ozeroff, J. Králová, & B. Moser-Mercer (Eds.), *Translators' strategies and creativity* (pp.127–136). Philadelphia: John Benjamins.

Nord, C. (2000). *Translating as a text-production.* Paper given as part of the Innovation in Translator and Interpreter Training Symposium, 17–25 January 2000. http:/www.fut.es/~apym/symp/nord.html.

Nowell, R. C., & Stuckless, E. R. (1974). An interpreter training program. *Journal of Rehabilitation of the Deaf, 7*(3).

O'Loughlin, K. (1995). Lexical density in candidate output & semi-direct versions of an oral proficiency test. *Language Testing, 12*(2), 99–123.

Ozolins, U., & Bridge, M. (1999). *Sign language interpreting in Australia.* Melbourne: Language Australia.

Padden, C. (1980). The Deaf community and the culture of Deaf people. In S. Gregory, & G. Hartley (Eds.), *Constructing deafness* (pp.40–45). Milton Keynes: Open University Press.

Page, G., Elkins, J., & O'Connor, B. (Eds.) (1979). *Communication through reading: Proceedings of the 4th Australian reading conference.* Adelaide, SA: Australian Reading Association.

Page, J. (1993). In the sandwich or on the side? Cultural variability and the interpreter's role. *Journal of Interpretation, 6*, 107–126.

Paneth, E. (1957). *An investigation into conference interpreting, with special*

230   *reference to training interpreters.* Unpublished masters dissertation,
       London University.
Patrie, C. (1993). A confluence of diverse relationships: Interpreter
       education and educational interpreting. In *A confluence of diverse
       relationships: Proceedings of the 13th National Convention of the Registry of
       Interpreters for the Deaf* (pp.3–18). Silver Spring, MD: RID Publications.
——(1994). Entry level to the profession. Response paper #1: The
       readiness-to-work-gap. In E. Winston (Ed.), *Mapping our course: A
       collaborative venture. Proceedings of the 10th National Convention of the
       Conference of Interpreter Trainers* (pp.53–56). USA: CIT.
Paul, P.V., & Quigley, S. P. (1990). *Education and deafness.* London:
       Longman.
Pergnier, M. (1978). Language meaning and message meaning: Towards
       a sociolinguistic approach to translation. In D. Gerver, & H. W.
       Sinaiko (Eds.), *Language interpretation and communication* (pp.199–204).
       New York: Plenum Press.
Perner, J. (1988). Developing semantics for theories of mind: From
       propositional attitudes to mental representations. In J. Astington, P.
       L. Harris, & D. R. Olsen (Eds.), *Developing theories of mind.* Cambridge:
       Cambridge University Press.
Perren, G. E., & Trim, J. L. M. (Eds.) (1971). *Applications of linguistics: Selected
       papers of the 2nd International Congress of Applied Linguistics, 1969.*
       Cambridge: Cambridge University Press.
Peterson, R. (2000). Metacognition and recall protocols in the interpret-
       ing classroom. In C. Roy (Ed.), *Innovative practices for teaching sign
       language interpreters* (pp.132–152). Washington, D.C: Gallaudet Univer-
       sity Press.
Phillip, M. J. (1994, April). *Professionalism: From which cultural perspective?*
       Paper presented to the Issues in Interpreting conference, University
       of Durham.
Plant-Moeller, J. (Ed.) (1992). *Expanding horizons.* Silver Spring, MD: RID
       Publications.
Pollitt, K. (1997). The state we're in: Some thoughts on
       professionalisation, professionalism and practice among the UK's
       sign language interpreters. *Deaf Worlds, 13*(3), 21–26.
——(2000a). Critical linguistic and cultural awareness: Essential tools in

the interpreter's kit bag. In C. Roy (Ed.), *Innovative practices for teaching*
sign language interpreters (pp.67–82). Washington,, D.C: Gallaudet
University Press.

——(2000b). On babies, bathwater and approaches to interpreting.
Deaf Worlds, 16(2), 60–64.

Pratt, C., & Garton, A. F. (Eds.) (1993). *Metalinguistic awareness: The
development of children's representations of language.* Chichester: Wiley.

Prillwitz, S., & Vollhaber, T. (Eds.) (1990). *Sign language research and
application. Proceedings of the International Congress on Sign Language
Research and Application, March 1990.* Hamburg: Signum Press.

Qian, H. (1994). Looking at interpretation from a communicative
perspective. *Babel: International Journal of Translation, 40*(4), 214–221.

Quigley, S. (1965). *Interpreting for deaf people: A report of a workshop on
interpreting.* Washington, D.C: US Department of Health, Education
and Welfare.

Riccardi, A. (1998). Interpreting strategies and creativity. In A. Beylard-
Ozeroff, J. Králová, & B. Moser-Mercer (Eds.), *Translators' strategies and
creativity* (pp.171–179). Philadelphia: John Benjamins.

Richards, J., Platt, J., & Platt, H. (1992). *Dictionary of language teaching and
applied linguistics.* Singapore: Longman.

Roberts, R. (1987). Spoken language interpreting versus sign language
interpreting. In K. Kummer (Ed.), *Proceedings of the 28th annual
conference of the American Translators Association* (pp.293–307).
Alburquerque, NM: Learned Information Inc.

Roberts, R., Carr, S. A., Abraham, D., & Dufour, A. (Eds.) (2000). *The
Critical Link 2: Interpreters in the Community. Selected papers from the 2nd
International Conference on Interpreting in legal, health and social service
settings, Vancouver, BC, Canada, 19–23 May 1998.* Philadelphia: John
Benjamins.

Romaine, S. (1995). *Bilingualism* (2nd ed.). Oxford: Blackwell Publishers.

Roy, C. (1987). Evaluating performance: An interpreted lecture. In M.
McIntire (Ed.), *New dimensions in interpreter education: Curriculum and
instruction. Proceedings of the 6th National Convention of the Conference of
Interpreter Trainers, November 6–10, 1986* (pp.139–147). Silver Spring,
MD: RID Publications.

——(1989a). *A sociolinguistic analysis of the interpreter's role in the turn*

232   *exchanges of an interpreted event.* Unpublished doctoral dissertation, Georgetown University.

——(1989b). Features of discourse in an American Sign Language Lecture. In Lucas, C. (Ed.), *The sociolinguistics of the Deaf community* (pp.231–252). New York: Academic Press.

——(1992). A sociolinguistic analysis of the interpreter's role in simultaneous talk in a face-to-face interpreted dialogue. *Sign Language Studies, 74,* 21–61.

——(1993). The problem with definitions, descriptions and the role metaphors of interpreters. *Journal of Interpretation, 6,* 127–154.

——(1996). An interactional sociolinguistic analysis of turntaking in an interpreted event. *Interpreting, 1*(1), 39–68.

——(2000a). *Interpreting as a discourse process.* Oxford: Oxford University Press.

——(2000b). Re: More words of advice, anyone? *IEPFAC email discussion list.* listserv@admin.humberc.on.ca.

——(2000c). Training interpreters—Past, present and future. In C. Roy (Ed.), *Innovative practices for teaching sign Language interpreters* (pp.1–14). Washington, D.C: Gallaudet University Press.

——(Ed.) (2000d). *Innovative practices for teaching sign language interpreters.* Washington, D.C: Gallaudet University Press.

Russell, D. (2000). *Interpreting in legal contexts: Consecutive and simultaneous interpretation.* Burtonsville, MD: Sign Media.

Ryan, E. B., & Giles, H. (1982). *Attitudes towards language variation: Social and applied contexts.* London: Edward Arnold.

Sacks, H. (1974). An analysis of the course of a joke's telling in conversation. In Bauman & Sherzer (Eds.), *The ethnography of speaking* (pp.337–353). Cambridge: Cambridge University Press.

Sanderson, G., Siple, L., & Lyons, B. (1999). *Interpreting for postsecondary deaf students: A report of the National Task Force on Quality of Services in the Postsecondary Education of Deaf and Hard of Hearing Students.* Northeast Technical Assistance Centre, Rochester Institute of Technology.

Saur, R.E. (1992). Resources for deaf students in the mainstreamed classroom. In S.B. Foster, & G.G. Walter (Eds.), *Deaf students in postsecondary education* (pp.96–113). London: Routledge.

Schank & Abelson (1977). *Scripts, plans, goals and understanding: An inquiry into human knowledge and structures*. Hillsdale, NJ: Erlbaum.   233

Scheibe, K. (1986). Creative problem solving. In M. McIntire (Ed.), *New dimensions in interpreter education: Task analysis, theory and application* (pp.152–173). Silver Spring, MD: RID Publications.

Scheibe, K., & Hoza, J. (1986). Throw it out the window! (The code of ethics? We don't use that here): Guidelines for educational interpreters. In M. McIntire (Ed.), *Interpreting: The art of cross cultural mediation* (pp.128–134). Silver Spring, MD: RID Publications.

Schein, J. D., & Delk, M. R. (1974). *The Deaf population of the United States*. Silver Spring, MD: National Association of the Deaf.

Schembri, A. (1996). *The structure and formation of signs in Auslan (Australian Sign Language), Renwick College Monograph No. 2*. North Rocks, NSW: North Rocks Press.

Schembri, A., Napier, J., Beattie, R., & Leigh, G. (Eds.) (2000). *Deaf studies, Sydney 1998: Selected papers from the Australasian Deaf studies research symposium, Renwick College, Sydney, 22–23 August 1998, Renwick College Monograph No. 4*. North Rocks, NSW: North Rocks Press.

Scherer, K., & Giles, H. (Eds.) (1979). *Social markers in speech*. Cambridge: Cambridge University Press.

Schick, B., Williams, K., & Bolster, L. (1999). Skill levels of educational interpreters working in public schools. *Journal of Deaf Studies and Deaf Education, 4*(2), 144–155.

Schiffrin, D. (1993). "Speaking for another" in sociolinguistic interviews. In D. Tannen (Ed.), *Framing in discourse* (pp.231–263). New York: Oxford University Press.

Scott Gibson, L. (1992). Sign language interpreting: An emerging profession. In S. Gregory, & G. Hartley (Eds.), *Constructing deafness* (pp.253–258). Milton Keynes: Open University Press.

——(1994, April). *Open to interpretation: The cult of professionalism*. Paper presented to the Issues in Interpreting conference, University of Durham.

Seleskovitch, D. (1976). Interpretation: A psychological approach to translating. In R. Brislin (Ed.), *Translation: Applications and research* (pp.92–116). New York: Gardner Press.

——(1978). *Interpreting for international conferences*. Washington, D.C: Pen and Booth.

234   ———(1992). Fundamentals of the interpretive theory of translation. In J. Plant-Moeller (Ed.), *Expanding Horizons*. Silver Spring, MD: RID Publications.

Shaw, R. (1997). Many stones to form an arch: Co-operation and consideration as the cornerstones of successful interpretation. *Journal of Interpretation*, 7(1), 23–38.

Sherwood, B. (1987). Third culture: Making it work. *Journal of Interpretation*, 4. 13–24.

Simon, J. H. (1994). *An ethnographic study of sign language interpreter education*. Unpublished doctoral dissertation, University of Arizona.

Sinclair, J., & Coulthard, R. (1975). *Towards an analysis of discourse*. London.

Sinclair, A., Jarvella, R. J., & Levelt, W. J. M. (Eds.) (1978). *The child's conception of language*. Berlin: Springer-Verlag.

Siple, L. (1993). Working with the sign language interpreter in your classroom. *College Teaching*, 41(4), 139–142.

———(1995). *The use of additions in sign language transliteration*. Unpublished doctoral dissertation. State University of New York.

———(1996). The use of additions in sign language transliteration. In D. M. Jones (Ed.), *Assessing our work: Assessing our worth, Proceedings of the 11th National Convention of the Conference of Interpreter Trainers* (pp.29–45). USA: CIT.

———(2000, July). *Working with the sign language interpreter in your classroom*. Paper presented to the International Congress of Educators of the Deaf, Sydney.

Smith, M. (2000). Enhancing self-regulation in ASL/English interpreting: Promoting excellence in interpreter education. In *CIT at 21: Celebrating Excellence, Celebrating Partnership. Proceedings of the 13th National Convention of the Conference of Interpreter Trainers* (pp.89–102). Silver Spring, MD: RID Publications.

Stauffer, L. (1994). Entry level to the profession. Response Paper #2: A response to the readiness-to-work-gap. In E. Winston (Ed.), *Mapping Our Course: A collaborative venture. Proceedings of the 10th National Convention of the Conference of Interpreter Trainers* (pp.57–59). USA: CIT.

Steiner, B. (1998). Signs from the void: The comprehension and production of sign language on television. *Interpreting*, 3(2), 99–146.

Sternberg, M. L. A., Tipton, C. C., & Schein, J. D. (1973). *Curriculum guide*

for interpreter training. Unpublished manuscript, New York University, 235
Deafness Research & Training Centre.

Stewart, D., Schein, J., & Cartwright, B. E. (1998). *Sign language interpreting: Exploring its art and science.* Boston: Allyn and Bacon.

Stokoe, W. (1969). Sign language diglossia. *Studies in Linguistics, 20,* 27–41.

Stokoe, W., & Kuschel, R. (1979). *A field guide for sign language research.* Silver Spring, MD: Linstok Press.

Strong, M., & Rudser, S. F. (1992). The subjective assessment of sign language interpreters. In D. Cokely (Ed.), *Sign language interpreters and interpreting* (pp.1-14). Burtonsville, MD: Linstok Press.

Stuckless, E. R., Avery, J. C., & Hurwitz, T. A. (Eds.) (1989). *Educational interpreting for deaf students: Report of the National Task Force on Educational Interpreting.* New York: Rochester Institute of Technology.

Sunnari, M. (1995). Processing strategies in simultaneous interpreting: "Saying it all" versus Synthesis. In J. Tommola (Ed.), *Topics in Interpreting* (pp.109–119). Turku, Finland: University of Turku, Centre for Translation & Interpreting.

Sutcliffe, T. H. (1975). Interpreting at higher levels of thought. In R. M. Ingram & B. L. Ingram (Eds.), *Hands across the sea: Proceedings of the 1st International Conference on Interpreting* (pp.205–211). Silver Spring, MD: RID Publications.

Sutton-Spence, R., & Woll, B. (1998). *The linguistics of British Sign Language.* Cambridge: Cambridge University Press.

Svartvik, J. (Ed.) (1973). *Errata.* Lund: CWK Gleerup.

Swabey, L. (1992). Interpreting in community settings: A comparison of sign language and spoken language interpreters. In Plant-Moeller, J. (Ed.), *Expanding horizons: Proceedings of the 12th National Convention of the Registry of Interpreters for the Deaf, August 1991* (pp.106–119). Silver Spring, MD: RID Publications.

Tannen, D. (1979). What's in a frame? Surface evidence for underlying expectations. In R. Freedle (Ed.), *New directions in discourse processing* (pp.137-181). Norwood, NJ: Ablex.

——(Ed.) (1984a). *Coherence in spoken and written discourse.* Norwood, NJ: Ablex.

——(1984b). *Conversational style.* Norwood, NJ: Ablex.

——(1993). *Framing in discourse.* Oxford: Oxford University Press.

236   Taylor, M. (1993). *Interpretation skills: English to American Sign Language.* Edmonton, Alberta: Interpreting Consolidated.

———(2002). *Interpretation skills: American Sign Language to English.* Edmonton, Alberta: Interpreting Consolidated.

Tommola, J. (Ed.) (1995). *Topics in interpreting.* Turku, Finland: University of Turku, Centre for Translation & Interpreting.

Tunmer, W. E., & Bowey, J. A. (1984). Metalinguistic awareness and reading acquisition. In W. E. Tunmer, C. Pratt, & M. L. Herriman (Eds.), *Metalinguistic awareness in children: Theory, research and implications.* Berlin: Springer–Verlag.

Tunmer, W. E., & Herriman, M. L. (1984). The development of metalinguistic awareness: A conceptual overview. In W. E. Tunmer, C. Pratt, & M. L. Herriman (Eds.), *Metalinguistic awareness in children: Theory, research and implications.* Berlin: Springer-Verlag.

Tunmer, W. E., Pratt, C., & Herriman, M. L. (Eds.) (1984). *Metalinguistic awareness in children: Theory, research and implications.* Berlin: Springer-Verlag.

Turner, G. H. (2001). Interpreting assignments: Should I or shouldn't I? In Harrington, F. J., & Turner, G. H. (Eds.), *Interpreting interpreting: Studies and reflections on sign language interpreting* (pp. 67–73). Gloucestershire: Douglas McLean.

Tweney, R. (1978). Sign language and psycholinguistic process: Fact, hypothesis and implications of interpretation. In D. Gerver & H. W. Sinaiko (Eds.), *Language interpretation and communication* (pp.99–108). New York: Plenum Press.

Ure, J. (1971). Lexical density and register differentiation. In G. E. Perren, & J. L. M. Trim (Eds.), *Applications of linguistics: Selected papers of the 2nd International Congress of Applied Linguistics* (pp.443–452). Cambridge: Cambridge University Press.

Viera, J. A., & Stauffer, L. K. (2000). Transliteration: The consumer's perspective. *Journal of Interpretation*, 83-100.

Wadensjö, C. (1998). *Interpreting as interaction.* London: Longman.

Wardhaugh, R. (1992). *An Introduction to sociolinguistics.* Oxford: Blackwell Publishers.

Wells, J. (1996). Educational interpreting: Consumer awareness, rights and responsibilities project. In D. Jones (Ed.), *Assessing our work:*

Assessing our worth (pp.149–178). USA: CIT.

West, E. A. (1994). Dialogue videojournals: Connecting teacher and student through interactive communication. In E. Winston (Ed.), *Mapping our course: A collaborative venture, Proceedings of the 10th National Convention of the Conference of Interpreter Trainers, March 1994* (pp.217–225). USA: CIT.

Wilcox, S., & Wilcox, P. (1985). Schema theory and language interpretation. *Journal of Interpretation, 2*, 84–93.

Winston, E. (1989). Transliteration: What's the message? In C. Lucas (Ed.), *The sociolinguistics of the Deaf community* (pp.147–164). Washington, D.C: Gallaudet University Press.

——(Ed.) (1994). *Mapping our course: A collaborative venture. Proceedings of the 10th National Convention of the Conference of Interpreter Trainers.* USA: CIT.

——(Ed.) (1999). *Storytelling and conversation: Discourse in Deaf communities.* Washington, D.C: Gallaudet University Press.

Winston, E. A., & Monikowski, C. (2000). Discourse mapping—Developing textual coherence skills in interpreters. In C. Roy (Ed.), *Innovative practices for teaching sign language interpreters* (pp.15–66). Washington, D.C: Gallaudet University Press.

Witter-Merithew, A. (1982). The function of assessing as part of the interpreting process. *Professional Interpreting, Journal of the Registry of Interpreters for the Deaf, 1*(2), 8–15.

——(1987). Claiming our destiny, Part I. *RID Views*, Winter 1987.

——(1988). Claiming Our Destiny, Part 2. *RID Views*, Spring 1988.

Woodward, J. (1972). Implications for sociolinguistics research among the Deaf. *Sign Language Studies, 1*, 1–7.

——(1973). Some characteristics of Pidgin Sign English. *Sign Language Studies, 3*, 39–46.

Wray, A., Trott, K., & Bloomer, A. (1998). *Projects in linguistics. A practical guide to researching language.* London: Hodder Headline Group.

Zimmer, J. (1989). Toward a description of register variation in American Sign Language. In Lucas, C. (Ed.), *The sociolinguistics of the Deaf community* (pp.253–272). New York: Academic Press.

Index